MODERNIZING TRADITION

MODERNIZING TRADITION

Gender and Consumerism in Interwar France and Germany

ADAM C. STANLEY

LOUISIANA STATE UNIVERSITY PRESS

BATON ROUGE

PUBLISHED BY LOUISIANA STATE UNIVERSITY PRESS
Manufactured in the United States of America
First printing

DESIGNER: Michelle A. Neustrom
TYPEFACES: Adobe Garamond Pro, Market Deco
TYPESETTER: J. Jarrett Engineering, Inc.
PRINTER AND BINDER: Thomson-Shore, Inc.

Portions of chapters 1, 2, and 4 first appeared, in somewhat different form, in "Hearth, Home and Steer-ing Wheel: Gender and Modernity in France after the Great War," *The Historian* 66 (Summer 2004): 233–53, and are reprinted by permission of Blackwell Publishing. Part of chapter 4 first appeared as "Eve's Conquest of the Steering Wheel: Gender and the Automobile in Interwar France," *Automotive History Review* 43 (Spring 2005): 4–23, and is reprinted by permission.

LIBRARY OF CONGRESS CATALOGING-IN-PUBLICATION DATA

Stanley, Adam C., 1974–
  Modernizing tradition : gender and consumerism in interwar France and Germany / Adam C. Stanley.
    p. cm.
  Includes bibliographical references and index.
  ISBN 978-0-8071-3362-0 (cloth : alk. paper) 1. Consumption (Economics)—Sex differences—France—History—20th century. 2. Consumption (Economics)—Sex differences—Germany—History—20th century. 3. Women—France—History—20th century. 4. Women—Germany—History—20th century. I. Title.
  HC79.C6S73 2008
  306.30943'09042—dc22

                              2008007959

For Caryn,
who has stood beside me
every step of the way

CONTENTS

ILLUSTRATIONS

ACKNOWLEDGMENTS

Having accumulated seemingly innumerable debts to so many people over the past several years, I scarcely know where to begin. I must thank Alisa Plant at Louisiana State University Press, whose insight, support, advice, patience, and encouragement have been invaluable. She embodies everything that a writer dares to hope for in an editor, and I have been exceptionally fortunate to have had the privilege of working with her. Many thanks are due to Susan Brady for her diligent and meticulous editing of the manuscript, as well as to the anonymous reviewers of my manuscript for LSU Press, each of whom provided very sound and constructive recommendations for revisions to the work.

This book grew from my doctoral dissertation at Purdue University, and many people there have had an influence on this project. I owe an immeasurable debt of gratitude to my mentor, Whitney Walton, whose wisdom and guidance consistently challenged me to think in new directions and to pursue new avenues of inquiry. In addition, James Farr, Nancy Gabin, William Gray, and Gordon Mork made selfless contributions of time and effort. The diversity of their perspectives provoked me to address a myriad of issues that might else have gone overlooked.

I would like to thank all of the personnel at libraries and archives in Europe and the United States who made my research travels more fruitful than I could have anticipated. In particular, I would like to thank the staff of the Library of Congress in Washington, D.C.; the Landesarchiv Berlin, Staatsbibliothek zu Berlin (both East and West sites), and Geheimes Staatsarchiv in Berlin; and, in Paris, the Archives de Paris, Bibliothèque Forney, Bibliothèque

Historique de la Ville de Paris, Bibliothèque Marguerite Durand, and Bibliothèque Nationale de France. I also wish to thank the members of the library staff of the University of Wisconsin–Platteville, especially Lori Wedig in the Interlibrary Loan Office.

A number of current and former colleagues at Purdue University, the University of Wisconsin–Platteville, and several points beyond have likewise taken the time to involve themselves in my work, and they deserve recognition as well. Special thanks are due to Ryan Anderson, Susie Calkins, Brian Carter, Cullen Chandler, Mark Edwards, Stephen Harp, Sally Hastings, Clark Hultquist, Michael Morrison, Rebecca Nedostup, Paula Nelson, Joelle Neulander, Michelle Patterson, David Rowley, Sandrine Sanos, Thilo Schimmel, Yesuk Son, Nancy Turner, Karol Weaver, and David Welky. I also must acknowledge my undergraduate mentors at Millikin University—Steve Dodge, Kevin Murphy, and the late J. Graham Provan—who inspired me to become a historian in the first place. Moreover, I must thank Kathy Faull, the administrative assistant in UWP's Department of Social Sciences, who never failed to respond to my endless queries and requests with the highest degree of patience and professionalism.

My family has been a source of unending encouragement. My parents and parents-in-law were ever ready to lend assistance and emotional support in whatever manner possible. Last, to Caryn, Alissa, and Quinn, I cannot begin to express how much your love and understanding has meant to me. I hope that the completion of this project can in some small measure make worthwhile all of the sacrifices you have made for me along the way.

MODERNIZING TRADITION

INTRODUCTION

GENDER IN THE POSTWAR ERA

In the aftermath of the Great War, European society found itself in an extraordinary state of flux. Politically, economically, and socially, almost all of Europe was undergoing profound changes and experiencing unprecedented instability. Popular anxiety and dismay at such upheaval concentrated in particular on gender. The expanded roles in society enjoyed by women during World War I, coupled with the emasculation felt by numerous soldiers, placed concerns over appropriate social roles for men and women at the forefront of European cultural discomfiture. For many, disorder in the realm of gender represented a microcosm of Europe's larger disarray. This disorder could be alleviated, according to popular thinking, by a reorganization of notions of masculinity and femininity to reflect more closely the prewar gender (and, by extension, wider social) order, nostalgically remembered as an almost utopian bastion of stability and order.[1] At the same time, however, given the dramatic changes Europe had undergone since 1914, conceptions of gender would have to be reconstructed along modified lines, not simply reasserted in their precise prewar formulations.

Affecting European society as a whole, this postwar crisis was acutely felt in France and Germany, both of which were left devastated by the human and economic costs of World War I. Political and financial uncertainty as well as perceived social disorder deeply troubled the citizens of both nations. The war had effected sweeping transformation in both countries, and once the armistice brought military peace, French and Germans alike began to reflect on a world that seemed so different from the one that had existed before 1914 as to be almost unrecognizable. In the postwar era, gender became the focal point around which French and German cultures attempted to modify and neutralize the impact that war had had on their societies. Such a strategy, according to Elaine Showalter, is not uncommon in times of massive upheaval and concomitant societal anxiety. She writes that in times of "cultural insecurity," there is often an intensification of "the longing for strict border controls around the definition of gender," as well as other categories such as race and nationality. If such categories can be preserved along traditional lines, it is thought, then "apocalypse can be prevented and we can preserve a comforting sense of identity and permanence" amidst widespread change and upheaval.[2]

A focus on gender as the key to controlling the pace of change and recapturing a fleeting sense of tradition and order was therefore not entirely novel in the wake of World War I. However, the historically specific effects of that war on European society certainly heightened the need for maintaining long-standing notions of gender since men's and women's roles, it was widely perceived, were thrown severely out of balance during the war. The Great War in many ways had dramatically altered the boundaries of the masculine and feminine not only in France and Germany but in all of Europe. Prewar Europe had been divided, at least in the popular imagination, between a male-monopolized public realm and a feminine private sphere. Discursively, men were free to engage and participate in the life of the public and political world, while women were expected to remain largely isolated within the home. The war had severely shaken this tidy cultural paradigm. As men headed off to the battlefront in ever greater numbers, more and more women were called upon to replace them in public-sphere jobs, especially in factories that supplied needed war materiel. By taking on these occupations, women were able to appropriate erstwhile masculine public spaces and roles to an unprecedented extent. In the German Krupp arms factories, for example, the number of female employees leapt from two thousand or three thousand to as many as twenty-eight thousand during the war years.[3] Meanwhile, battlefield conditions led to a feeling of emasculation among many European soldiers. Although such sentiments were not unheard of among those who had returned home defeated in previous conflicts, in World War I this feeling extended to all sides, due in large part to the nature of trench warfare.[4] On the front lines, men found themselves confined in close quarters, huddled in underground bunkers, and crammed into narrow trenches. In this environment, men's access to any semblance of a public realm disappeared. Troops languished under the kinds of confined conditions associated in popular consciousness with femininity, while women on the home front were enjoying greater access to and freedom in the public sphere than ever before. The fear ran rampant that as women were becoming more masculinized—literally and figuratively—men were becoming feminized.[5]

As the war drew to a close, the landscape of European society and culture seemed completely altered. Millions of troops had died or been incapacitated in the fighting, while many others were about to be demobilized and faced the prospect of reintegration into a very changed society—a process that promised to exacerbate tensions. Women were viewed as having achieved, or at least as being well on their way toward, equality with men on a number of levels.[6] Initially, there was hope for a simple return to the bygone ways of the prewar era, to an "*ancien régime* that was still salvageable."[7] In reality, the situation proved to be far less straightforward, and it soon became apparent that the building of a postwar culture would necessarily involve considerable "restructuring and renovation" in order to account for real changes in society.[8] In other words, France and Germany would have to blend change with tradition in the aftermath of the World War I. Nonetheless, the prevailing ideological emphasis remained upon the restoration of an idealized, allegedly "natural" gender order with women as homemakers under the authority of a male, on the one hand, and men as breadwinners and the dominant figures in the public world, on the other—a dichotomy that remained stable in popular ideology across the two interwar decades.[9] Moreover, this heretofore bourgeois ideal was being adopted increasingly as a model by the upper echelons of the working-class ranks as well.[10] It was not just men, but many women as well, who subscribed to such notions, approving at least tacitly of a gender system that relegated them to the household.[11]

THE "MODERN WOMAN"

Females who did not subscribe to such traditional precepts of gender difference risked being classified in popular parlance as a "modern woman." The "modern woman" was a symbol of postwar anxieties—a cultural construct encompassing everything that society found dangerous or threatening about women's expanded roles and visibility in the public sphere. Visualized discursively as a sexually promiscuous, smoking, independent, and working woman, she was known in France as *la femme moderne* or *la garçonne,* while in Germany the term "new woman" (*neue Frau*) was more commonly employed for the same figure.[12] The conception of the "modern woman" was rooted in two interlocking beliefs: first, that women were ignoring their traditional duties as mothers in favor of sexual liberation; and second, that women were coupling this neglect of motherly responsibility with outright abandonment of their "proper" domestic sphere to work outside the home. These traits were seen as perpetuating the destabilized nature of postwar society and even as a threat to the nation's continued existence.

modern woman

"Modern women" were most easily identifiable by their appearance, which often was described as "masculinized." Forgoing the long hair and ornate modes of dress thought appropriate by "respectable" society, these women preferred short, bobbed hair, and dressed in a more functional style commensurate with an active, working life. Their outfits deemphasized their feminine physical features; when combined with their short hair, this style created a boyish or androgynous look, not at all expressive of a traditional conception of "respectable" womanhood.[13] Indeed, for women who consciously dressed in this manner, this was entirely the point: their clothes signified—both to them and to those who criticized them—a larger political statement, a "visual language of liberation."[14] To masculine society, it was a sign of women's defiance, of their refusal to live according to the dictates of "proper" femininity, instead choosing to look and act like men. The elimination of sexual difference entailed by the short hair and unisex-style clothing of the "modern woman" symbolized the collapse of larger social and cultural boundaries. Fashion itself came to be perceived as an attack on the values, norms, and social practices that had constructed femininity in terms of domestic and maternal functions.[15]

Perhaps the most famous *femme moderne* in interwar Europe was a fictional one—Monique Lerbier, the title character of Victor Margueritte's best-selling and widely translated 1922 novel, *La garçonne.*[16] Growing up in a comfortable bourgeois family, Monique is shattered when she learns that her beloved fiancé, Lucien, seeks to marry her only for her father's wealth. Utterly heartbroken, Monique "is thrown into a frenzy of anger and makes love to the first man who picks her up on the street."[17] When her parents insist that she marry Lucien despite his dishonest pretensions, she cuts her hair and runs away to Paris, where she intends to live and work as an independent woman. Soon, she "is dancing in a jazz club, drinking cocktails, and engaging in an openly sexual affair with a woman."[18] Monique finds, however, that her new lifestyle as a "modern woman" brings her only emotional emptiness, and soon she begins yearning to have a child. Striking up a completely moral relationship with an injured veteran named Blanchet, she nurses him back to health, and, when he is able to forgive her for her past transgressions, she grows her hair long again, gives up her independent lifestyle, and marries him.[19]

An intriguing German counterpoint to Margueritte's novel is Vicki Baum's 1928 novel, *stud. chem. Helene Willfüer*.[20] Written by a woman, *Helene* demonstrates a different viewpoint on the "modern woman," one that shows an impetus toward reasserting the redemptive and traditional characteristics of this transgressive figure. Helene is a graduate student in chemistry who becomes pregnant during the course of her studies. While her education, employment (after graduating, she works as a chemist), and sexual liberation directly point toward the "modern woman," Helene is at the same time associated with motherhood, thereby mitigating the perceived societal dangers inherent in her professional life. Moreover, not unlike Monique's redemption near the end of *La garçonne,* Helene eventually realizes that she loves her former professor, providing a message of hope for her future as a "proper" woman.[21]

As the existence of a discursive figure like the "modern woman" suggests, an ideology emphasizing a feminine devotion to home and hearth alongside a masculine monopoly on public and political life persevered into the interwar years. The so-called "separate spheres" ideology has lately come under attack at the hands of several historians who, with good reason, point out that public and private were not nearly as clear-cut in practice as many earlier writers believed.[22] Women were, of course, working and moving about outside the home in greater or lesser numbers throughout the span of modern European history. While certainly it would be foolish to debate the accuracy of these recent conclusions regarding the (lack of) existence in practice of clearly demarcated gendered spheres, one must be cautious not to throw out this significant discursive tool altogether. In a study such as this one whose focus is to be found at the level of cultural ideology, the idea of separate spheres can still be quite informative, for despite its failure to withstand scrutiny at ground level, there can be little doubt that this ideal was still a powerful, widely circulated one in European society throughout the interwar decades, and still had a significant effect on the ways in which gender constructions were formulated, even if those formulations did not always translate perfectly in practice.

Similarly, some scholars are skeptical as to whether women's increased visibility in public life was as drastic as the constitution of this image of the "modern woman" would lead one to suspect. Regardless, the important point as far as it concerns this study is the ideological currency of the image, and in that context, the "modern woman" was an undeniably powerful figure. With respect to France, Charles Rearick perceptively notes that, after World War I, despite the myriad of monuments that appeared and honors that were bestowed on soldiers and civilians alike who contributed to the war effort, no public tributes were paid to the women who worked in wartime factories to provide vital war materiel for the front lines; by the early 1920s, these women too closely resembled the discursively unacceptable "modern woman."[23] Thus the image of *la femme moderne* or the *neue Frau* was a powerful one in cultural consciousness, but, importantly, one that was not beyond perceived redemption. In response to the image of the "modern woman," French and German society sought to reassert women's primary roles as housewives and mothers— women who remained in the domestic sphere to fulfill their wifely and motherly responsibilities.

GENDER, CONSUMPTION, MODERNITY, AND THE NATION

Writing the history of women and gender in the interwar years was long overlooked in French and German historiography, and the project of examining cultural constructions of femininity in interwar Europe started only relatively recently.[24] During the last two decades, a number of works published by historians of France have begun to explore cultural discourse on women and gender after the Great War, but there are still important interpretive and methodological issues that need to be addressed.[25] The scholarly terrain is similar in German historiography, where academic attention long subordinated questions of gender in the Weimar Republic and Nazi Germany to wider political issues, most especially the well-known *Sonderweg* debate.[26] The fact that scholars were slow to give extensive attention to questions of gender in the interwar years is all the more confounding given that issues relating to women and gender were "central to people's political consciousness, to state policy and political ideologies."[27]

Among the most important works to appear in this field in the past decade are those of Robert Frost, Mary Louise Roberts, and Katharina von Ankum. Drawing largely from literature directed at specifically female audiences, Frost analyzes the ways in which electrical appliances contributed to the redefinition of housewifery in interwar France. In particular, Frost's work is significant for its establishment of a connection between household labor and modernity in French cultural discourse.[28] Similarly, the essays in *Women in the Metropolis: Gender and Modernity in Weimar Culture,* edited by Katharina von Ankum, draw on sources such as film and fictional literature in order to highlight discursive connections between modernity and gender in the Weimar era in Germany.[29] Roberts examines the reconstruction of gender conceptions in France in the decade following the end of the Great War. Building upon sources such as contemporary fiction, Roberts demonstrates the existence and cultural currency of a number of different discursive models of femininity in postwar France, including *la femme moderne.*[30]

One area of interwar gender scholarship that has shown signs of promising debate is the so-called "reconstruction" of gender ideologies following the Great War. Historians such as Mary Louise Roberts and Susan Kingsley Kent, writing about France and Great Britain, respectively, have led the way in explicitly describing the formation of gender norms after the Great War as a "reconstruction" of gender.[31] This argument states that, given the turbulent effects of the war on gender roles, European cultures had to reconstruct their notions of gender in the aftermath of the conflict, for these ideologies had been torn apart by the realities of wartime conditions. More recently, however, Susan Grayzel contends, in her examination of motherhood ideologies in wartime France and Britain, that there would have been no need for a reconstruction of gender ideology following World War I because that ideology did not in fact break down during the conflict itself. Despite the fact that thousands of women left the home to work in previously male-dominated jobs, Grayzel argues, the prevalent conception of women remained the mother figure. The war, therefore, had a conservative rather than innovative effect on cultural attitudes toward women, heightening the association of women primarily with maternity.[32]

My goal is to reassert the value of exploring gender discourse after the Great War in terms of a reconstruction. My contention is that the gulf separating the views of Grayzel from those of Roberts and Kent is not as wide as it may at first glance seem. Most importantly, we should take into account that culturally constructed categories are intrinsically dynamic and shifting. To use an extreme example, an early-nineteenth-century discourse on motherhood would certainly not involve an identical set of meanings as a post-1945 motherhood ideology. Thus, that the image of *la mère* remained prominent in

French cultural discourse during the war, as Grayzel convincingly shows, does not negate the possibility that the significations of those cultural meanings had changed, potentially dramatically, by the 1920s. In addition, we also should keep in mind the very significant transition from wartime to peacetime, which entailed an important cultural reevaluation of gender roles. Grayzel concedes that a key reason that discursive constructions of women remained dominated primarily by the image of the mother during the war was that French and British societies recognized that women's encroachment into the public realm was temporary—a patriotic necessity engendered by the migration of male workers to the battlefront. In the postwar context, however, if women were perceived still to be dominating the masculine world of factories, a noticeable change in cultural attitudes from those of wartime could indeed result. It would be apparent that this participation in the public sphere was not, at least for the women in question, intended to be a transient, patriotic endeavor, but one undertaken for personal reasons and perhaps meant to be permanent. At this point, cultural discourse would have to reinterpret women's work in factories and visibility in the public spaces discursively assigned to masculinity; no longer heroic, such work would now be portrayed as a culturally unacceptable transgression. Indeed, this was the situation in the immediate aftermath of World War I that helped to give rise to the construction of the "modern woman."

This debate is of central import for my purposes because I argue that interwar French and German popular discourse sought to contain the allegedly liberated lifestyles of women by carrying out a reconstruction of definitions of femininity that combined elements of the new and modern with idealized tradition. Women were defined primarily as wives and mothers, but in a manner that granted a degree of discursive access to the modern, particularly through newly available consumer goods. Thus being a housewife or a mother could be portrayed as an empowering, even liberating lifestyle for a woman. At the same time, discursive messages reinforced patriarchal and paternal authority, making it clear that women still were subordinate to men. Moreover, popular images of gender also depicted women engaging in activities outside of the home, such as vacationing and driving, but even in these cases, the ultimate ideological intent was similarly to accommodate such modern and liberating pursuits with traditional conceptions of womanhood. Women could participate in such affairs as tourism and driving only insofar as it remained consonant with their traditional duties and connected them to familial roles or cast them as reliant on masculine supervision. The gender discourse that emerges in the pages that follow, therefore, is one that hinges on a push-and-pull between the forces of tradition and the advance of modernity. Women were caught conceptually between these two poles as French and German social ideologies took into account the reality of women's expanded roles and activities, but simultaneously sought to limit as much as possible the context and conceptual boundaries of such behaviors and actions.

Historical works such as those discussed above have made significant contributions to the development of scholarly literature on gender discourse in interwar Europe, yet they largely remain restricted to one national culture and only a segment of the interwar years. In this project, I attempt to address the historiographical need for a study that bridges national boundaries and encompasses the whole of the interwar period. France and Germany are particularly suitable as areas of research in this respect for these two nations arguably encountered more wartime and postwar upheaval than any other major belligerent states. As a result, the discursive emphasis on restoring an idealized gender order after the Great War, which was common across much of Europe, was most immediately evident and even amplified in those two countries. Using a cross-national framework of analysis, I attempt to bring issues of national identity as related to gender, consumption, and modernity into sharper relief. While there were distinct national inflections embedded within the two countries' discourses of masculinity and femininity, one of the important findings of this study is the widespread similarity in these nations' popular gender imagery. The strategies and themes invoked in formulating constructions of gender demonstrate the common framework shared by French and German popular gender discourse. In such a context, there is considerable value in incorporating a perspective that goes beyond a single nation-state, for my work suggests the possibility of a common, continentwide ideology of gender, replete no doubt with national particularities, but nonetheless rooted in undeniably congruent ideals regarding men's and women's roles.

Mixing old and new, at least where gender was concerned, involved accommodating new realities of women's opportunities and roles in society with age-old categories of femininity, such as housewifery and motherhood. Most prominently, consumerism and newly available modern technologies played a crucial role in the reconstruction of gender ideals following the Great War. Gender, consumption, and modernity were inextricably intertwined in French and German discourse in the 1920s and 1930s, as consumer culture and the accoutrements of modernity formed a central foundation for definitions of gender in popular ideology. This book connects these threads together into a unified narrative of the ways in which modern consumer goods were utilized to delimit the boundaries of masculinity and femininity. In the interwar years, gender, consumption, and notions of the modern were at the forefront of popular discourse, and therefore a study that encompasses each of these areas can be very revelatory of wider cultural attitudes circulating in interwar France and Germany. Women were defined as consumers more strongly than ever in this era, and French and German discourse in the interwar years utilized modern consumer culture as a means to relegate women to traditional categories of femininity, melding notions of tradition and change in interwar gender constructions and maintaining long-standing gender definitions and conventions in the face of shifting social and cultural realities. Women were granted discursive access to the modern—in every arena from household appliances and medical goods to automobiles and tourist activities—but only to the extent that such connections tied women to their roles as wives and mothers or emphasized their subservience to and dependence on masculine guidance, expertise, and authority.

This book analyzes such cultural constructions of gender in France and Germany between the world wars through an examination of various consumption-related sources. Among these are advertisements (as well as a few articles, stories, and cartoons) from the popular press of each nation. I have incorporated publications from across the political spectrum of each country.[33] In addition, my study utilizes diverse promotional materials generated and distributed by French retailers and manufacturers in the 1920s and 1930s. Included in this latter group are advertising flyers, mailings, and catalogs, as well as the annual calendar books, or *agendas,* distributed by French department stores. These *agendas,* which were explicitly directed at female consumers, frequently contained not only a calendar schedule for each day of the year, but also often were filled with cartoons, snippets of wisdom or advice, short stories, and other content deemed of interest to women. Together, these consumer-driven sources reveal a cultural emphasis on retaining tried-and-true classifications of femininity, with a particular focus on home and hearth, while at the same time accommodating elements of change and modernity into visions of women's roles in society so long as these did not challenge an idealized, traditional gender order.

Evidence of the powerful currency of such discursive images can be found in their staunch consistency across the entire chronological span of the two interwar decades. Change in the 1920s and 1930s was often rapid and seemingly unavoidable, and France and Germany were in many ways very different countries in 1939 than they had been in 1920. Nevertheless, with some minor exceptions, the nature of gender images in popular discourse remained very much the same throughout these years, showing relatively little change. Regardless of political regime and economic circumstance, portrayals of men and women in any given year were often indistinguishable from any other time during the period from 1920 to 1939. One of the important contributions of this study is to note and document this consistency of definitions of masculinity and femininity in the interwar era. The ability of traditional gender ideologies to hold firm among disparate elements of the population, people at all points on the political spectrum (including publications of the political Right, Left, and Center), and highly differentiated political regimes should form in future scholarly endeavor a vital point for analysis and questioning of cultural attitudes about gender. The fact that gender conceptions did not change dramatically over the course of these two decades—years when virtually every other aspect of society and culture seemed to be in almost constant flux—attests to the extraordinarily powerful constancy of these gender conceptions in French and German society.

In addition to this chronological and political uniformity, the similarity of French and German gender ideology across geographic-national lines is also a significant finding of this study. The images of gender examined in the following pages are often striking in their transnational similarity. While incorporating an analysis in which distinct national ideologies can indeed be discerned, what emerges most noticeably in this study are the highly similar frameworks within which such images were contained in each nation under consideration. Contrasts between them were a question of degree, not of kind. Each state's popular notions of gender dealt with and responded to largely the same set of questions and concerns. This is likewise an important jumping-off point for future studies of gender constructions in Europe, for it suggests the possibility—the likelihood, I would contend—of a broad consistency in cultural conceptions of gender across wider swaths of Europe as a whole. At the same time, it must be noted that precise definitions of masculinity and femininity in France and Germany were not completely identical. Despite the broad, transnational consistency in frameworks of gender notions, there were also differences in the two nations' gender constructions that highlight issues of national identity and distinctiveness.[34] Yet this book demonstrates that although each state had its own particularities in defining and carving out its gender ideals, an overwhelming cultural emphasis on restoring an idealized gender order was the primary impetus behind French and German gender images that appeared in popular discourse in the 1920s and 1930s.

Along similar lines, in both France and Germany there was a pronounced cultural need to emphasize the ways in which maintenance of "proper" gender roles would benefit the nation, helping to protect and strengthen the national body politic in both an internal and external sense. That is to say, adherence to cultural dictates of gender was thought to ensure both the internal recovery of the nation in the turbulent interwar years as well as the ability to defend and protect the state from potential outside threats. Thus gender was very closely connected to the nation in interwar gender ideology, as the reestablishment of an idealized gender order was equated with restoring national stability and greatness, and this was largely defined as dependent on women's adherence to cultural norms of femininity. According to popular thinking, such an adherence necessitated above all that women reject the temptation to become "modern women," and live instead devoted to home and family, as a means both of finding personal happiness as well as of restoring national order and strength.

As suggested above, the development and heightened prominence of consumer culture was inextricably linked to interwar definitions of gender. Yet scholarship on the history of consumerism, particularly with respect to interwar Germany, has sometimes developed only rather slowly and haltingly.[35] Even some scholars who have explored the history of consumerism downplay the importance of consumption in the interwar era given the absence of a true consumer economy anywhere in Europe.[36] After all, even in the best interwar economic years, the amount of consumer goods purchased by French and German citizens was relatively small compared to American consumption levels. In that light, it is difficult to argue that France and Germany had been completely transformed by 1939 into societies of mass consumption. In spite of this stark reality, the issue of consumerism is nonetheless vital to an analysis of popular discourse in interwar France and Germany, for my interest lies in the establishment of a consumer *mentality* rather than a consumer *economy.* As scholars such as Robert Frost and Gerard Sherayko illustrate, the lack of actual purchases in the interwar era is less important than the adoption of a consumerist mind-set by Europeans.[37] People viewed themselves as potential consumers of goods whether or not they could actually purchase them, and as such "a consumer culture was already in place in the 1920s even if many people could not directly partake of all its wonders."[38] In large part, this can be attributed to ever more ubiquitous calls to consume: "An individual could no longer walk down the street, ride a trolley, go to the movies or read a favorite magazine without being confronted with enticements to consume. The very physical landscape, at least in urban areas, began to be transformed as this new emphasis on consumption exerted its mark."[39] These seemingly omnipresent seductions to consume helped to ensure that, regardless of whether individuals could or did buy particular goods, they were participating in a consumer culture. Germans and French alike formulated self-identities as consumers, regardless of whether or not they actually could afford or did purchase commodities ranging from automobiles to washing machines and refrigerators.

This consumer culture had significant consequences for individual as well as collective identities in the interwar years, a point raised by Alon Confino and Rudy Koshar.[40] Perhaps most notably, it blurred distinctions of class and locale. Gerard Sherayko maintains that the wide dissemination of consumer images allowed villagers in isolated, rural regions to be connected at the level of popular ideology with urban culture.[41] It touched all age groups, and also had an effect on class. Peter Stearns argues that the participation in this culture of consumption (again, at the level of mentality rather than actual spending) by the working classes is particularly noteworthy; he highlights a working-class tendency to acculturate middle-class standards as far as consumption was concerned.[42] Each of these examples is germane, for they all point to a homogenizing tendency across social and regional lines, thanks largely to the pervasiveness and uniformity of consumer culture and the consumerist imaginary. The singular power of consumer culture was such that it could be utilized not only to formulate self-identities, but also to contribute to national identities and even the legitimization of political regimes.[43] John Breuilly argues that, due mainly to the blossoming of consumer culture (along with, it should be mentioned, the experience of war), the Weimar Republic was the first German regime to transcend regional loyalties and become a true national society.[44] Focusing on Nazi Germany, Nancy Reagin demonstrates that the Nazi government hoped to utilize consumer goods as an avenue through which Germans would become unified in their support for the regime. Although the exigencies of the Four-Year Plan were to hinder this goal, it was thought that mass consumption of consumer goods could serve to promote a sense of common experience and national identity among Germans.[45]

Although the entire nation was involved intimately in the culture of consumption, it was women who were most closely identified and associated with the new consumer culture, and who were seen—with dubious accuracy, perhaps, but again the important point is the widespread perception—as the purchasers of consumer goods.[46] Indeed, conceptions of womanhood in the interwar period involved inextricable links to consumption and commodities. Women were repeatedly defined in their discursive guises as mothers or housewives through commercial products, whether it was a vacuum cleaner to maintain the household or a nutritional item to ensure the health of one's children. Consuming, then, was vital to the interwar reconstruction of femininity, and advertisements for commodities that appeared in the French and German press or were printed by retailers and manufacturers are crucial to analyzing discursive images of women after the Great War.

Likewise vital to an examination of interwar gender ideology is the intersection between consumption and modernity. Scholars agree that consumption is utterly central to modernity: "Consumption is not some interesting but insignificant byway in the development of modern life, it is intrinsic to the dynamic organization of economic society and to the human experience of being and becoming modern."[47] In the interwar era, many saw burgeoning consumer culture, especially advertising, as the very essence of modernity.[48] This new modern culture, however, was not met with universal enthusiasm. Many observers in interwar France and Germany traced the roots of modernity and mass culture directly to the United States, which was largely judged an overly standardized and too homogeneous society. Anxieties about the loss of national distinctiveness or uniqueness in the face of an overwhelming Americanizing modernity caused considerable fear and frustration in many sectors.

In response, both the French and Germans attempted to reconcile the modern with historic national tradition and identity as a means of negating the worst aspects of its homogenizing effects. In Germany, while cognizant of the economic benefits that could result from modernism and its impact on consumer culture, many "feared a loss of German uniqueness," and "predicted a leveling and homogenization of culture" as a concomitant aspect of American-style consumer culture.[49] This feeling was particularly acute in Germany, as Wilfried van der Will contends, because the modernization process had come later to Germany and thus had taken place much more rapidly than elsewhere, with less time for adjustment by society at large to changes wrought by modernity. As a result, modernism seemed an overpowering force that was creating in some sense an "intolerable shock" in the speed with which it brought massive change.[50] As such, a main tenet of Nazi ideology was to emphasize "the recovery of those supposedly traditional values which modern civilization had destroyed."[51] It was, in Jeffrey Herf's words, a "reactionary modernism" that sought to reconcile modernity with elements of German national tradition.[52] Meanwhile, many French reacted to modernity in ways very similar to their eastern neighbors. French commentators "responded to modernity's threat and its promise by reinventing their social environment in ways that brought together the alien and the familiar, the innovative and profoundly conservative, since modernity was palatable only when it could be presented as a renovation of time-honored customs."[53]

Not uncommonly, such ambivalent visions of modernity were dichotomized along gendered lines, to the point that men were seen as representing the apogee of modernity's offerings to European culture, while women signified the dangers of the modern. This, too, will be the subject of further elaboration, but for the time being, it is important to keep in mind this perceptual division, as it noticeably colored gender ideologies in interwar France and Germany. Cultural unease with modernity was most frequently expressed in the form of feminine independence, decadence, and even criminality.[54] At the same time, just as contemporary novels suggested that the "modern woman" was ultimately redeemable, constructions of women were accompanied by the view that women could serve as a potential salvation for national society in a modern age. As Vibeke Rützou Petersen argues with respect to popular fiction in Weimar Germany, it was on women rather than men that the future of the nation was scripted and in many ways on whom it depended.[55] Women's roles in society would to a great extent determine the course of the nation, at least according to popular thinking, and thus images of women came to exemplify the uneasy oscillation between tradition and modernity.

It is significant that modernity was specifically associated with the media and the department store, the two main realms from which my primary documents are drawn. Detlev Peukert's analysis of what he calls the crisis of classical modernity in the Weimar Republic demonstrates that media products and images are absolutely central to, even dominant in, modernist culture.[56] The media, from which I draw advertisements as well as occasional cartoons and articles, represent a privileged site of popular ideology in modern culture, and offer fertile and revealing territory for the study of cultural discourse. Moreover, the department store was widely seen across Europe from the late nineteenth century onward as emblematic of modernity. Replacing the small shops and local merchants that had dominated European modes of consumption previously, these new stores were an expression of the modern that thousands of people encountered on a daily basis.[57] As such, the publicity documents that they generated are of inestimable value in a cultural history of modernity and consumer culture.

THE FRENCH AND GERMAN PRESS

Given the importance of the media to emerging attitudes toward modernity as well as to the development of the new consumer culture—not to mention the importance of the press as a source for this study—it is appropriate at this point to delineate briefly the nature of the popular press in the interwar period in France and Germany.[58] As Lyn Gorman and David McLean note in a more general context, beginning in the late nineteenth century, the press became more closely tied than ever with a mass readership. This was a development in many ways linked to the increasing importance of advertising (although technical developments facilitating increased production also played a key role); as ad revenue grew, becoming the lifeblood of press finances, there was a concerted effort by press publications to appeal to a larger readership. Elite opinion became less prized, and the press began to direct itself at a very wide-ranging audience. At the same time, a reliance on advertising revenue to support press ventures meant that pricey subscriptions were no longer required, and papers could be sold much more cheaply than before, allowing for a wider readership of daily and weekly publications.[59]

This mass audience increasingly included women, as illustrated by the presence of "women's pages" in many press publications. Numerous French and German newspapers and periodicals had a regularly appearing page for women, though often not in every issue (the norm for daily publications, for example, was usually to print women's pages once per week, often on Sundays). These one- to two-page sections would be clearly identified as being for women so that there was no mistaking their intended audience. Arguably the most famous of these women's pages was "Die Deutsche Frau" (The German Woman), which was printed weekly in the pages of the Nazi newspaper, the *Völkischer Beobachter*. Other publications in both France and Germany also had such pages, which appeared under headings such as "Women's World" (*Germania*) or "For You, Madame" (*Gringoire*). The content of these sections, as one might expect, was geared toward topics considered to be of interest or importance to women, from issues of housework to fashion, health, leisure, and many other subjects.

The new mass audience of men and women provided a shared frame of reference for readers. Noting that many scholars see the mass-circulation newspaper as the archetypal modern form because it was, in an important sense, the very first commodity produced for mass consumption, Vanessa Schwartz describes the attempts of French publishers from the late nineteenth century onward to reach a reputed "universal" reader, connecting readers in a veritable community in a way not otherwise physically or geographically possible.[60] In addition, Schwartz makes an important point about Paris as the hub of Frenchness. Explaining the focus in her work on Paris, she writes, "Paris had enormous power to 'represent.' When it came to 'modernity,' Paris stood for things French."[61] My work follows from this important observation, as the French publications that I have utilized in this study are drawn from the Parisian press. Such an approach does not completely ignore the dissemination of cultural discourse in the provinces, for most major Parisian papers' circulations carried well beyond the capital itself, and although the provincial readership of some Parisian papers was declining, major publications were still widely read outside Paris as well.[62]

Meanwhile, in Germany, no single city represented the national culture in the same way that Paris did for France. Certainly Berlin was an important site of publication, and every major nationally circulated newspaper had an office there, but prior to 1933 the German press was more "decentralized" than most.[63] The German publications included in this study were published in different parts of the nation and were selected to reflect the lack of a single newspaper publishing center in Germany. In both Germany and France, however, the mass circulation press was perceived in important ways as a quintessential expression of modernity.[64]

THE NATURE OF ADVERTISING

Within the pages of these French and German press publications were numerous advertisements for a multitude of goods. Advertisements were essential to the cultural reconstruction of femininity after the Great War. Other works on the history of gender in interwar Europe have tended to overlook this vast array of meaningful documentation of cultural attitudes. Considerable scholarly work on the relationship between advertising and society, however, demonstrates the validity—perhaps even the imperative—of drawing from such materials extensively in the context of understanding the ideas of a culture.

The advertising industry in the interwar years was in many ways at the peak of a process of modernization that marked a departure from advertising methods and techniques employed earlier. Although the process did not develop along identical lines in any two places, a rather analogous process can be seen in France, Germany, elsewhere in Europe, and even in the United States. At the outset, it is worth noting the assertion of Ruth Schwartz Cowan, who defines the "advertiser" as not just the advertising agent who promoted a particular product, but a combination of this entity along with the manufacturer of the product and the publication that printed the promotion.[65]

In the decades leading up to 1920, the advertising business had changed in significant ways. Most visibly, in both Europe and America, the process whereby advertisements were constructed changed from one in which in-house elements at a publication or business frequently devised their own advertisements to one wherein outside, full-fledged advertising agencies were coming to play an increasingly powerful role in the design and preparation of advertising materials.[66] The rise of such agencies and the growth of the advertising industry also indicated a greater willingness on the part of retailers, manufacturers, and the press to produce and to print advertisements, facilitating the expansion of advertising discourse into the very center of European consumption and, in many ways, the very core of popular discourse as well.[67] Those who worked in advertising began moving toward greater professionalization (and became, as scholars have noted, the archetypal standard bearers of modernity).[68] In part, this process was spurred along by the increasing presence of American advertising agencies, which set up offices in a variety of foreign locales, France and Germany among them, starting in the 1920s to serve their (still largely American-based) corporate clients.[69]

Despite the impact of American models on European consumer culture, it cannot be said that French or German advertisements were merely imitations of their American counterparts. The emphasis on creating a distinctly national avenue to modernity helped to ensure this, and advertisers consciously avoided copying American-style advertising too closely, believing such messages would not be particularly effective anyway, and instead forged new styles, techniques, and modes of salesmanship based on what were considered French or German tastes, traditions, and business models.[70] Thus advertisements from interwar France and Germany are not simply poor copies of American ones, but rather are quite revealing of the attitudes and value systems of the French and Germans in the 1920s and 1930s.

Gerard Sherayko explores the increasing impetus toward professionalization and greater cultural legitimization on the part of German advertising agents in the Weimar era. Founding an Association of German Advertising Professionals, advertisers communicated about the latest developments and trends in their industry via their own specialized periodicals and books.[71] In the 1920s, German advertising executives even went to the United States to familiarize themselves with American marketing methods and ideas.[72] Nonetheless, the advertising landscape in Germany remained something of a "dilettantish free-for-all," with frequent allegations of misleading or outright false advertising, and as a result many in the German advertising industry welcomed the intrusion of the Nazi authorities in 1933, hoping that the new government would instill greater order and standards in the industry as well as raise the prestige of advertising through publicity and propaganda campaigns.[73] Although Hartmut Berghoff argues that, overall, the Nazi government did not fulfill German advertisers' aspirations, he notes that greater strides in professionalization were made. The Nazi-created regulatory entity for the industry, the Advertising Council for the German Economy, created an advertising college for young German would-be admen, and encouraged companies to employ "professional" ad agents rather than handle ads themselves (from the state's perspective, this was another way to create job opportunities for Germans, according to Berghoff).[74] Still, Berghoff highlights the contradictions between such emphasis on advertising, on the one hand, and the Nazis' disdain for capitalism and their discouragement of conspicuous consumption, on the other, concluding that on the whole advertising did not achieve higher standing during the 1930s.[75]

In France as well, efforts at professionalization and greater public acceptance were made in the 1920s and 1930s. For instance, advertising organizations were founded, trade journals published, and professional schools created.[76] While in reality ad representatives were a hodgepodge representing several different occupations and talents (for example, artists), Marie-Emmanuelle Chessel argues that the notion of professionalization still applies to the interwar advertising business.[77] Clark Hultquist describes the French advertising industry as pyramidal in structure, with one major national agency, Havas, at the top; a handful of moderately sized ad companies below that; and numerous small

agencies—some of them one-person operations—occupying the bottom.[78]
This is not to suggest, though, that American agencies such as J. Walter Thompson were able to come in and dominate French advertising. Indeed, Hultquist argues that that company's Paris office struggled mightily to entice French-based corporations to sign with Thompson in the face of stiff competition from French ad agencies like Havas. In the final analysis, Hultquist classifies Thompson's efforts in France during the interwar years as only marginally successful.[79]

Still, as Julia Sneeringer points out in the German case, determining precisely who was responsible for the production of advertisements remains a difficult task due to the underdeveloped nature of the German advertising industry. She notes that companies usually did not retain detailed information about their advertising, not even recording the individual in charge of advertising at the company or, if outside advertisers were hired, what ad agency was commissioned.[80] It is clear that American advertising agencies such as J. Walter Thompson that were doing business in Europe were indeed attempting to engage in "scientific" research (that is, market research like consumer surveys and interviews) in order to learn about consumer tastes, tendencies, and markets.[81] Yet even in this case, as Jeff Merron notes, company records do not provide a link between the results of such research, on the one hand, and the formulation of actual advertisements, on the other.[82]

The growing ranks of professional advertisers who were greatly concerned with gauging public tastes and desires elicited alterations in the form and content of advertisements. Advertisements became more consumer-oriented rather than being product-centered, as heretofore many ads had been. Before 1920, advertisements were most often text-only announcements that dryly explicated the uses and quality of a product.[83] For the new, prototypically modern ad agent, this was an ineffective means of connecting to the audience, and so advertisements became much more focused on what a particular good could mean in the context of the lives, fears, hopes, or desires of a consumer rather than simply extolling the particulars of a product. Visual illustrations showing people using the product became much more common and central to ads after 1920, engaging the reader on a new level, catching the eye, and helping to ensure that ads were read. Moreover, by deemphasizing the importance of text and simplifying the words that did remain, ads became accessible to a wider audience than ever before. The purpose of advertisements became not just to provide information about a product, but to persuade readers to buy it.[84] Advertisements evolved into "an attempt to associate the product with an ideal, with what the advertisers believed the reader wants to become. The shift is away from the mundane item for sale to the interpreted aspirations of the readership."[85]

This shift to aspirations and desires in advertising materials likewise effected greater emotionality in ads. The sum of visual illustrations, simplified language, and appeals based on hopes or anxieties created a new type of advertisement in which the reasoned, relatively objective tone of earlier text-only advertisements was replaced by ads that sought to provoke a response from the reader based on emotion and impulse. This is noteworthy, for it further explains the centrality of identifications of women with consumption in the 1920s and 1930s. Gerard Sherayko, in fact, argues that at least some of the changes in advertisements in Weimar Germany, such as more frequent use of illustrations, were made by advertising professionals precisely because of the widely held belief that women were the main purchasers of goods, and thus ads were directed more toward a female audience.[86] The connection of femininity with emotionality (as opposed to perceived rational masculinity) was a long-standing, widespread, and powerful association in Europe.[87] This is significant for, as I will discuss, this dichotomy of masculine reason and feminine emotion was utilized as a means to deny feminine agency and discursively subjugate women to men in advertising discourse. While they were at the center of consumer culture, women were still far from empowered by this fact.

This new type of advertisement is quite significant for other reasons as well. As Roland Marchand claims, the shift from information-oriented, text-centered ads to those that emphasized visual appeal and consumer desire was what made advertising modern and, not unimportantly, made advertisements of immense value to cultural historians.[88] In modern society, advertising materials play an important role in the process of negotiating cultural attitudes, as "advertisements serve not only as tools for business success but also as factors in competitions for cultural authority."[89] Advertisements must bear specific markers of cultural attitudes in order to function effectively. Signals sent by ads "depend for their signifying process on the existence of specific, concrete receivers, people *for* whom and in whose systems of belief, they have a meaning."[90] Thus effective advertising is dependent upon the exploitation of existing ideas and images, since "demands could not be created from thin air, and advertisers had to keep careful tabs on existing culture in order to figure out how to pitch their wares."[91] As such, advertisements are inextricably linked to the cultures of which they are a product, and analyzing them can reveal wider societal ideologies, norms, and mores.

Advertisements rely on what Judith Williamson calls "alreadyness"— making consumers feel as though they are already a part of the group that a particular product represents.[92] Yet this does not mean that interwar advertisers appealed to all social groups in different and mutually exclusive ways. Advertisers often set their images in more upscale environments than their presumed audiences inhabited on a daily basis. Advertisers utilized these more wealthy settings because they believed the public preferred an idealized, distorted image of itself in advertisements, one that demonstrated a more comfortable and extravagant existence than was the reality for most consumers.[93] This is not to suggest that advertising images bore no relation or resemblance to the values and desires of middle-class and even lower-class audiences. To the contrary, advertisements consistently worked to echo and reinforce existing and widely held social ideologies. Even though the representations of reality may have been more upscale than most readers' actual financial situation, the ideals and aspirations contained within those same ads still accurately reflected those of the culture as a whole.[94]

Even in the related case of propaganda, reinforcing contemporary values and building upon existing social ideologies, rather than fabricating new ones, were powerful considerations.[95] In the Nazi regime, as David Welch shows, Propaganda Minister Joseph Goebbels devoted significant attention to public opinion, even receiving regular reports about the mood of ordinary Germans on various topics.[96] This is not meant to equate propaganda with advertisements, but merely to highlight the partly analogous ways in which they can be conceived. Propaganda demonstrates further the importance of sending a message that resonates with one's audience, and as such the validity of advertising as an indicator of cultural attitudes and values, even under Nazism, cannot be overlooked.

Advertisements should be considered no less useful source material than any other type of contemporary primary documents. Perhaps one cannot document the specific effects of an advertisement on an audience or its precise relationship to "reality," as Roland Marchand contends, yet the same uncertainty exists for any number of other historical sources.[97] In many ways, "ads actually surpass most other recorded communications as a basis for *plausible inference* about popular attitudes and values."[98] After all, advertisers have historically concerned themselves with understanding their audiences' fundamental beliefs, and incorporating those ideas into their messages so that their advertisements function most effectively, and have spent comparatively hefty sums of time and money to assess how audiences generally respond to them.[99]

The cultural significance of advertising grew exponentially in the twentieth century. Prior to that, the types of discourses that most frequently touched ordinary people's lives were things like sermons, political rhetoric, and advice of senior family members, but in the twentieth century those forms of communication became to at least a certain extent devalued, and as that happened, the authority of such discourses at the popular level lessened considerably. Meanwhile, advertising was one of the forms of discourse that became ever more central to people's daily experience, and the "space left as these influences have diminished has been filled largely by *the discourse through and about objects.*"[100] A corollary of the increasing centrality of advertising discourse in people's lives was a heightened commonality in frames of reference across larger regions.[101] Unlike the words of one's clergyman or father, the messages carried by advertising materials in the twentieth century reached a broad—increasingly, a mass—audience, establishing common cultural signals in very often a nationwide sense, and in a powerful enough way so as to remain stable and resilient over time and the course of political and economic events.[102] My study found such consistency in French and German advertising content regardless of the particular social group that read or sponsored the printing of a given publication. The pages that follow are filled with examples of advertisements with quite similar imagery and ideology regardless of the political orientations or intended audiences of the publications in which they appeared.

Chapters 1 and 2 analyze definitions of housewifery and motherhood, respectively, exploring the reformulations of these age-old categories of femininity in the interwar years. In chapter 3, issues of fashion, health, and beauty become the focus. In each of these arenas, the public sphere was reclaimed in popular discourse as a solely masculine domain, while definitions of femininity emphasized women's "natural" place in the domestic realm. Despite this powerful and widespread ideal, some publicity images did indeed depict women in the public sphere. As is shown in chapters 4 and 5—the former dealing with automobiles, the latter with employment and leisure—such portrayals were designed in such a way so as actually to reinforce the concept that women were not fit to operate and move about independently in public beyond their domestic duties and obligations, or without male guidance and approval. In such imagery, the modernized yet traditional woman attained fullest discursive expression.

CHAPTER ONE

DUTY AND EMPOWERMENT

Constructing Modern Housewives

Following the Great War, the political, economic, and social upheaval wrought by the conflict was traced, in part, in the popular imagination to an imbalance in gender roles caused by women's perceived appropriation of erstwhile masculine public spaces and roles during the war. As a result, a strong discursive focus on constructing an image of femininity more in keeping with traditional, prewar notions of womanhood developed in France, Germany, and, indeed, much of Europe. Thousands of women in each of the major belligerent nations had left the confines of the household to work in places like munitions factories to support the war effort, but postwar cultural ideology sought to define women's roles along far more familiar lines. One of the most important aspects of this interwar reconstruction of femininity was housewifery. Women were expected to remain in the domestic sphere to manage the affairs of the house. Such thinking sought to offset the worrisome image of masculinized "modern women" who worked and lived independently, allegedly attempting to deny men their primacy of place in the public sphere.

Interwar popular ideology in both nations revived an ideal of femininity in which women were expected to act as housewives. The array of functions and meanings attached to housewifery, however, was re-created in popular discourse in the wake of the Great War. One notable change was the new availability of technological consumer goods for the home during the interwar years. Items ranging from vacuum cleaners and refrigerators to improved laundry detergents were to play a pivotal role in the reconstruction of femininity around the ideal of housewifery in interwar France and Germany. Thanks largely to the availability of such goods, the discourse regarding interwar house-wives included a critical element separating it from prewar ideologies of house-hold work: an emphasis on rationalization and efficiency. Rationalization was a rapidly spreading concept in the 1920s that, focusing mainly on industry, promoted increased production through technological advancements, a re-organization of the methods of labor (such as the assembly line), and improved worker efficiency and discipline.[1]

In the case of Germany, Mary Nolan traces the application of rationalized ideology into the discourse of housework, noting its prevalence as a concept to which German housewives were to aspire. In fact, in Germany it was to lower-class women that much of the Weimar-era discourse on the rationaliza-tion of housewifery was directed. This discourse acknowledged that economic necessity would often require working-class women to engage in paid labor in order to supplement the family income. Since their jobs posed a major ob-stacle to spending time on housework, efficient and timely performance of their tasks as housewives was even more necessary.[2] Although grounded in a traditionally defined domestic, sphere, rationalization offered a path to mo-dernity for housewives.[3] Indeed, a number of women did adopt the precepts of rationalization in the organization of their household work, particularly by taking advantage of new domestic appliances.[4] Given the social reality that women were indeed aware of and involved with items of modernity, albeit in a domestic setting, popular discourse had to account for this change in order to create a coherent image of femininity in the postwar era.[5]

Thus the language of workplace rationalization was utilized in both France and Germany to encourage women to remain in the domestic sphere. This was a crucial discursive task: if women who had become accustomed during the war to working with items of modernity in industrial factories were to be con-vinced to return to the home full-time, a reconstruction of the discourse re-garding the traditional domestic sphere was required. The private realm would no longer be one of mindless tasks and tedious work; instead, new items of household technology would transform the women who used them into do-mestic engineers who could work with items of modernity as professionals, just as they had in wartime factories. The ideological focus centered upon con-vincing women that a return to the hearth would not, despite the home's as-sociation with tradition, be completely grounded in the past. Instead, people who toiled within the home were now performing work just as modern and professional as anyone else.[6] These newly available, efficient, modern tools of domestic labor would purportedly make household chores rationalized, pleasurable activities that were easy to perform. Women could utilize items of modernity and feel like professional workers but, since these items still tied them to the household, without raising cultural fears about "modern women."

As scholars such as Robert Frost and Eugen Weber caution in the French case, though, the pervasiveness of this ideology did not necessarily imply that such appliances were, in reality, present in most homes. In Germany, Detlev Peukert likewise maintains that mass consumption of new domestic technology did not come to fruition until after World War II. For example, whereas electrification was viewed in the United States as absolutely essential to the household in the interwar period,[8] a 1928 survey in Berlin found that less than half of all homes were equipped with electricity.[9] Indeed, in many ways household technology was not as important in the German vision of the rationalized home as it was in other countries, particularly during the Nazi era. Given the Nazi program of rearmament and autarky, fewer manufacturing efforts focused on household technologies.[10] Nevertheless, the important point lies not in the widespread existence of particular practices, but in the wide dissemination of the ideas themselves.[11] Even if housewives did not own particular pieces of domestic technology, knowledge of them was well established in interwar France and Germany by, for example, public exhibitions that showcased these goods.[12] Whether or not they could afford them, French and Germans alike developed a consumer mentality, aspiring to acquire such products and to live the lifestyles discursively embodied in them.

At the same time that this ideology of enjoyable housework empowered housewives by transforming housework into a modern, rational set of tasks, there was also a significant element of duty embedded in the discourse of housewifery. The labor-saving aspects of household technology might make the housewife's chores easier and quicker, but they also imposed larger responsibilities on the housewife related to the service of family and state.[13] Being an efficient housewife was a duty a woman performed for a higher purpose, not something she chose for personal reasons. Empowerment in housewifery discourse, then, was not an avenue toward complete liberation, but instead toward intensified duties and responsibilities grounded in traditional concepts of gender ideology. Mary Nolan claims that, at least for many, rationalization "was seen as the modern way to attain [an] old-fashioned ideal of home and family."[14]

In this chapter, I analyze the discourse of housewifery in interwar France

and Germany in order to highlight this dualistic nature of housewifery ideology. At the same time that women were presented an empowering image of
dignified, pleasurable housewifery in which they seemingly worked at their
leisure, a countervailing set of ideas reminded women that housewives still
owed a number of duties to family and nation that were of the utmost importance. Underlying all of these ideals were two key issues of the interwar
era that contributed to contemporary notions of housewifery. First, there was
the increasing social concern with women—especially middle-class women—
engaging in paid labor (see chapter 5). Second, a crucial factor in creating the
need to redefine the nature of housework (along with technological items)
was the disappearance of domestic servants from many wealthy French and
German households after World War I. This new lack of domestics meant
that "respectable" women would have to perform the chores of the house
themselves.

THE DECLINE OF DOMESTIC SERVICE

Housewifery ideology became particularly significant after World War I in
light of the decline in domestic service. In the nineteenth and early twentieth
centuries, domestic service had been one of the most common types of employment for lower-class females, but in the immediate aftermath of World
War I, a number of factors converged to make the employment of domestics
much less common.[15] Expanded occupational opportunities for working-class
women after the war were a key factor in this regard, as domestic service was
almost universally regarded as the lowest and least desirable form of paid labor.[16] In addition, acute financial dislocation during the interwar years, from
the earliest days after World War I through the Great Depression in the 1930s,
inhibited considerably the ability of the middle and upper classes to afford servants.[17] The German inflationary crisis of the early 1920s is well known, but
France also endured (albeit far less catastrophic) inflationary problems of its
own immediately after the war.[18] Other factors also played a role in the reduction of servants, from a bourgeois view of servants as an intrusion on a family's
privacy, to a reduction in the average bourgeois family size that mitigated the
need for a servant, to a cultural vilification of servants as untrustworthy.[19]

Taken together, these factors led to a significant decline in domestic service in both France and Germany in the interwar period. This situation was
potentially threatening to "respectable" women, who now were going to have
to handle the housework—and all the perceived indignity and drudgery that

But what was it?

came with it—on their own. This helps to explain why the appearance of new domestic technology in interwar France and Germany was so crucial. Housework had to be transformed discursively into an activity that "respectable" women could perform without sacrificing their status or dignity—which for middle- and upper-class women had long been contingent on having servants and thus not doing household chores themselves.[20] As Sibylle Meyer points out in the German case, in reality middle-class women in the years leading up to World War I did engage in some housework to complement the efforts of maids.[21] Nonetheless, popular ideology before the Great War in both Germany and France held that "respectable" women did not participate actively in the chores of the house. After the war, however, this was precisely what they were to do. This shift was reflected in advertisements and publicity materials from both nations, which, as they phased out images of domestic servants, began appealing directly to *ménagères, maîtresses de maison,* or *Hausfrauen* as the mantle-bearers of household labor early in the 1920s.

In the earliest postwar years in France and Germany, a number of publicity materials for specific products and stores still focused on domestic servants as the people responsible for housework. In Germany, for example, a 1922 advertisement for Kunze soap shows a domestic servant carrying an oversized package of the product.[22] Meanwhile, a 1921 ad for Bamberger & Hertz stores pictures a domestic servant washing a shirt and trousers by hand in a large washing basin.[23] In this latter advertisement, it is noteworthy also that the work being performed is the traditional, rather tedious work historically ascribed to domestic servants; there is no washing machine, and the servant must clean the clothes manually. At times, advertising images associated servants with modern technological products, but these were exceptional cases rather than the norm.[24] Generally, ads with servants focused on nontechnologized and nonrationalized methods of housework.

Images of servants in German ads diminished over the first half of the 1920s. While some ads, for example those of O-Cedar (a company that produced goods such as floor polish), still continued to feature domestics prominently as late as 1926,[25] already by that year advertisements in Germany that pictured servants had declined considerably. Plus, even where domestic servants did appear in advertisements from the middle of the 1920s onward, their role was often merely that of a foil to the emerging rationalized housewife. An interesting transition took place in popular imagery wherein the *Hausfrau* began to confront and displace servants. This process is illustrated by an advertisement for Versale washing detergent from 1927, in which a smiling housewife thrusts a package of Versale in the face of an aghast and haggard-looking domestic servant, who is carrying a washing board in one hand and a scrubbing brush in the other.[26] The implication was clear: a major shift in the nature of household labor was under way. No longer a grueling exercise requiring intense physical exertion, housework was now a pleasant activity the *Hausfrau* could be happy to perform.

In an interesting reversal, domestic servants began to reappear in the imagery of the German popular press in the late 1930s, although certainly not to the same extent as before, particularly in the Nazis' own newspaper, the *Völkischer Beobachter.*[27] There are two likely reasons behind this shift in imagery. First, as Jill Stephenson notes, given the pronounced emphasis on military production in the late 1930s in Germany, a return to the employment of domestics could potentially reduce demand for the manufacture of labor-saving technological devices for the home.[28] Second, the Nazi push to get more women into the workforce (see chapter 5) may well have made the prospect of a domestic servant attractive to women who would now be employed outside the home and thus have less time for their domestic work.

In France in the early 1920s, the first postwar depictions of household work, like their German counterparts, pictured domestic servants in ads for products such as Layton eggs and L'Ozi soap.[29] Two cartoons from the annual calendar of the Bon Marché in 1923, moreover, not only refer to work being done in many cases by servants, but also highlight the increasing reasons employers have for dissatisfaction with their domestics. In the first cartoon, a very rotund servant is being chastised by a dismayed man (who is rather portly himself) for having gained thirty kilos since being hired.[30] Even more noteworthy is the second cartoon from the 1923 *agenda,* which suggests incompetence among domestics. The cartoon shows a husband, wife, child, and their guest seated at a table having a meal. The husband and wife look mortified as the visitor, pointing to the dishware, says that he can tell that Madame has changed servants, because the fingerprints on the plates are different than they used to be.[31]

Even though domestic servants continued to appear in ads for products like Phoscao and Banania brands of sugar as late as 1926 and 1927,[32] by that time the number of images featuring servants was diminishing considerably. From 1928 onward, in spite of the occasional exception,[33] portrayals of servants were comparatively scarce. Indeed, from the middle of the 1920s onward, indications of the switch in household labor from domestic servants to housewives were evident in French discourse. An article entitled "The Domain of the Kitchen" from the *agenda* of the Bon Marché from 1925 declares that the situation has changed from bygone days when an "army of domestics" made lavish residences possible.[34] The same store's 1933 calendar also addresses this issue in a paragraph of text under the header "The Crisis of Domestics." Explaining the flight of servants from French households, it assures housewives that completing domestic chores themselves is perfectly acceptable, because knowing how to perform household tasks has now become "a sign of intelligence."[35] The following page of the *agenda* includes another paragraph, this one entitled "The House without Domestics." It discusses various new technologies available to the French housewife, such as vacuum cleaners, that were replacing "the deficiency of domestics."[36] Once again in this case, the issue of servants' shortcomings plays a key role in legitimizing the household labor of "respectable" women.

As in Germany, the middle of the first postwar decade in France witnessed a number of images transforming servants into merely an obsolete foil for the emergent efficient housewife. In the top-left corner of an O-Cedar ad, a box next to the word "YESTERDAY" contains a drawing of a servant scrubbing a floor on her hands and knees. Meanwhile, an opposing image in the main part of the ad, labeled "TODAY," shows a smiling *ménagère* mopping a floor with little effort. The text of the advertisement emphasizes the time and energy that can now be saved in doing household chores, thanks to products like O-Cedar.[37] Moreover, there were some suggestions that new, more efficient tools of housekeeping available to the housewife would actually fill in as modern domestic servants. An advertising brochure distributed for Calor electric washing machines, for instance, assures Madame that owning the item will allow her to "possess" an "ideal servant."[38]

EMPOWERING THE NEW HOUSEWIFE
Identifying, Educating, and Glamorizing

As the imagery surrounding servants was fading, a set of publicity images associating housewives with household labor independent of domestics became apparent starting in the immediate postwar period in both France and Germany. This process involved identifying housewives as the new bearers of the burdens of domestic labor and appealing directly to them without reference to servants. At the simplest level, such a process meant utilizing labels that would be applied to housewives throughout the interwar period. In Germany, the term *Hausfrau* was invoked repeatedly in advertisements, often in bold or large print, identifying the audience to whom such messages were directed. The term was printed frequently in advertisements for companies ranging from margarine producers to sewing machine manufacturers and even to department stores.[39] Even more numerous were ads that, while not necessarily using the word *Hausfrau,* depicted German housewives performing household work such as cooking, cleaning, serving the family at the table, and sewing.[40] The situation in France was much the same, with added complexity provided by the existence of two different terms for identifying housewives: *ménagère* and *maîtresse de maison.*[41] As in Germany, an array of products advertised to women in France invoked specifically one of these two terms.[42] In another close parallel to the German case, more ubiquitous than these ads were ones picturing housewives engaged in some facet of domestic work, even if neither *ménagères* nor *maîtresses de maison* were directly mentioned.[43]

Given that these housewives were about to begin doing the household work themselves for the first time (at least according to popular thinking), it should not be surprising that, beyond appealing directly to housewives, publicity images also sought to help educate these women about their new domestic tasks. Quite commonly, recipes were offered to the new housewife, providing her with ideas and instructions on the preparation of dishes that she would be cooking for the first time without domestic help.[44] German advertisements for products such as gravy, margarine, and spices often included instructions for various dishes that could be made with the products in question.[45] In addition, on the women's pages of some German publications, recipes would also be included, often on a thematic basis, such as ideas for Christmas dishes.[46] Such recipes were printed less frequently in French advertisements,[47] but the pages of the annual *agendas* of the *grands magasins* perennially were filled with recipe ideas for the French housewife.[48] The incorporation of recipes was so commonplace that occasionally a store's *agenda* offered creative spins on suggesting recipes, such as the 1924 *agenda* of the Galeries Lafayette, which contained various thematic collections of recipes, among them "The Beautiful Poultry of France" and "250 Ways to Prepare Fish."[49]

Other educational messages for the French and German housewife appeared as well in the decades of the 1920s and 1930s. The Galeries Lafayette *agenda* for 1923, for instance, includes between the months of July and August a half-page interlude under the heading: "Attention! Is this egg fresh?" An accompanying paragraph carefully explains, with the help of a series of illustrations, how to judge the freshness of an egg by submerging it in water and taking note of its buoyancy (when it sinks, an egg is fresh, according to the text; if it floats, it is no longer fit to eat).[50] Other *agendas* provided tips on home interior décor and entertaining guests in one's home.[51]

Other methods of educating the new housewife allowed for more active participation on her part. A good example can be found in the German case in a series of "instructional days" sponsored by the Thügina Company in Leipzig in 1921. In an advertisement for the event, the large- and bold-printed term *Hausfrauen* headlines the ad. The text of the advertisement promises a free opportunity for housewives to learn how to use their kitchen appliances more effectively by coming to educational sessions run by the company in its "model kitchen."[52] A similar service was offered in Paris by the Bon Marché, as detailed in the store's 1925 *agenda*. Part of an article on running a modern kitchen refers to a demonstration service wherein every Saturday the store sponsored a live demonstration of the operations of a new kitchen appliance. The article refers to the weekly demonstrations as a veritable "school for housewives" that has drawn the interest of "all women."[53] Thus a body of educational opportunities of this type existed for the betterment of French and German housewives in the interwar period. Such information, advice, and lessons served not only to acquaint housewives with the duties for which they were now to be responsible, but also presented those duties in an attractive and empowering way, even to the point of offering instructional sessions at which women could gain a pseudo-professional training.

In a similar way, empowering language and imagery frequently glamorized housewifery by likening it to professional occupations. For example, a 1927 article on housekeeping in the German monthly *Westermanns Monatshefte* compares the work of housewives to that of doctors and businessmen.[54] An ad from 1934 for the Fink Company also makes such a comparison (fig. 1). On the left side of the ad, a depiction of a man depositing money into a safe appears under the words "A safe in the office." On the right side of the ad, below the words "An 'Eisfink' [a Fink refrigerator model] in the kitchen," is an image of a woman depositing food into a refrigerator, equating her labor and equipment with those of a professional, office setting.[55]

Another method of glamorizing housewifery in the interwar period rested with the construction of new items of domestic technology as intrinsically "modern" and innovative, thus uplifting housewifery from what was so re-

FIG. 1. Ad for the Fink Company, *Westermanns Monatshefte*
(September 1934, advertising section)

cently defined as tedious, manual labor befitting only a lower-class servant
into a profession on the cutting edge of modernity in which women of virtually any social stature could proudly participate. Ellen Furlough writes of
French interwar housewives that "their status within the household was to be
enhanced as rational agents of progress and arbiters of domestic modernity."[56]
First and foremost, such ideology was asserted by emphasizing that the products in question were "modern" items, or that they transformed a domestic
interior into a "modern" home, especially with respect to electrical items.[57]
In a similar manner, a German ad for Lindberg vacuum cleaners declares the
Lindberg brand to be "a more splendid vacuum." The header of the ad, entirely in capital letters, is "PROGRESS."[58] Thus modernity and progress were
made an inextricable part of housewifery, casting aside long-standing cultural baggage about denigration and drudgery as unavoidable consequences
of housework.

Closely tied to this focus on modernity and progress were intimations in
both countries that housework no longer epitomized unchanging tradition,
but was instead centered upon innovation. Some French advertisements focused on the novelty of being able to serve cold drinks in hot weather, thanks

to newly available refrigerators. A 1936 ad shows two women sitting at a dining table discussing GEM refrigerators as they drink (presumably cold) beverages from glasses on the table. One of the women declares: "My husband is delighted: he loves so many fresh drinks!"[59] Likewise, a 1927 Frigidaire ad shows a smiling woman glancing out her window on a warm day as she puts ice in a glass she is holding (fig. 2). The ad's focus is the delight that her guests will experience from being able to have fresh, cold drinks in summer.[60]

In Germany, this discourse of innovation was focused less on individual items of domestic technology than on the impact of those technological goods and rationalization methods as a whole, particularly in the kitchen.[61] This was made clear in a German article on housekeeping from 1927 that addresses the innovations and steps necessary to create a "modern" kitchen. Rather than being devoted primarily to technological inventions, the article focuses instead on rationalized methods of organizing and administering the kitchen, from the promotion of more "practical" kitchen utensils and appliances to an illustration detailing the need for uniformity and standardization in sizes of jars

FIG. 2. Frigidaire ad, *Le Matin* (23 September 1927)

and lids.[62] A discussion of the rationalization of the kitchen was likewise at issue in a 1939 article from France. The article encourages housewives to organize the physical layout of their kitchens in such a way as to minimize the time and effort needed to perform tasks in it.[63]

The Joy (and Liberation) of Being a Housewife

An interwar advertising brochure for Calor electric washing machines vows that, upon reading the testimonials from reputedly actual customers contained within the booklet: "You will be delighted to learn that now you can liberate yourself from all the worries of laundering by using the Calor Electric Washer in your home"[64] That statement encapsulates the repeated intimation of publicity materials that modern technological goods were transforming the chores of the home into an easy, simple, and even enjoyable set of tasks. French and German advertisements for household products ceaselessly stressed that, by using the advertised product, a housewife could complete her domestic labor more easily and quickly than before. More often than not depicting a happy, smiling woman obviously enjoying the benefits of the goods in question, ads for products like vacuums, refrigerators, stoves, and water heaters proclaim that they greatly simplify housework and ease the domestic tasks of the housewife.[65] Other ads promise similarly that particular domestic chores related to the advertised products will ensure that housework can be done without difficulty, fatigue, or any need to monitor the operation of a product (such as a washing machine or stove).[66]

With the departure of servants and the availability of new items of domestic technology forcing a rethinking of the nature of housework, a key part of the ideology of modern housewifery was its distinctly unintensive nature. A French ad for Persil laundry detergent from 1938, in which two women discuss the subject of doing the laundry, makes this point. The first woman is attempting to counsel the second woman, who cannot achieve the same degree of whiteness in her laundry as the first woman. The second woman insists that she already scrubs her wash "energetically," and asks what more she could possibly do. The first woman, declaring that "it's not the work that counts," reveals that by using Persil, one's laundry will become cleaner than ever before, and without any intensive labor.[67] Similarly, a 1931 ad for Electro-Lux floor polishers shows a woman scrubbing the floor on her hands and knees. The ad's header reads: "Scrub no more." The text of the ad assures the woman that she can avoid all of the common physical problems associated with traditional housework by acquiring an Electro-Lux floor polisher, which will reduce significantly both the amount of labor she has to perform and the intensiveness of it.[68]

From Germany, a similar advertisement for Burnus laundry detergent makes the same point. In the ad, which tells its story in three boxes with illustrations and text, one *Hausfrau* lends her expertise and advice to another, who still scrubs her wash by hand. In the first frame, the wise housewife enters as the second woman is hunched over her laundry with scrubbing brush and washboard. Asking why the second woman still would do her wash in this manner, the first woman instructs her to use Burnus. In the final two frames of the ad, the second woman tries Burnus under the guidance of the first woman, and indeed her wash comes out cleaner than ever before, with only "half the work" of manual washing.[69] Another ad, this one for Henko laundry soap, is quite similar in tone. In it, a woman standing at a washing basin with a washing board rubs her brow, obviously tired and perspiring from her labor. In front of her, a smiling woman declares, "You do not need this anymore, Frau May!" and explains the labor-saving benefits of Henko.[70] Thus modern housework seemed to offer a real liberation for French and German housewives from the tedium and indignity of old-fashioned, labor-intensive domestic chores.

A further element of this aspect of housewifery discourse was the suggestion that these technologies did not just save work, but actually accomplished nothing less than magical or miraculous acts.[71] A 1937 article from France, which discusses a recent exposition featuring gas-powered appliances, refers to gas as a "magician" due to its ability to "tame" the chores of the household.[72] A couple of ads for Sauter electric stoves make similar points; the focus of these ads is the housewife's ability simply to insert food into the oven and then return later when the cooking is done, having in the interim done no work or expended any energy on the cooking process. One of the two ads refers to the stove's ability to do the cooking completely by itself as nothing less than a "miracle."[73]

In fact, advertisements from both countries suggested that household labor was now so easy to perform that even a child could do it. The best example from Germany is an ad for Cirine floor polish that, while addressed to the "dear *Hausfrau*," features an image of a small girl polishing a floor (fig. 3). The text of the ad declares that this work is "mere child's play."[74] Such phrasing

FIG. 3. Ad for Cirine floor polish, *Illustrirte Zeitung* (18 February 1926)

also is employed in a French ad for Electro-Lux vacuums and floor polishers; the ad states that the polishers have made an "intolerable chore" into "child's play."[75] Further, a number of French ads, while not referring to children in words, feature them as the subjects of illustrations in their ads, thus implying that these young people can operate products such as ovens and irons (which they are indeed shown using in some ads).[76]

Along with the labor-saving nature of modern housewifery came a time-saving element as well. In a Burnus detergent ad from Germany, for instance, a housewife named Anna disputes the time it takes to do the wash with a for-hire washing woman. The "Waschfrau" says it takes her two days do all of the washing, but Anna reveals that she can do it all in a single day with Burnus.[77] Moreover, an ad for iMi cleaner, under the header "How many hours does a *Hausfrau* have in the day?" also discusses the product's time-efficient nature, explaining that, without iMi, a *Hausfrau* could start cleaning very early in the morning, but still not finish completely by the end of the day.[78] In France, the language was often quite similar. A 1937 O-Cedar ad promises that, with its broom, one can "complete in one hour the work of an afternoon."[79] Another ad for O-Cedar brooms shows a woman smiling as she looks up from her sweeping toward a clock. The header of the ad reads: "8 O'clock! Her housework is already done."[80]

These two related threads of savings of time and savings of effort coalesced into a discussion of the newfound free time of the housewife, since her household chores would allegedly neither take very long to perform nor drain her energy. Several scholars have argued that in reality, such ideology often proved misleading, since due to the perceived efficiency of items of domestic technology, women were expected to perform more household chores, and to do so more frequently, than had been the case before 1920.[81] Regardless, in the popular imagination, a strong belief persisted in the time- and labor-saving nature of modern housewifery, especially in France, where an emphasis on leisure time was an important part of the discourse of modern housewifery (at least for middle-class housewives; working-class wives would not earn free time by modernizing their housework, but simply would make balancing their waged labor and household responsibilities more manageable).[82] A Calor washing machine ad from 1936 encourages women to keep leisure time in mind when considering buying a washer: "Think, Madame, about numerous hours of leisure that you are going to earn each week."[83] Although there was less emphasis on the leisure time of housewives in Germany, an example is provided by an ad from 1926 for Erdal, a shoe-shining product (fig. 4). It shows a smiling *Hausfrau* sitting in a chair reading a newspaper. The ad states that "a prudent *Hausfrau* always finds time for relaxation."[84]

Despite not promoting as strong a vision of leisure and relaxation for housewives, German discourse, like French commentary on the subject, insisted that modern housewifery would bring joy and happiness to the housewife. German ads for laundry detergents, for instance, report the "pleasure" that wash day has become and the "enthusiasm" of *Hausfrauen* for such products.[85] The most visually striking ads of this variety assert and display the excitement of numerous *Hausfrauen* for new domestically related goods, such as a 1930 ad for iMi in which housewives are anxiously reaching out of every window and balcony of an apartment complex, thrilled at the arrival just outside the building of a figure carrying a crate filled with iMi cleaner.[86] In France, an ad for Sauter electric ovens similarly notes the "pleasure" with which women can cook thanks to the technological advancement and quality of the product.[87] Further, an article on the uses of electricity for housework promises that electricity in the home will make Madame's domestic life happier.[88] By establishing the easy, time-saving, and labor-saving nature of modern house-

FIG. 4. Ad for Erdal, a shoe-shining product, *Illustrirte Zeitung*
(21 January 1926)

work, French and German discourses promoted a vision of housewifery largely grounded in the joys and liberation from tedious, old-fashioned housekeeping inherent in being a modern housewife.

Making the Home Attractive

Another important means by which French and German cultural ideology (especially the former) sought to empower the modern housewife was through the construction of the modern domestic sphere as a place where women's traditionally perceived aptitudes regarding taste, style, and beauty could shine through in full force. In a sense, this aspect of housewifery ideology suggested that domestic labor in the interwar years represented a key improvement over paid employment, as the realm of the housewife was to be an attractive and aesthetically pleasing environment.

Perhaps the most straightforward method of promoting a vision of pleasing household aesthetics was to tout the beauty that a product would bring to the home. Most commonly, a cleaning product claimed to create a beautiful home interior. Such was the case in a 1937 ad from Germany for Seifix floor polish, in which a smiling woman is pictured mopping the floor. Identified by the ad as Frau Schwan, she shows off her newly cleaned floor by declaring: "This is the beauty of Seifix."[89] French examples were often quite similar. A 1934 advertisement for Arthur Martin ovens describes their all-white exterior as "beautiful."[90] Similarly, an ad for GEM refrigerators discusses the aesthetic merits of the appliance at considerable length. Taking the form of a conversation between two women having a drink at a table, the ad touts the product's pleasant appearance, including references to its porcelain finish and chrome-plated latches and hinges.[91]

Along similar lines, other ads from both France and Germany invoke aesthetic value by referring to a particular consumer good as being stylish, in good taste, or elegant.[92] One example from Germany is a 1920 ad for Degea irons, which calls the items "tasteful."[93] A 1937 ad for furniture-seller Rosipalhaus assures the reader that its furniture will help to create an "elegant" apartment.[94] French publicity materials utilized "elegance" and "elegant style" as selling points as well.[95] Similarly, a 1933 article dealing with electricity and housework declares that an electric water heater can be installed in the home "without harming the aesthetic of the room" where it is placed.[96] Ads for Singer sewing machines occasionally mentioned the aesthetically pleasing cases in which Singer machines were housed. One such ad states that, with Singer's encased models of sewing machines, "your sewing machine will brighten your interior" rather than detract from its appearance.[97] Even laundry areas could be constructed as visually pleasing, as an article from *L'Illustration* from 1937 demonstrates. In its discussion of a recent exposition at which a model laundry was featured, the article highlights the "charming" appearance of the laundry room on display, and directly connects it with the happiness of the housewife, asking rhetorically about such aesthetic values in a laundry (and, by extension, in the domestic interior as a whole), "is that not the dream of every *maîtresse de maison?*"[98]

In addition to such aesthetic pleasure in the home, French and German advertisements promoted, as a corollary to their vision of an attractive home interior, the importance of comfort in it. The significance of this emphasis on comfort as part of beautifying the home cannot be overlooked. In his analysis of the marketing of electricity to American housewives in the early twentieth century, James Williams argues that, in spite of the cost- and labor-saving features of electricity, officials in the electrical industry felt that perhaps the strongest selling point to American housewives about the desirability of electrical power was the "'coziness and comfort'" it could provide.[99] For instance, a 1937 advertisement from Germany for Rosipalhaus, a furniture dealer, shows a smiling husband and wife—she sitting in a chair looking through a book, while he stands bending over her shoulder. The ad promises that, with Rosipalhaus furniture, "you could scarcely imagine your home more comfortable and more beautiful."[100] French sources shared this emphasis on comfort. In a full-page ad for Lux, above an image of a woman placing items into a refrigerator appears the word "comfort" over which, in smaller type, "Electro-Lux" is superimposed. The ad promises, among other things, that Lux vacuum cleaners, refrigerators, and floor polishers will increase the comfort of the home interior.[101] A 1932 article on electricity in the household, moreover, discusses notions of "modern comfort" by contrasting them to evidence from the ruins of Pompeii. The article quickly determines that, despite the existence of heating systems and running water in the age of the Roman Empire, the recent emergence of electricity as an important component of the home interior has made modern French concepts and accoutrements of comfort "without any doubt very superior" to Roman-era ideas and realities on the subject.[102]

Closely related to such images of comfort in the home were instances in which the silence of appliances, particularly refrigerators and vacuum cleaners, was held out as a central selling point. Creating a comfortable household involved also making the interior pleasant to the ears. A good example from Germany is a 1938 ad for Siemens refrigerators. Quite simple in design and execution, the ad succinctly promises silent operation, in addition to vibration-free and automatic functioning.[103] In the French case, ads for Electro-Lux, Frigidaire, Kelvinator, and Crosley refrigerators all made the same kinds of assertions about silence and automatic operation.[104] The French company that most frequently invoked silence as a hallmark of its technological devices was Lux, which actually built an entire advertising campaign around the issue. "Under the Sign of Silence" became a company slogan that was printed prominently in Lux vacuum cleaner and refrigerator ads.[105]

A couple of French advertisements go so far as to relate the use of modern domestic goods with the beauty, elegance, and charm of the housewife herself. A 1923 Lux detergent advertisement, for example, shows a woman bedecked in a formal dress holding a box of Lux soap in one hand and a piece of cloth in the other. The ad declares that "the elegant woman" cleans with Lux.[106] The im-

FIG. 5. Ad for Sauter electric stoves, *Gringoire* (13 May 1932)

pression from this advertisement that modern housework is eminently compatible with remaining a "respectable" woman—formalwear and all—is inescapable. Further, an ad from 1932 for Sauter electric stoves depicts a frazzled housewife who, after using an old gas stove, finds her hands and cheeks blackened (fig. 5). The ad informs her that using such an outmoded appliance is "not good for your hands or your complexion."[107] Thus, in this case, one could salvage her personal appearance thanks to the wonders of Sauter electric cookers. No longer was housework the sole purview of allegedly untrustworthy, immoral servants; rather, it had been transformed by items of modernity into a profession in which the housewives administering the household retained beauty, charm, and elegance—that is, the quintessential elements of "respectable" femininity.

Perfecting Quality, Finalizing Happiness

The final significant way in which French and German ideology empowered the modern housewife between the world wars was through presenting new products as absolutely perfect, signaling to the interwar housewife that her tasks could be done with similar perfection, improving exponentially on the notorious inefficiency of domestic servants. Claims of perfection extended to various household products.[108] A French ad for Cornue cookers from 1928 shows a woman standing beside the appliance, and claims that it "cooks and glazes to perfection" without requiring any human intervention during the cooking process.[109] An ad for Sanitor washers that also features a female figure declares that the machines accomplish their work "in a perfect manner."[110] In the German case, a couple of advertisements for Persil soap likewise stake a claim to perfection *(Vollendung)*.[111]

The products that claimed perfection most frequently were laundry detergents. Advertisements for various brands of these soaps routinely promised perfectly white linens and perfectly clean clothes for the housewife using the product in question. In Germany, detergent manufacturers such as Persil, Henko-iMi, and Burnus printed advertisements of this variety.[112] In the French case, the most commonly advertised brand of this type was Persil.[113] At its apex in the late 1930s, this form of Persil ad usually involved an image of a woman with her husband, children, or a friend, in which a piece of white fabric or clothing that she has washed with Persil has gotten so radiantly white that it makes other purportedly white fabrics appear gray in comparison.[114] The implication that such cleanliness could bring the housewife happiness is made directly in a couple of Lux ads from the late 1930s. In each of them, a series of images with accompanying text reveals how a distraught woman, unhappy with the state of the cleanliness of her laundry, gains happiness from the capabilities of Lux. By the end of each ad, women who had been in tears at the start become smiling, proud housewives.[115] These ads show how centrally a woman's ability to perform her housework weighed on her self-worth in popular ideology; according to interwar French and German cultural ideology, a modern housewife, with the help of high-quality household goods, could enjoy a more general happiness in life.

Certainly much of this ideology was simply grounded in exaggerated claims by the advertiser intended to sell the product. I would argue, however, that in these examples, something more significant also is evident. French and German discourses were further empowering the new, modern housewives of the interwar age by assuring them of the perfectibility of their own domestic labor (again, perhaps an exaggerated claim to make, but that is precisely the point), thus completing the process of transforming housewifery from an onerous burden into an empowering career.

IMPARTING THE DUTIES OF THE NEW HOUSEWIFE

Coexisting with the discourse of empowerment in both France and Germany was a simultaneous countervailing emphasis on the modern housewife's duties to family and nation.[116] Such messages of duty and responsibility could be made quite subtly, and even melded with empowering language and ideals. New items of technology might make housework itself more enjoyable and even effect a feeling of liberation, but the modern housewife, according to popular ideology, was performing this work ultimately not for her own self-fulfillment, but for the betterment of others. Those who were figuratively to profit from household rationalization were foremost husbands and children, the national economy, and the state, not housewives themselves. Housewives' happiness was merely incidental, despite the ceaseless discursive emphasis on such joys and wonders for the housewife.[117]

The conclusion of the discussion of leisure for housewives provides evidence of this. As mentioned previously, there was less emphasis on leisure for housewives in German popular ideology. New domestic products for women in the interwar era were not seen primarily as leading to increased leisure time for the *Hausfrau* to relax and enjoy, but rather their time- and labor-saving nature was expected to provide German housewives, middle-class and working-class alike, with more time to devote to the needs of their husbands and children.[118] In France, although there was a stronger vocabulary of housewifely leisure, evidence there also suggested that attention to children would be an intrinsic part of household rationalization. An advertising brochure for Calor electric washing machines notes that the product will allow the *maîtresse de maison* to enjoy "numerous hours of leisure" that can be devoted "to your children, to your family, to reading, to your preferred leisure activities."[119] Thus French materials paid some heed to the issue of children and the family as an outgrowth of the housewife's newfound free time, but made it clear that this was to coexist with leisure time.

It should be noted that notions about duty and responsibility pervaded housewifery discourse throughout the interwar years. Changing economic conditions and differing political regimes could certainly result in alterations in specific parts of this ideology or shifts in emphasis, but the overall nature of this discourse remained remarkably stable given the political, economic, and social turmoil that was inescapable in interwar Germany and France. A good example of a shift in emphasis that did not alter the fundamental nature of housewifery ideology can be seen in the transition from Weimar Germany to the totalitarian Nazi regime. As Nancy Reagin effectively shows, the context of self-sacrifice by German housewives changed after 1933. During the Weimar Republic, housewives' responsibilities were cast in terms of benefits that would accrue to their families. With the advent of Nazism, and especially with the Hitlerian government's focus on national autarky, the benefits of rationalization were seen as accruing to the nation as a whole. Indeed, the goals and ideas of a number of Weimar housewives' groups were so compatible with Nazi ones on this subject that, as Reagin shows, the Nazi government was able to absorb such groups under its banner (and grant them greater funding). Thus the shift in emphasis between the Weimar and Nazi periods did not necessarily suggest a reversal in policies and ideologies vis-à-vis the housewife; indeed, the ideas were so closely linked that there was a relatively seamless integration of Weimar housewives' groups into the Nazi fold.[120]

The Healthiness of the Hearth

A box of text printed on the title page of the 1933 *agenda* of the Bon Marché illustrates the way in which the emphasis on empowerment could coexist with that of duty for housewives. Addressed to the *maîtresse de maison,* the text states:

> The house! . . . Kingdom of the woman . . .
>
> It is still necessary that the sovereign of this kingdom is not at all content with ruling it, but that she also knows how to govern it. For her role is not at all preoccupied solely with the affection of her entourages and the tributes we pay to her. It should be, to the contrary, that of a true manager, conscious of the complicated administration that falls to her, concerned with expending in it her devotion and her activity, jealously guarding the order, health, and peace of the *foyer.*[121]

Several pages later, the same *agenda* states that the term *maîtresse de maison* signifies not just women's mastery in the home, but also that she has "a special and very delicate mission to accomplish" there, for "every woman has the *obligation* of organizing her home, maintaining it and managing it."[122] One of the most important parts of this obligation was her responsibility to keep the home clean and healthy for the well-being of the family. In turn, this ideology of hygiene aimed to benefit the state as well; due to the loss of life suffered in

World War I and perceived low birth rates in the interwar era, natality was a central concern of both French and Germans. A hygienic hearth could assist the maintenance of population levels in this context, and thus would serve to strengthen the nation as well.[123] Yet the concern for household cleanliness was certainly not new; Mary Lynn Stewart provides a fascinating analysis of the "'sanitary domain'" that French officials sought to create as early as 1880.[124] What was different in the interwar period was in large part the new and improved technologies that seemingly made it more possible—and allegedly enjoyable and "liberating" for the housewife—to achieve this goal.[125]

The importance of ensuring a hygienic environment in the home as a means of protecting the health of those within it was emphasized frequently in French and German advertisements for products such as refrigerators, soaps, and vacuums, all of which were thought to contribute to a "hygienic" household.[126] One 1939 advertisement for iMi cleaner, which states that "the kitchen is the calling card of the *Hausfrau,*" pictures a sparkling kitchen as well as an image of a housewife bending over to study the floor intently. The ad's header poses the following question to German *Hausfrauen:* "Could you eat lunch off of the floor?"[127] If the answer was no, the housewife risked bringing potentially catastrophic ill-health into her home, as a French ad for Lux vacuum cleaners makes clear. The ad touts the cleaning abilities of the Lux vacuum, assuring that it disinfects effectively. The ad equates not purchasing a Lux vacuum with welcoming germs and sickness into the home: "Electric cleaning is a necessity of the first order. By avoiding the purchase of a 'LUX VACUUM'—which lasts ten years—you prefer to risk daily illness, infectiousness, epidemic."[128]

The issue of avoiding ill-health was raised with respect not just to cleanliness, but to keeping foods in the home fresh as well. Many refrigerator ads from both countries emphasized the need to prevent food from spoiling, offering refrigerators as a health-saving solution to spoilage and freshness concerns.[129] In some French ads, specific references were made to children or the family, reminding French housewives that health was not an abstract issue, but one that directly influenced those closest to them.[130] Closely related to the need to serve unspoiled foods was a renewed emphasis on providing the family with foods that were high in nutritional value.[131] In an ad from Germany for Palmin vegetable oil, a housewife carries a hot dish. Exactly what she has cooked is not specified, but the ad nonetheless states: "Quite wholesome—that is important!"[132] Moreover, an advertisement for the fruit industry that pictures two *Hausfrauen* declares that a "clever" housewife knows that fruit is not only tasty, but also contributes to a healthy diet.[133] In the French case, the best example is an advertisement for a drink called Ovomaltine. The ad's header reads: "Nature and science in the service of health." The text of the ad proclaims Ovomaltine as the highest expression of nutrition, as it combines the best elements of natural foods, milk, and eggs, as well as new scientific capabilities to enhance the content of vitamins and other nutritional essentials.[134]

Submission to Masculine Authority

The housewife's duty to submit to masculine authority was also emphasized during the interwar period. While the belief that women were to be submissive to masculine authority certainly had been common in the pre–World War I era, this feature of gender discourse became a powerful imperative in the wake of the Great War. Women's increasingly visible involvement in the public sphere during the war elicited a postwar backlash. Cultural discomfort escalated over the perception that promiscuous, independent women were usurping discursive masculine authority in the public arena.[135] Immediately after the war, it was widely held that women's gains during the conflict, as well as the fact that many women had run the household completely on their own while men were away fighting in battle, had increased the power of wives vis-à-vis their husbands' authority in the home. The fear endured that women would appropriate patriarchal authority in the household even after their husbands had returned.[136] As a result, both French and German popular discourse dealt with the issue of gender authority in the home, seeking to reestablish masculine authority over women. This cultural task was frequently linked to issues of housewifery. The modern housewife, empowered though she may have been in some areas, had a firm responsibility to accept masculine authority.

This process had several facets and took a number of forms. Most directly, the authority of the husband over the housewife within the home was made clear. In a French ad for Pèr'Lustucru pasta, for example, a two-frame cartoon making up part of the advertisement is instructive. In the first frame, the housewife brings a plate of pasta to the table where her husband and child are sitting. Visibly angry, the husband scolds his stunned and saddened wife, complaining that he "has had enough" unappetizing pasta. In the second frame, set at some time in the future, the housewife sits with guests, happily telling them that her husband loves to eat pasta now that she buys Pèr'Lustucru, for it is light and tasty.[137] A Frigidaire ad further makes clear the contrasts between the primacy of the husband's pleasures in the home and the housewife's responsibility to facilitate them. Specifically addressed to men, this advertisement informs Monsieur of the various "pleasures," from chilled drinks and ice to delicious foods, that he will be able enjoy with the advertised refrigerator throughout the year, regardless of the weather. Meanwhile, in a section of the ad labeled "for your wife," the language, although couched in a pleasant tone, focuses on the wife's domestic duties rather than her own desires, such as constantly having healthy foods in the house and the need to cook a variety of dishes.[138] This theme was also evident in a German ad for iMi cleaner from 1939. The ad depicts a man, Herr Becker, sitting leisurely with legs crossed as he reads a newspaper. The ad explains that Herr Becker's wife has made him happy by getting the balcony of their domicile so clean with iMi that it is now his favorite place in their home, and as such he takes his newspaper there each morning to read it.[139]

Other publicity materials were more subtle in attempting to reestablish male authority over housewives. Rather than promoting husbandly authority directly, some sought to establish a general masculine dominance over women with respect to the tasks of housewifery. For example, an ad from Germany for Persil detergent features an image of a housewife standing at a retail counter. Behind the counter and literally elevated above her stands a man in a coat and tie. The woman's question to him forms the ad's header: "Means of rejuvenation for the wash . . . is there such a thing?"[140] The man's response forms the bulk of the ad's text; he informs her that by using Persil detergent, she can get her laundry cleaner and ensure that her fabrics last for a long time without being damaged in the washing process.[141] In the French case, a 1934 ad for Electro-Lux vacuum cleaners pictures a man carrying a vacuum (fig. 6). The advertisement is unique in its utilization of the first person—the ad is essentially dictated to the reader by the male figure. The pictured man, who offers to bring demonstrations into the homes of interested parties, promises that, among other things, "I bring comfort and health to your home, by new devices, new methods."[142] Thus in this advertisement as well, a masculine figure purveys knowledge of a new item of domestic technology to an intended female audience. Along similar lines, an illustration and accompanying text from the 1928 *agenda* of the Galeries Lafayette depicts a man looking at the reader and talking—the look on his face suggests an instructional lecture. The page's header, "The perfect *ménagère* should know how to . . . ," precedes a

FIG. 6. Ad for Electro-Lux vacuum cleaners, *Gringoire* (9 March 1934)

list of various cleaning tasks at which the modern housewife must be adept, along with brief instructions about effectively cleaning floors, laundry, furniture, and other items.[143] Such images highlight the notion that men sought to reassert their authority over housewives in part via control over the knowledge and understanding of the new domestic goods around which cultural definitions of housewives were built.

Such use of an image of a masculine expert in promotional materials was not uncommon in the interwar period. With respect to the United States, scholars have noted the cultural belief that women were technologically incompetent, and would thus need to rely on masculine experts.[144] Certainly such ideas were at work in the ads cited above, but an additional element was unmistakably present as well. The issue was not simply the perceived lack of feminine aptitudes regarding the nature and operation of new technology-based items, but rather the discursive need to subjugate housewives to masculine authority as well. This is made clear by a brief tale printed in the 1938 *agenda* of Printemps. An accompanying illustration shows a silhouetted image of a man sitting in a chair in the living room while reading his newspaper; opposite him on the couch is his wife, who looks visibly worried and distressed. The story begins with the husband reminding his wife that an abbé will be visiting their home for dinner the following week. Acknowledging that she indeed remembers the appointment, the wife expresses her concern that "we are in the midst of Lent," and as such a "sparse meal is necessary," yet one that at the same time is duly appropriate for a visit from such an esteemed guest. The story narrates that, as Madame continues to be deeply concerned about this quandary, "Monsieur makes an effort to break the storm: 'Look therefore in the Agenda of Printemps, there will perhaps be an idea there.'"[145] The store's self-promotion notwithstanding, the housewife in this case comes across as far from empowered, a long way removed from the happy and confident *maîtresse de maison* suggested elsewhere in popular discourse. Instead, she is utterly and helplessly distraught over an issue centrally related to her tasks as a housewife, and needs her husband's intervention to alleviate her anxiety and show her a solution to her problem. This story does not deal with any technological issues; therefore, the explanation of male expertise cannot be attributed to any masculine dominance over technical knowledge. Instead, this tale illustrates the emphasis on restoring a sense of masculine authority over the housewife, to the point that in this story the husband is made into the more knowledgeable and reasonable of the pair where an issue related to housewifery is concerned.

Adherence to Economy

One of the other responsibilities of the modern housewife in France and Germany was to guard the balancing of the household economy. In France, this aspect of housewives' duties was often linked with the reintroduction of masculine authority between the world wars. An article from the 1922 *agenda* of the Grands Magasins du Louvre entitled "The Art of Balancing Your Budget" is accompanied by an illustration of a woman sitting at a desk, poised to write in a ledger in front of her, as a man stands before her talking, apparently instructing her as to how to go about this task.[146] Additionally, in the 1923 *agenda* of the Nouvelles Galeries "A La Ménagère," a page introducing *nouveautés* for the spring assures the reader that, when she shops at this store, "your husband will praise your perspicacity and your economy."[147] Thus in this arena as well, the message clearly being sent was that women were no longer on their own in the home, as many had been during the war, but were now answerable to their husbands for the state of the household economy.

German advertising did not provide a similar example of masculine authority being established over the household economy. This was likely due to the fact that throughout the interwar years in Germany, concerns about economic management and housewives centered less on individual households and more on the macroeconomic view of national fiscal well-being. The emphasis on maintaining a stable household economy was closely related to concerns about the national economy during both the Weimar Republic and the Nazi years.[148] Still, the rise of the Nazi dictatorship intensified the pressures on the modern German housewife to oversee the household economy effectively. In the context of the Nazi drive for autarky, virtually all aspects of household economy were further imbued with national importance.[149] In advertising, the most common way in which concerns over the management of the household economy were showcased was by referring to the affordability of various household-related products. The need to avoid the purchase of excessively priced goods was particularly acute in German discourse in the 1930s.[150] Discussion of the price of products, of course, is to be expected in advertisements; however, in both France and Germany, ads often went beyond merely indicating a product's low price in order to lure buyers. Rather, advertisements often cited the household economy and its needs in promoting their products.[151] On a related note, French and German ads also promoted as a corollary to purchasing low-priced goods the affordability of gas- and electrically powered items of domestic technology due to their low consumption of energy. Ads for products such as water heaters, stoves, and refrigerators frequently made such claims in both nations.[152] In addition to purchasing goods at low prices, housewives in both France and Germany were exhorted to conserve goods as long as possible—from foods that could stay fresh longer in refrigerators to clothes that could last longer thanks to improved detergents.[153]

Avoiding Americanization

The concern for preserving the national economy extended to cultural fears over the spread of American values into French and German cultures. Indeed, the final set of duties for the housewife in both countries was to avoid being seduced by the temptations of full-fledged Americanism, despite a general recognition of American economic prowess. As Ellen Furlough claims in the French case, "Americanization was accepted when it could be recast as 'French' or when its techniques and meanings already existed in a French variant."[154] France and Germany wanted to emulate American economic growth, but only selectively and on their own terms, without accepting wholesale the unwanted and potentially threatening aspects of Americanism.[155] Evidence indeed indicates that housewives in the 1920s and 1930s were quite cognizant of the American example, and sought in some ways to imitate it.[156] An advertisement from the early 1920s for O-Cedar shows a smiling housewife cleaning a floor with the O-Cedar Polish Mop. Referring to the "new manner" of housework, the ad touts the fact that this product was currently being utilized in millions of homes in both Britain and the United States.[157]

Such enthusiasm was tempered by increasing fears that adopting American economic methods might also invariably entail accepting the social values and cultural hegemony of the "Market Empire," as Victoria de Grazia describes it.[158] As Mary Nolan convincingly shows in regard to Germany, a common view held that American housewives were creating materially rich but emotionally barren homes that were completely devoid of tradition or culture. The postwar household required most centrally not material goods, but rather *Geist,* or spirit, a term used in relation to housework to connote traditional feminine virtues, such as morality and selflessness. The most technology-filled household, it was felt, would be worthless without the guiding principles provided by an appropriate *Geist.*[159] The diametric opposite of *Geist* was "the soulless materialism that many believed had permeated the rationalized American home, family, and society at large."[160] Thus modernity was to be copied from America only partially; both rationalized factory laborer and rationalized housewife would "combine American techniques with a German *Geist* and thereby avoid the soullessness and materialism that ostensibly permeated home, family, and society in the United States."[161]

The need for a distinct national avenue toward modernity was expressed in publicity materials in a couple of ways. Most straightforwardly, it took the form of highlighting the French or German production—a "made in France" or "made in Germany" tenor—that lay behind the creation and construction of the advertised goods. In France, many companies producing household-related items noted that their goods were "French products," thereby assuring the consumer of their quality and appropriate spirit, at least in production.[162] In Germany, such assertions of home manufacture were even more important given the concern with national self-sufficiency throughout the interwar period, culminating with the Nazi drive for autarky. Even in the Weimar era, housewives' associations regularly sponsored "buy German" campaigns as a means of encouraging housewives to consume only German-made goods.[163] Not surprisingly, then, German ads also evinced an affinity for promoting the German construction of household-related products, often focusing on the traditional notion of German quality work.[164] In fact, a couple of German ads specifically decried and disparaged foreign-made competition. One such ad, for Siemens vacuum cleaners, cautions the reader to be wary of foreign-produced imitations of Siemens vacuums currently on the German market.[165] At the same time, however, though they condemned the purchase of foreign-made products, ads for French- and German-made goods occasionally tried to augment their prestige by suggesting or explicitly proclaiming their international reputation. Such a tactic allowed for the possibility that French or German modernity, as embodied in domestic technology at least, was so well developed that it now was becoming an accepted standard of modernity not just in the home country, but beyond its own borders as well. As an example, a German ad for ATA cleaner from 1930 proclaims that its product is known worldwide.[166] Conveying the same message in a more visually striking manner are two French ads for Electro-Lux—one for its refrigerators, the other for its vacuums—that utilize an image of the globe to suggest the international stature and reputation of the products in question.[167]

The two decades separating the world wars witnessed a significant restructuring of women's roles as housewives in France and Germany. In the wake of the upheaval of the Great War and consequent fears of "modern women," cultural ideology in both countries sought a restoration of order through more familiar roles for women. One of the crucial guises in which women had long been constructed, as housewives, was a central focus of this postwar gender discourse. Definitions of housewifery differed significantly from prewar conceptions, due to the decline in numbers of domestic servants and the appearance of new domestic technologies such as vacuum cleaners and washing machines. With middle-class women, like their lower-class counterparts, now completing the chores of the household themselves, significations underlying the nature of housework were dramatically altered in some respects in order to transform household labor from drudgery and tedium into a set of tasks befitting a "respectable" woman. French and German discourse constructed modern housewives empowered by the wonders of new pieces of household technology—which reputedly made housewives' work immeasurably easier, were unceasingly innovative and virtually infallible, and allowed for elegance and comfort in the home. At the same time, however, the empowering aspects of modern housewifery were superseded by intensified obligations and duties for housewives, among them safeguarding the health of the household, submitting to masculine authority, bearing the burdens of the relative well-being of the national economy, and avoiding a wholesale acceptance of soulless, overly materialistic Americanization. In these ways, French and German gender ideology between the World Wars constructed a vision of modern housewifery that, resting on the twin pillars of empowerment and duty, glorified housewives' tasks and importance while intensifying traditional conceptions of femininity.

CHAPTER TWO

WOMEN'S "DELIGHTFUL DUTY"
The Discourse of Motherhood

The 1920 and 1922 *agendas* of the Bon Marché opened with the same appeal to French women: "Mothers, young women, have children! France asks it of you and nature imposes this delightful duty on you."[1] Similar sentiments were echoed in Germany, where, as in France, a perceived "crisis of the family" meant that motherhood was viewed as a duty of the highest national importance. A strong connection between femininity and maternity was nothing new, as women had long been discursively defined primarily on the basis of childbearing and child rearing, in France and Germany as well as across Europe.[2] After the Great War, however, fears of depopulation and a weakened home country transformed motherhood into a cultural imperative on which the very survival of the nation was believed to depend.[3]

Motherhood was a national issue precisely because French and German observers across a wide political and socioeconomic spectrum feared that the modern age was endangering the age-old tradition of mothering as adult women's primary task. In a sense, women becoming mothers had been taken almost for granted before the Great War; in its fighting and aftermath, though, the conflict raised a frightening specter to French and German societies: women were taking on increasingly independent lifestyles, at least in the popular imagination, consciously forgoing a life of motherhood in favor of greater personal freedom and selfish interests. Even married couples across Western Europe were deliberately ending their childbearing years prematurely, through contraception, abstention, and other methods—a familial choice, Wally Seccombe argues, originating most often with wives rather than husbands.[4] In the eyes of contemporaries, modernity in the family represented not positive change, but rather a detrimental and potentially permanent shrinking of family size and blurring of gender roles.[5]

In such an environment, fears of shrinking families and, by extension, reduced national populations prompted vociferous objections from cultural commentators. A commonly voiced fear in both France and Germany was that, should current trends continue unabated, disaster for the country would soon follow. In both Weimar and Nazi Germany, this tragedy usually took the form in popular ideology of the "death of the nation," suggesting that, in the absence of an improvement in demographic numbers, the German "race" would soon fail to reproduce itself and essentially become extinct.[6] In France, meanwhile, the anticipated catastrophe was France's impending inability to maintain its status as a major world power due to falling population numbers.[7] Eventually, it was feared, the nation would be left impotent to repel an allegedly hostile, aggressive, and virile Germany to the east.[8] As a result, there was great emphasis in France and Germany upon producing children for the good of the state. Both nations' state apparatuses became much more intimately involved in matters affecting reproduction and the maintenance of the family. States would now play a greater role than ever before in regulating reproductive behavior, seeking to encourage the growth of larger families.[9]

Given such concerns about demographic figures, the array of meanings attached to femininity became tied more strongly than ever with motherhood. Women, allegedly increasingly independent and promiscuous, were to be controlled reproductively by the state because they purportedly no longer willingly served as mothers, thus threatening the nation with potentially disastrous consequences. Ute Frevert notes, with respect to interwar Germany, the commonly held view that women "were aspiring to the individualistic ethic of the modern age and failing to meet their obligations as mothers of the nation."[10] Government involvement in reproductive behavior was supported virtually unanimously in France and Germany, as a number of scholars have shown, even if there were disparate visions of how the problem was to be solved.[11] The ubiquity of the notion of motherhood as an imperative for women in interwar France and Germany was reflected frequently in publicity materials and the popular press. In these images, the "duty" of motherhood was counterbalanced by an emphasis on the "delightful" nature of having and raising children. An ideology of the pleasures of motherhood, while certainly extant, was superseded in most cases by maternal responsibilities, such as the maintenance of infant health, the perpetuation of the nation, and submission to paternal authority.

THE DEMOGRAPHIC CRISIS OF THE INTERWAR PERIOD
Public Policy and Public Opinion

Demographic concerns in both France and Germany had their roots in the pre-1914 era. It was the carnage of the Great War, though, that galvanized such fears profoundly, and thrust them into the public limelight to a heretofore unseen degree.[12] In France, pronatalism took firm hold of the political landscape in the immediate aftermath of World War I. Marie-Monique Huss discusses the widespread adherence to pronatalist ideology, noting that politicians from the radical Left to the conservative Right largely supported pronatalist measures because of both the demographic decline and moralizing fears regarding independent female sexuality.[13] A well-known 1920 law prohibiting abortion and banning the sale and advertisement of contraception sought to halt the precipitous drop in the birth rate.[14] Testifying again to the unanimity of political views on the subject, Elinor Accampo asserts that even most feminists supported the law.[15] The opposite end of the interwar decades witnessed the passage of the French Code de la Famille in November 1938 and July 1939. These laws, which reinforced and stiffened the penalties for abortion and contraception, enjoyed widespread public support.[16]

In spite of efforts to reverse population trends, French birth rates remained low throughout the 1920s and 1930s. In 1929, France experienced a year of negative population growth, as deaths exceeded births by about 8,600 people.[17] That shocking demographic fact became commonplace a few years later, as deaths exceeded births in France in every year from 1935 through the end of World War II.[18] As Marie-Monique Huss writes, pronatalists "seemed to have convinced parents more easily of the urgency for France to have pronatalist legislation than of the necessity for them as parents to have children."[19]

Better demographic numbers in Germany did not preclude concerns being voiced there over the reproductive rate, and there was still a widespread consensus across political lines that the birth rate had to be improved for the good of the nation.[20] The new Weimar government left intact (although strictures were eased after 1926) the Wilhelmine-era law outlawing abortion and the advertisement of contraception—paragraphs 218–220 of the Penal Code.[21] Stefana Lefko contends that even the Federation of German Women's Associations (BDF, Bund Deutscher Frauenvereine) opposed the legalization of abortion and the dissemination of contraception during the 1920s, fearing that these would lead to "indiscriminate" sexual relationships.[22] After a brief spike in births in the first postwar years, the German birth rate declined throughout the rest of the Weimar era, reaching a nadir of 14.7 per 1,000 inhabitants in 1933, the lowest rate in Europe for that year.[23]

At no point did the definition of women as mothers come into clearer focus than with the Nazi regime beginning in 1933. Encapsulating the importance of motherhood to Nazi ideology, Hitler himself emphasized that the mother was "the most important citizen" in his regime, and it was her duty to reproduce for the benefit of the nation.[24] Like other interwar governments, the Nazi regime quickly set about establishing a series of reproductive laws soon after coming to power. In part, Nazi decrees in this regard involved retractions and reversals of liberal Weimar practices, such as closing down Weimar-era sexual advice centers.[25] Nazi attempts to stimulate the German birth rate met with only modest success. From Germany's figure of 14.7 births per 1,000 inhabitants in 1933, the Nazis oversaw a consistent yet limited rise in the birth rate over the rest of the decade, which culminated, in 1939, in a rate of about 20.4 births per 1,000.[26] The modest nature of the increase may suggest that the rise in the birth rate was due less to fundamental lifestyle changes on the part of Germans than simply to the improvement of economic conditions after 1933.[27]

Thus the interwar years witnessed in both France and Germany a continued stagnation in birth-rate statistics, with the modest exception of Nazi Germany, despite a myriad of public efforts and popular pronatalist sentiment. French and German governments in the 1920s and 1930s were largely unable to restore desired maternity levels, and in part because of this, both countries continued to purvey the importance of motherhood throughout the interwar period in a variety of ways.

Incentives and Honors

A number of incentives and honors were bestowed on French and German mothers in the interwar years. The Weimar Republic, for instance, offered a series of maternity benefits and protections that encouraged women to bear children. As early as September 1919, it had codified benefits designed to cover completely the costs of delivery.[28] Later Weimar legislation granted twelve weeks of maternity leave, including protection from dismissal.[29] The Nazi government also pursued various welfare measures as a means of assisting German mothers. In 1935, Hitler's regime instituted family allowances for large families in difficult economic straits. By 1938, such payments covered some 2.5 million German children.[30] In addition to such direct payments, the Nazis provided support through a welfare organization created in February 1934 known as the Hilfswerk Mutter und Kind. This organization provided a number of services to struggling mothers, and offered information and advice to women at maternal assistance centers.[31]

In France, incentive efforts for motherhood also often took the form of family allowances. In the 1920s, a number of industrialists began voluntarily granting such allowances to their employees through *caisses de compensation,* mechanisms designed for the purpose of collecting and distributing funds.[32] By 1930, completely on a voluntary basis, this system had expanded exponentially, with more than thirty-two thousand French companies affiliated with one of hundreds of *caisses.*[33] The family allowance system was so widespread, successful, and politically popular that, in 1932, the French government passed a law making it mandatory for all employers to provide family allowances through one of the *caisses.* By 1939, the system covered more than 5.6 million workers and, in that year, paid out nearly 4 billion francs.[34]

In addition to such incentives, both France and Germany showered mothers with various honors. In France, for example, a French version of Mother's Day was established in 1920 as a means to honor and recognize the importance of mothers to the nation.[35] On the first occasion of this holiday, the French government forged medals to give in honor of mothers of large families.[36] Similarly, in Germany the Nazi regime in 1938 established the Honor Cross of the German Mother for women with at least four children.[37] Members of the Hitler Youth were instructed to salute women whom they saw wearing the medals.[38] During the Nazi years, mothers of large families (of "racially valuable" stock) were given the designation *kinderreich* (rich in children) upon the birth of a fourth child, and were entitled, among other perks, to reduced public transportation fares, occasional free theater tickets, and going automatically to the front of the line in shops and government offices.[39] Germany also began celebrating Mother's Day in the early 1920s.[40] The purpose of a German Mother's Day, as Karin Hausen notes, was not simply to allow individual families to honor their maternal figures, but for the entire nation to celebrate motherhood as an ideal.[41]

THE JOYS OF BEING A MOTHER

Both France and Germany attempted to make motherhood an attractive option to women by emphasizing the joys and pleasures of being a mother. This emphasis on explicating the pleasures of motherhood as a means of trying to convince women to bear children should not be surprising. As Elisabeth Badinter argues in the context of influential Freudian models that circulated in twentieth-century intellectual thought, to many French and German commentators, simply asking a would-be mother to be devoted to her children was not enough. The very success of her relationship with her children, and thus the success of the upbringing she was to give them, was thought to hinge upon the mother finding pleasure and enjoyment in her maternal role.[42] This view was certainly reflected in French and German publicity materials, which throughout the interwar period contained seemingly innumerable images of mothers taking pleasure in their maternal tasks.

In France, depictions of the joys of motherhood occurred in numerous forms. A number of advertisements from the popular press, for products ranging from sugar and milk to laundry detergents and refrigerators, portrayed mothers and their children happily together, frequently sitting at a table or on a chair or sofa.[43] The pages of French *agendas* also included such images.[44] The opening series of text from the Bon Marché *agendas* from 1920 and 1922, as cited at the start of this chapter, implores women to have children and discusses the store's maternity benefit. This introductory text tells readers that every mother will stay young and happy by having children, even to the point where a "radiant halo" will crown a mother's forehead, shining with "brighter splendor" with the arrival of each child.[45] Thus the focus of the text highlights that same message: becoming a mother will bring happiness to a young woman.

Other images from French publicity materials contained similar implications. One way in which the joys and happiness of being a mother was emphasized was through the dissemination of images of mothers and children sharing tender moments of affection. Quite often such images—utilized most frequently in advertisements for nutritional and medicinal products for children—showed mothers breastfeeding their newborns, lovingly nursing a sick child, or sharing a delicate embrace with their infants.[46] It is clear from the expressions on the mothers' faces that they are enjoying a rewarding experience with their children. An article from the Grands Magasins du Louvre *agenda* for 1921 helps to make this point. The article, entitled "Reflections on Little Girls and Little Boys of Today," discusses the important shift that it claims has taken place in relations between parent and child. Whereas in the past, the article states, parent-child relationships were marked by parental severity and coldness toward children, affection and tenderness by parents toward their children is now the norm. As evidence of this fact, the article notes the replacement in common usage at home of the formal terms *père* and *mère* with the informal *papa* and *maman* (essentially the equivalent of referring to one's parents as "Daddy" and "Mommy" rather than "Father" and "Mother"). At the end of the article, mention is made of the increased happiness that parents now actively seek to bring to their children's lives, by extension contributing to a greater degree of happiness for the parents themselves.[47]

Publicity materials from interwar France also portrayed mothers and their children happily playing together. Advertisements from the popular press for goods as varied as nutritional items, laundry soaps, and cameras deployed such images showing smiling or laughing mothers playing lightheartedly with their equally jovial children.[48] A 1925 catalog of the Palais de la Nouveauté shows a similar image. The catalog as a whole consists of a series of illustrations of fictitious scenes within homes, below which on each page appears a list of goods shown in each picture that are for sale at the store. One of these hypothetical vignettes, under the heading "The Compliment," shows a smiling mother sitting on a chair in her bedroom as her two young children stand before her; one of the children is reading aloud to her, while the other holds a bunch of flowers intended for mother.[49] There is no sign or mention of the scene representing any special occasion; to the contrary, its tone is that of a playful everyday setting repeated thousands of times over each day by happy mothers and children everywhere. Meanwhile, some images depicted mothers and children happily playing together in settings such as parks or beaches.[50] The pristine countryside and beachside locales that formed the milieu of these advertisements were not merely incidental; rather, they tied women more closely to deeply held notions about tradition. Charles Rearick demonstrates that in the turbulent interwar era, the French idealized peaceful, nonurban settings in opposition to the fast-paced, coldly rational, business-oriented world of the city. The provinces were constructed in the French popular imagination as places of natural beauty where the traditions of the prewar world still lingered.[51] Taken together, such depictions of mothers playing with their young ones, whether set in the home or outdoors, were perhaps the purest expression in publicity materials of the simple, unadulterated pleasures that a mother was bound to experience.

German advertisements from the 1920s and 1930s exhibited similar characteristics. Just as in France, the most common type of ad consisted rather simply of a smiling mother and child together.[52] For instance, ads for foods and food-related goods, particularly margarine, show happy mothers and their offspring happily eating or preparing food.[53] In some cases, German images belied any comparison to French ones, such as ads for the Nazi welfare organization Hilfswerk Mutter und Kind that center upon familial images of mothers and children (fig. 7).[54] Most striking about these ads in contrast to French ones is that German images—especially those from the Nazi years, when the government's emphasis on having large families became almost obsessive— occasionally pictured two, three, or even four children in each ad, while in French materials, depictions of more than one child were relatively scarce, and having as many as three included in one image was exceptionally rare.

FIG. 7. Ad for Hilfswerk Mutter und Kind, a Nazi welfare organization, *Westermanns Monatshefte* (September 1934, advertising section)

Like their French counterparts, German advertisements often pictured mothers and children together sharing moments of tenderness and affection, promoting the closeness intrinsic to the mother-child relationship as a further means of expounding the joys of motherhood. Ads for shampoo and underwear, among other goods, showed such images of mothers caring for or lovingly holding their children.[55] In the German case, however, one of the most common uses of such imagery occurred in various ads for Nazi welfare organizations such as the Hilfswerk Mutter und Kind. The emphasis on maternity in the advertisements of Nazi welfare programs can be explained in part by the fact that these programs were intimately linked in Nazi Germany to a veritable cult of maternity.[56] The discourse of motherhood in the Nazi era provided the perfect symbolic counterpoint to welfare organizations; the image of the mother tending to and nurturing her children could be analogized easily to the German state doing the same for the financially underprivileged. A 1934 advertisement for the Hilfswerk Mutter und Kind, for instance, presents an image of a mother holding steady a young infant just learning to walk, helping him to stay on his feet, much as the Hilfswerk program was designed to help struggling German families stay on their feet in difficult economic times (fig. 8).[57] A number of ads for the Nazis' Winterhilfswerk program (WHW) contained images evoking the same ideals, frequently showing women tenderly holding a small child while other, older siblings cling to their mother.[58] As in French materials, a number of German ads connected women to nature and tradition by depicting mothers and children in idyllic outdoor scenes in park areas or on beaches.[59]

Overall, while there was certainly no shortage of images of French mothers happily involved with their children, more such ads—and a greater variety of them—seem to have come from Germany in the 1920s and 1930s. This is perhaps best contextualized by Ute Frevert's observation that, particularly in interwar Germany, there was a feeling that women lacked "motherliness," that they did not adequately display love and devotion to their children.[60] An explanation for this feeling may be found in the work of Elizabeth Domansky, who contends that, to a much greater extent than France or Britain, the traditional family virtually ceased to exist in Germany during the Great War.[61] In that context, "motherliness" may well have seemed a lost virtue, and thus the cultural imperative surrounding it may have been felt more keenly in German culture. The concern over this particular aspect of maternity seems to have been amplified in Germany, and as such greater emphasis on it emerged in

FIG. 8. Ad for Hilfswerk Mutter und Kind, *Simplicissimus* (15 July 1934)

popular imagery. Nonetheless, both nations' publicity materials clearly demonstrated a concern for imparting upon women the inherent joys and delights of motherhood.

THE DUTIES OF MATERNITY

Notwithstanding the promotion of the joys of being a mother, an emphasis on unselfish maternal duties and responsibilities was even more prevalent in French and German popular discourse between the world wars. These obligations were generally given primacy over those of the joy and happiness of maternity. The vital role to be played by women in their children's development was made explicit in the 1932 *agenda* of the Bon Marché. The theme of that year's *agenda*, in fact, was children and motherhood, which itself reveals the importance attached to maternity in French culture, particularly in the economic and demographic crisis years of the 1930s. The Bon Marché, according to this *agenda*, wanted to use the calendar book for 1932 as an opportunity to "pay tribute to young French moms." On the title page of the *agenda*, a message appears entitled "To the young moms of France." The text begins with a blunt notice to mothers: "It is on you above all, Madame, that the future of your child depends." Indeed, the text suggests, a newborn's "first cry" is actually "a call for help," and the way in which the young mother responds will determine if "the destiny of your little one will take a good or bad direction." The text does try to assure the young mother, though, that she can ably handle this significant burden—"you know better than anyone how to awaken its little brain, open its heart, develop its character."[62] This message to French mothers, which could just as easily have appeared in Germany, where similar discursive ideals held sway, illustrates a great deal about the responsibilities placed on the shoulders of mothers in the interwar period. It makes clear that the child's overall development is first and foremost the duty of the mother—it is she, and no other, who must bear the weight of this obligation, and who would ultimately decide the very course of her child's life. Even the mother-knows-best reassurance in the text reinforced the sole responsibility of mothers in matters of child rearing.

Such evidence supports the notion that, in the era between the world wars, European societies generally defined women more strongly than ever as the moral, physical, and social guardians of their young ones.[63] Indeed, in Elisabeth Badinter's analysis of Freudian-based morality, she argues that being a devoted mother meant that, above all else, a woman must be focused

FIG. 9. Cartoon from *Gringoire* (15 February 1929)

upon her child to the point of exclusion of all other, nonmaternal concerns. In particular, the presence of allegedly masculine desires—for a career, for example—led to internal conflicts that made good mothering a virtual impossibility. Only by giving herself completely over to the upbringing of her offspring (thereby, not coincidentally, also avoiding the pitfalls of the "modern woman") could a mother ensure the harmonious development of her child.[64]

All too often, however, French and German observers felt that women were neglecting such all-consuming duties, spending too much time on less important, more peripheral concerns than their children. This is clearly illustrated by a cartoon from the front page of *Gringoire* in 1929 (fig. 9). In the cartoon, as a man stands in the street observing the action with a look of consternation, a woman near him expresses horror at the plight of a small, obviously undernourished stray kitten. Bending toward the kitten, the woman exclaims, "the poor dear!" Meanwhile, the woman's focus on the kitten has caused her to ignore and overlook completely two young children standing behind her just a few feet away. They look every bit as poor, malnourished, and haggard as the feline, but the woman has—quite literally, in the spatial arrangement of the cartoon—turned her back on them to lament the cat's problems.[65] The symbolism in this cartoon is unmistakable: women have been neglecting their maternal responsibilities, choosing instead to devote themselves to relatively unimportant matters. The cartoon is also noteworthy for the male figure's passive role in it. A vaguely disapproving look is all that he can muster in response to the situation unfolding in front of him, conveying yet again the message that women were in a sense the sole guardians of children, the only ones qualified to help them develop into healthy and happy beings.

Infant Care and Health

In response to such concerns, both French and German popular discourse constructed images of women as cognizant of and adhering to these duties and responsibilities of motherhood, emphasizing their burden of responsibility in this regard as well as their capability of performing their maternal duties successfully. In both France and Germany, particular emphasis was placed on preserving the health of one's children and ensuring their physical development, whether in the course of mundane daily tasks or in matters declared to be of life-and-death importance.[66]

German advertisements illustrate this range of images relating to the maternal duty of preserving children's health and closely guarding their physical development. In one case, even an ad for a sunlamp appealed to pregnant mothers to use the product as a means of helping to ensure the "thriving" of the soon-to-be-born child.[67] A series of advertisements from the mid-1930s for Osram light bulbs, moreover, appealed directly to mothers to buy the advertised product to protect their children's eyesight. Usually featuring an image of a young child reading or writing, such ads proclaim it to be the mother's duty to buy a light bulb that provides adequate light for her children's sake.[68]

One of the main points of emphasis in German discourse connecting maternal responsibility to infant health was cleanliness.[69] For example, several ads for products such as laundry detergent and clothing items depicted happy mothers and children together, with children either showing off clean clothing or mothers happily working to clean dirty ones for their children.[70] One such ad for Benger's underwear, which pictures a father, mother, and child standing together, declares the importance of health quite explicitly. Under the header "Health is a prerequisite!" the ad discusses the importance of clean, warm, protective undergarments in the preservation of one's health, saying that health must come before all other hopes and wishes of the family.[71] Other German ads highlighted the importance of keeping children's bodies physically clean in order to ensure their good health. Often including an image of a smiling mother and children, ads for goods such as shampoo and soap sent these types of messages, reminding mothers that it was just as critical to keep their children's bodies clean as it was to maintain the cleanliness of the household around them.[72]

One final key element of German ideology regarding children's health was food and nutrition. Advertisements for various foods and food-related goods emphasized the need to provide children with fresh or nutritious foods so that they could grow and remain healthy.[73] Indeed, feeding one's children formed an inextricable part of the view of a mother's worth in the popular imagination, as Rosalind Coward argues. A mother's ability to feed her children adequately has often been viewed as a key guidepost to interpreting the ability of a mother to perform her maternal duties satisfactorily.[74] Feeding her family was viewed as a way in which a mother could facilitate not just the maintenance and growth of her children, but through which she could also build upon familial bonds of love, trust, and loyalty between mother and child.[75] As an example, in a 1939 ad for Kasseler "oats-cocoa," a mother and daughter are holding hands with arms outstretched, apparently engaging in a playful tugging match (fig. 10). The setting is scenic, even idyllic, as the two figures are surrounded by greenery, and mountains are visible in the distance behind them. The young girl, evidently holding her own in this lighthearted game with her mother, gleefully exclaims: "I am strong, Mommy!" Below the image, the ad responds to the girl's assertion, promising that, "Yes, Kasseler oats-cocoa makes you strong."[76] A less exuberant note is struck in another Nazi-era advertisement, this one for the Winterhilfswerk program. In it, a somber-looking mother slices bread from a loaf to give to each of her three children, who stand around her. The ad tells the mother that the WHW's assistance can "bring you joy."[77] Although the look on the woman's face does not suggest joy, the implication clearly is that she can attain it with the help of the state vis-à-vis the WHW; she will have enough to feed her children and thereby bolster her own happiness and sense of self-worth.

Like their German counterparts, French images touched upon the issue of clean laundry for one's children. Most notably, a plethora of laundry de-

FIG. 10. Ad for Kasseler "oats-cocoa," *Illustrirte Zeitung* (11 May 1939)

tergent ads appeared in the French press in the 1930s, focusing on the level of cleanliness that could be achieved in one's laundry by utilizing the advertised product. Such ads normally pictured a mother playing with her children, whose clothes were sparkling white after having been washed using the advertised detergent.[78] In a noticeable contrast to German ads, however, French images on household cleanliness lack almost any direct emphasis on the importance of cleanliness to the family's health. Instead, most such ads from France simply focus on the attractive appearance of clothes and linens washed with the various laundry soaps in question. Even a 1931 ad for Thomson electrical appliances that mentions the hygienic value of its goods does so only in passing. Depicting a woman ironing in a kitchen while her daughter watches, the ad focuses instead on the comfort that the appliances bring to the home.[79] Finally, in the context of keeping one's own children physically clean and free from illness, a 1927 advertisement for Palmolive soap that shows a mother and baby asserts the mother's duty to use soap, but on the grounds of maintaining the baby's youthful complexion (rather than the infant's cleanliness or health).[80] There is thus little indication of the emphasis on familial health and maternal responsibility in these instances.

The most ubiquitous French advertisements relating to maternity and infant health were ads for food products. As in Germany, these images suggested that a mother's duties centrally involved appropriately feeding and nourishing her children. In particular, foods designed for young children who were being or recently had been weaned from breast milk were frequently advertised, and generally depicted a mother and her children sitting together, often at a dining table. Such advertisements usually touted the importance of such foods for the health of a child at this quite delicate moment in life, and promoted not simply the nutritional value of the products in question, but their easy digestibility as well.[81]

Going one step further, some ads relating to food and nutrition display a concern with children's growth, strength, or weight. In a 1928 ad for the tonic Proton, for example, a small girl stands atop a small bookshelf, thus raising her height to the level of her mother standing beside her. The mother, holding the girl's hand to ensure that she does not fall, declares, "How you have grown!" The text of the ad promises that children given Proton will grow to be strong and healthy.[82] More blatantly, a 1935 ad for Blédine, a post-breastfeeding food, pictures a smiling mother holding a small infant. The ad contains a purportedly genuine letter of satisfaction to the company from a French mother. Her letter, as reproduced in the ad, discusses how strong and healthy all of her children have become thanks to Blédine. The letter even goes as far as to provide the age and weight of each of the mother's children.[83] Such a reference was not incidental or isolated; great importance was attached to the maternal duty of maintaining a child's proper weight based on contemporary medical guidelines. Ruth Schwartz Cowan analyzes this phenomenon with respect to the United States, noting the seemingly compulsive frequency with which mothers were expected to weigh their children, and suggesting that mothers were viewed in some sense as derelict if their children did not weigh as much as it was thought they should.[84] Indeed, the 1928 *agenda* of the Bon Marché contains an illustration of a mother and baby accompanied by a paragraph of text that instructs mothers to weigh their infants frequently, and provides a set of target weight guideposts for newborns by age.[85]

Thus feeding one's children was defined as crucially important, and this was true most especially for newborns. French publicity materials, in a number of references that have virtually no counterpart in the German case, emphasized greatly the importance of breastfeeding. Anne Cova notes that maternal breastfeeding was deemed so significant in interwar France that its encouragement was the subject of parliamentary discussions.[86] It was seen not only as an ideal source of nourishment for young infants, but also as promoting closeness and strong bonds between mothers and their children. Most common in this regard were advertisements for Nestlé baby cereal. Many of these ads followed a similar formula, wherein an image of a mother breastfeeding her baby accompanied text advising her to breastfeed her child if she could. If this were not possible, however, such ads advised that the mother's next-best option would be Nestlé (fig. 11).[87] The fact that a company would in essence discourage women from purchasing its product unless breastfeeding were not possible provides a clear idea of the importance of this ideal in French culture.

Some ads went even further, warning mothers of the dangers of not being healthy themselves. The expressed concern was that unhealthy mothers would, through breastfeeding, transmit poor health to their infants. Cure-all medicinal products touted in advertisements their ability to keep mothers strong and healthy, thus protecting their children from danger of illness. For example, a 1923 ad for Pilules Pink shows a mother breastfeeding her newborn. The ad states: "The sufferings, the fatigues of maternity have exhausted your strength." The mother is "weakened, worn out," but now more than ever it is

FIG. 11. Ad for Nestlé baby cereal, from *Le Matin* (12 July 1923) and *L'Oeuvre* (12 July 1923)

necessary that she not be so, because for several months to come, it will be on her health and vigor that "the life of your child will depend." The ad suggests that the mother take Pilules Pink in order to ensure that her body is prepared to handle this responsibility.[88] A 1927 advertisement for Proton tonic is similar in tone and content. Above the ad's header, "A weakened young mother," is an image of a woman breastfeeding an infant. The ad states: "Weakened by motherhood, the young mom is no longer in a condition to feed her baby normally. On her depends nonetheless the health of the dear little being who asks only to live. *Strengthen the Mother, strengthen the Child!*"[89]

Such grim warnings regarding the delicate balance between life and death for young infants were not uncommon. Indeed, in some cases French publicity materials raised the issue of the importance of preventing the deaths of infants. This is explained at least in part by Mary Lynn Stewart, who cites a general sensitivity in interwar France toward infant mortality, in particular preventable deaths, which were more common in France than in many other European countries, and were often blamed on poor maternal care.[90] In 1930, for example, an advertisement for silver tablets, depicting a mother trying to placate a baby who is crying and obviously in discomfort, makes the morbid claim that "more than 60,000 babies die each year from infantile diarrhea." Declaring silver tablets the only way to stop this diarrhea immediately, the ad counsels mothers always to have some of them on hand.[91] The *agenda* of the Bon Marché from 1932 also addressed the issue of infant mortality. On the opening calendar page covering 1 and 2 January 1932, a text box entitled "FOR MOTHER AND CHILD" appears, accompanied by an illustration of a smiling mother holding two toddlers. The text states that over 100,000 French children die each year, and asks rhetorically, "Is that not frightening?" In addition, such infant mortality is described as a major threat to "the future of our nation."

Maternity and the Nation

As the previous example illustrates, in addition to devoting themselves to the survival of their children, women were also expected to bear in mind the survival of the nation, for childbearing was constructed as a national duty owed to the state. In the case of 1930s Germany, Jost Hermand argues that some Nazi-era thinkers accomplished in their intellectual thought nothing less than "a maternalization of the national concept."[92] Women, specifically mothers, were closely linked to the roots of national identity in Germany, and exhorted to maintain the purity of the nation, both in the Weimar and Nazi periods. They were likewise expected to oversee the transmission of German culture and morality to their children.[93] Such references to German nationality and culture can be found in interwar advertisements. For example, a family of three is pictured in a 1934 ad for Benger's underwear, whose text celebrates this purportedly typical—and uniquely German—family: "'Him,' 'Her,' and 'the children'—the German family!"[94] A 1936 ad for the Hilfswerk Mutter und Kind, which depicts a mother and two small children sitting together, appeals to the traditional notion of the German *Volk*, stating simply that "a great *Volk* grows from strong mothers and healthy children."[95]

Similar messages regarding the nation can be found in French publicity materials. In a 1923 advertisement for Gloria milk, a mother and child sit at the table as a domestic servant walks past. The ad's header reads: "The Future of the Race." The text of the ad asks, "Will our children later be strong enough physically to withstand the tests that await them in life?" The ad continues by explaining how Gloria milk will help ensure that the answer to this question is yes.[96] By linking the well-being of children to the very survival of the nation—the future of the race[97]—this ad implicitly raises the issue of the French birthrate decline. By extension, its allusion to the strength of the child and the trials he might face speak also of the possibility of a future battle to be fought against an allegedly aggressive and virile German neighbor to France's east.

Finally, the passage quoted at the outset of this chapter from the 1920 and 1922 *agendas* of the Bon Marché is again instructive: "Mothers, young women, have children! France asks it of you and nature imposes this delightful duty on you."[98] This example brings together a number of threads of maternity discourse in the interwar era. Its focus on the nation being in need of women to become mothers, as well as on the delights and the duties incurred by women who take up this civic mantle of motherhood, illustrates that the ideology of motherhood between the world wars was not only about individual pleasures and responsibilities, but also centered upon national cultural imperatives. The underlying purpose of all of the joys and duties of maternity ultimately was to promote the interests of the nation.

Patriarchal Authority

The interwar mother in France and Germany had one final duty: submission to masculine authority. In both nations after the Great War, there was a widespread perception that, given men's extended absence from the home during the conflict, when millions went to the battlefront, women's position vis-à-vis their husbands had been greatly strengthened by this absence of fatherly authority, and that women would usurp patriarchal power even after the war ended and soldiers returned home.[99] Karin Hausen argues that this emphasis may have been even more pronounced in postwar Germany; she discusses the overthrow of the Wilhelmine government as a macroexample of the loss of patriarchal authority, substituting the Kaiser for the father on the national political stage.[100] Such concerns did not abate in the years after the war; instead, worries about a lack of patriarchal authority in the home continued into the 1930s.[101] Simon Gunn illuminates another aspect of this interwar concern about patriarchal control with respect to England, arguing that the increased importance in everyday life of consumption, which was generally considered a feminine engagement, also contributed to preexisting anxieties about a loss of masculine authority in the home and in society at large.[102] The continued allure of traditional notions of the family meant that there was considerable longing and nostalgia for an idealized image of family, at the head of which an authoritative father ruled over a loving wife/mother and obedient children.[103]

Such ideas did not translate, however, into numerous depictions of fathers in publicity materials. Instead, as Elisabeth Badinter notes, the expectation was that fatherly involvement would be practiced at a distance. In order to preserve the distinction between masculine and feminine familial roles (and thus preserve his authority), the father was not to participate in the day-to-day and moment-to-moment minutiae of child rearing.[104] Still, in some instances father figures were shown in publicity materials as a means of reestablishing masculine authority over mothers. In Germany, a 1939 advertisement for Hohenlohe oat products pictures a smiling father carrying a toddler on his shoulders. The text of the ad simply states: "What father likes, mother gladly cooks!"[105] While certainly innocuous enough in appearance, this ad nonetheless sends a clear message that the father is in control of the household and specifically in an authority position vis-à-vis the mother. Other German examples in this regard appear mainly in advertisements for life insurance. Such ads assert the father's authority over the all-important issue of financial protection and provision for the family. In one such ad, a family of four is sitting at the table; the father reads a newspaper while the mother appears to assist the two children with their schoolwork. The ad's header reads: "'Later' can be too late!" Explaining that one never knows how long or short a life will be, the ad declares that "every conscientious father" should acquire life insurance at an early date to protect his family in case of his death.[106]

Indeed, an ad that shows the effects of the father's failure to take this necessary step illustrates his centrality to the family. The ad, which shows a grieving mother and daughter next to the header, "What a widow needs," discusses the various expenses—funerary costs, cemetery plot, and so on—that will drive the mother and daughter into considerable debt because the father did not take the time to purchase life insurance.[107] Certainly, part of the intent of the ad is simply to show the difficulty in which an unexpected, premature death can leave a family, and thus encourage readers to purchase insurance. At a deeper level, however, the implication is that the mother and daughter have been left not simply in a difficult financial situation but, more importantly, spiritually adrift by the loss of the head of the household. Their grief is not just about their sadness at the father's death or the economic burdens that they will assume because of it, but about their seeming sense that the permanent loss of the husband has left an irreplaceable void in the guidance of the family for which the mother will never be able to compensate.

In France, there were likewise images addressing the need for a restoration of patriarchal authority, although these differed in form from German examples. Most commonly in the French case, the issue was raised in relation to children's health in advertisements for nutritional products. One such ad, for Nestlé baby cereal, shows a smiling mother sitting in a chair with a young, smiling child standing in her lap, facing her. The ad's header reads: "Papa is going to find you have grown!"[108] The implication is that the mother's performance of her maternal duty to keep the child strong and healthy is subject to the review of the father, who plays a supervisory role in the health and upbringing of the child. Although its message is undeniably subtle, this ad reinforces the notion that French culture was indeed concerned with the fate of patriarchal authority in the interwar years. Another ad for Nestlé baby cereal from the 1920s makes this point more directly (fig. 12). In the ad, a husband is

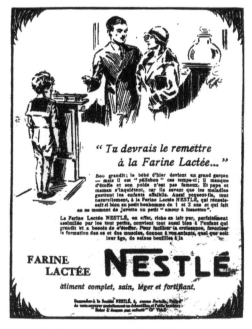

FIG. 12. Another Nestlé baby cereal ad, from *L'Oeuvre* (21 September 1927) and *L'Action Française* (20 July 1928)

pictured speaking to his wife, who is standing next to him. In front of them, their young son stands on a scale. The husband is telling the wife that she must once again provide the boy with Nestlé baby cereal. The text of the ad explains that the child is underweight, and must be given that product in order to grow and become healthy.[109] The ad obviously implies that the woman was not performing her maternal duties adequately, and had to be coached or scolded by a supervising father and husband. Thus this advertisement strongly promotes the assertion of paternal authority in the family.

In response to widespread cultural anxiety over falling birth rates and predictions of dire national catastrophes if that trend continued, French and German popular ideologies reconstructed the meanings of motherhood in the interwar years. While politicians and other public figures fought unsuccessfully to bolster demographic numbers through reproductive legislation as well as by offering incentives and honors for motherhood, publicity materials from France and Germany created a revitalized image of maternity. On the one hand, this new conception of motherhood delineated the joys and pleasures intrinsic to being a mother as a means of making the prospect of childbearing and child rearing more attractive to women. Images of women and children happily and even frivolously playing together and sharing tender moments of affection imparted the message that maternity could bring women happiness and fulfillment. On the other hand, maternity in popular imagery was rooted even more strongly in the duties and responsibilities of being a mother in an effort to direct women to the most important elements of their own actions with respect to the raising of their children. Women were exhorted to keep their children healthy and strong, in part to ensure the nation's continued existence and vitality—a crucial task in societies in which demographic crisis prompted concerns about the nation becoming extinct or being overrun by a more powerful enemy due to a lack of able-bodied fighters. Finally, amidst fears of women usurping masculine authority in the home in the wake of men's lengthy absence during the Great War, mothers were instructed to resubmit to patriarchal authority so that traditional notions of family could be restored in the turbulent interwar years.

CHAPTER THREE

GENDERING THE BOUNDARIES OF PUBLIC AND PRIVATE

Fashion, Beauty, and Health

While in some instances men and women were both depicted in ads in the private sphere (in their roles as fathers and mothers, for example) or in the public sphere (such as when they were shown driving), in other cases publicity materials from France and Germany demonstrated a powerful and sustained gendering of the public and private spheres throughout the two decades separating the world wars. In particular, publicity materials dealing with issues of fashion, beauty, and personal health illustrated a dichotomy between public-centered, healthy, active masculinity and household-oriented, traditional, frail femininity.

While the connections to technological goods are sometimes less direct in this chapter than in others, interwar discussions of gender as they related to fashion, health, and beauty still were bound up with notions of modernity in France and Germany. Nina Lerman points out, for example, the "technologies of identity" that illustrate strong links between gender and technology in such arenas.[1] While Lerman speaks largely about more recent cultural phenomena—such as plastic surgery and sex change procedures—the concept of "technologies of identity" can certainly be applied, albeit perhaps in less dramatic form, to the 1920s and 1930s, in which emerging ideals about feminine beauty, curative medical products, and controversial fashions played a quite analogous role. Although less technologically sophisticated than an early-twenty-first-century surgical operation, these interwar issues were no less associated with modernity for contemporaries.

Taken together, the images of fashion, beauty, and health in interwar

French and German publicity materials are strikingly revelatory of cultural ideologies of gender. The thrust of each of these aspects of social discourse was to assert a gendered definition of public and private along masculine and feminine lines, respectively. While the reality of French and German daily existence may have been far removed from such models, at the level of the popular imagination the dichotomy between a male-dominated public sphere and a feminine-defined private one continued to hold sway in the 1920s and 1930s, a distinction evident in the powerful gendering of public and private spaces in images related to fashion, beauty, and health.

PUBLIC QUALITY AND PRIVATE ELEGANCE
The Masculine Public Sphere

In the 1925 *agenda* of the Bon Marché, there appeared a cartoon entitled simply "Fashion" that encapsulates one of the central themes of interwar discussions of fashion. The cartoon shows a newly hired domestic servant entering a room where a husband and wife are standing with their backs to her. Needing to deliver a letter to Monsieur, the servant is confounded for, viewing them from behind, both husband and wife look exactly the same. The style of their clothing and hair are virtually identical, to the point that this new servant is unable to determine which one is the man and which the woman of the house.[2]

Fashion, especially women's fashion, was a subject of sometimes intense debate in the interwar period. The culturally vilified "modern woman," after all, was recognizable first and foremost by her masculinized hairstyle and mode of dress—short, bobbed hair and a functional wardrobe that deemphasized "natural" feminine physiological features. The way a woman dressed could be read as a symbol of her acceptance or rejection of wider sociocultural dictates regarding "proper" femininity. The fashions of the interwar period, as well as the specific styles of the "modern woman," have been examined at great length in both French and German historiography, and my intent here is merely to mention the importance of fashion in the interwar politics of gender rather than detail the particular aspects of those fashions.[3]

The gendered nature of numerous fashion advertisements and catalogs was most immediately evident in a subtle but extremely significant tactic: the contrasts between backdrops for men and women depicted in publicity materials. Simply put, men in fashion ads were frequently shown wearing advertised clothing items in public or social settings,[4] while women were generally portrayed without any background image or in a domestic scene, often sitting in a chair or standing in a living room.[5] Such images clearly demarcated public spaces as masculine domains.

Fashion images connecting men with the public sphere were sometimes quite diverse in their visual and textual strategies. In the French case, some sources, in addition to picturing men outdoors, also provided textual references to *la ville,* promoting vestments that men would find useful for getting around in the city, an allusion rarely seen in materials featuring women.[6] German advertisements contained fewer of these references to the city, providing instead a more visual focus on the city as the realm of men. A good example occurs in a 1924 ad for a store, Alfred Kauf. The ad pictures seven well-dressed men milling about just outside the retailer's storefront. All of the men appear quite comfortable in this milieu; most of them are reading or examining their surroundings. A solitary female figure is also included in the ad, although she is likely to be noticed only on second glance . Although placed spatially in the center of the advertisement, she is difficult to notice because of her location slightly in the background (meaning also that she is smaller in appearance to the reader). Unlike the men, she does not seem particularly confident as she stands outside the store in a long dress. While she certainly does not look distressed, it is clear from the image that the male figures in the ad are much more familiar with this public setting, and much more aware of how to act in it, than she is.[7] Thus even though the advertisement shows a woman in the public sphere, she is outnumbered by her male counterparts and is decidedly ambivalent, even apprehensive, in this public space. This ad provides just one example of the ways in which men were generally shown as the occupiers of the public sphere.

This monopoly of public spaces extended in large part to the world of work. As I discuss in chapter 5, French and German discourse did not condemn all female work out of hand—recognizing that many women left without husbands or marriage prospects by World War I would have to engage in paid labor in order to survive—but acceptance of female labor was far from complete or without limitations. Therefore, while some fashion ads did mention working in the context of women's fashions, it was most often men to whom discussions of labor vis-à-vis clothing were imparted. As one example, a 1926 advertisement from Germany for the store Peek & Cloppenburg pictures two men standing together in an outdoor setting; the ad's text refers to business suits for sale at the store.[8] In the French context, some ads employed similar imagery and references, but even more noteworthy are several interwar catalogs of one of Paris's best-known department stores, the Bazar de l'Hôtel de Ville (BHV). A number of the BHV's catalogs, from 1921 to 1938, contain in their sections on men's fashions a special category of "clothing for work." Such a category is entirely absent in the catalogs' sections devoted to women's fashions, where instead clothes are organized into categories such as blouses and coats.[9] Such materials suggested that the world of work, an integral part of the public sphere, was also a solely masculine affair.

The masculine appropriation of public spaces could be seen in other venues as well. Ads from both countries utilized images of automobiles in fashion ads, employing images of men in such instances far more often than women. Fashion advertisements from France and Germany show men standing beside or astride automobiles, or make textual references to advertised clothes as suitable for wearing while operating a vehicle.[10] As a conduit for travel in public spaces, the automobile in fashion ads was gendered masculine quite noticeably; even where women were depicted with cars, as will be seen in the next chapter, such images reinforced associations of femininity with domesticity. Other publicity materials depicted men in another public environment engaged in what was defined as a quintessentially masculine pursuit: hunting. Various fashion advertisements from both nations produced images of men hunting or made textual references to clothing that could be worn while hunting (fig. 13).[11] Needless to say, women were virtually never shown in such ads.

Other advertisements performed a similar discursive function. In particular, there are a number of ads that raise the issue of weather conditions, and place men in outdoor settings where weather will be of concern to them. For instance, a French ad from 1920 shows two men standing and talking happily in the midst of a downpour of rain; their coats (the advertised products) are keeping them dry and warm.[12] A German ad from September 1930, also for coats, shows a man wearing a coat and tipping his hat to something unseen to the reader. While the image does not provide a backdrop, the male figure's adornment and posture strongly imply an outdoor setting. Moreover, the text of the ad is quite notable. It focuses on being ready for the autumn's weather, and emphasizes the coat's ability to protect one from the elements.[13] In this case, too, the male figure is presented as being concerned about meteorological conditions, suggesting his involvement and movement in the public sphere.

In spite of the powerful currency of this dichotomy, there were exceptions

FIG. 13. Ad for the Belle Jardinière department store, *Le Matin* (24 August 1922)

to depictions of women in indoor settings in fashion advertisements, but even these were carefully constructed so as to reassert ultimately an emphasis on tradition. Ads from both France and Germany contain a few examples of women shown in public spaces; in almost every case, the backdrop is simply a pristine-looking locale in which nature is the unifying characteristic. Women were not portrayed hunting, driving, or going to work, but simply walking about in a natural, unspoiled area. In such ads, there is virtually always ample greenery evident in the backdrop that highlights the less urban character of these settings.[14]

Perhaps the best examples are found in an advertising brochure distributed by the Bon Marché in 1920 touting the latest fashions and furniture at the store. A couple of images in the brochure illustrate the close connection between femininity and nature scenes in those fashion advertisements that placed women in public spaces. One such example is an illustration that takes up both sides of two facing pages in the brochure. It shows six women wearing advertised articles of clothing. They are standing, carefree, in a very inviting nature setting; there are a couple of trees in the illustration, and in the background is a lake on which a sailboat is visible.[15] Another drawing in the brochure is similar in tone. It occurs on a page highlighting fashions for girls and young women, three of whom are shown in the drawing. The setting, as with the previous example, is an inviting outdoors area, replete with trees and, in the background, a body of water. The young ladies seem to be on a quiet, enjoyable, peaceful picnic; they are sitting around a table with some fruit as well as cups for coffee or tea.[16]

These examples of women pictured in the public sphere are thus fundamentally different from images of men in fashion ads, and in fact serve to dissociate the images from any overtones of "improper" femininity such as that commonly linked with the "modern woman" (namely, an independent lifestyle and sexual promiscuity). Instead, the pristine, nature-oriented settings in which women were depicted in the public sphere actually returned them discursively to an idealized, nostalgic past and rooted them firmly in the realm of tradition.[17]

One other type of advertisement that appeared in the interwar years suggesting feminine entry into the public sphere is also significant. These were ads that portrayed women's operation in the public sphere as dependent on male assistance or kindness, thus subverting any potential feminine independence in the public realm. A good example is an ad from Germany from 1921, which provides an edifying contrast with ads earlier discussed in relation to men and adverse weather conditions. In this ad, a fierce storm is in progress, and a lone woman caught unprepared for the rain is helped by a masculine figure, who shelters her with an umbrella.[18] Unable to fend for herself in the public arena, this woman is essentially rescued by an everyman who, unlike women, operates ably in the public world. Ads like this further delineated the public realm as a masculine preserve even as they depicted women in public settings.

Male Quality, Female Elegance

Another method by which both nations' fashion advertisements and publicity materials defined masculinity and femininity along distinct lines was through an emphasis on masculine interest in a product's quality and a countervailing feminine concern with elegance and beauty in fashion goods. At the simplest level, asserting a discursive connection between masculinity and an interest and aptitude for quality could be made by touting the production and durability of the clothes in question. A Galeries Lafayette catalog of men's fashions, for instance, consistently emphasizes the quality and durability of the advertised products.[19] A Burberrys ad from the French press, moreover, refers to the "excellent materials" from which the store's clothes are made,[20] while an H. J. Nicoll ad from 1920 claims that its clothing products are of a "superior quality."[21] Both ads depict masculine figures as their subjects. Advertisements for German stores were often similar. One from 1926 that pictures two men and a young boy assures the reader that the store's winter clothing is made only from the "best materials."[22] Other ads from Germany cite the high-quality production or sturdiness of clothing items.[23]

A number of French ads for men's fashions went to significant lengths to assure readers of the quality not only of the products, but also of the manufacturing process that created them. A 1936 advertisement for Burberrys sporting outfits, for example, shows a man dressed in a suit walking with a bag of golf clubs slung over his shoulder. In part, the text of the ad states, "The Burberrys sport suit is the work of experienced specialists, who join impeccable technique with lengthy experience." Therefore, the ad declares, "the Burberrys sport suit puts up with the roughest use without ever being deformed."[24] Similarly, a 1923 Burberrys ad that shows a man standing in front of a vehicle also appeals to sportsmen: "BURBERRYS places at the disposal of sportsmen the experience acquired by three generations of manufacturers who, SPORTSMEN THEMSELVES, have personally tried the clothes that they have designed and, based on their practical tests, have improved continually the qualities of hygienic protection and lightness, to such an extent that, throughout the entire world, the word BURBERRY is synonymous with PERFECTION."[25] In such ads, interest in the quality of clothing was thus strongly connected to masculinity.

Along similar lines, practical clothing was seen as inherently masculine, once again particularly in the French case. The best example of this comes from another Burberrys advertisement, this one from 1926, that shows two men leaving what appears to be a golfing clubhouse.[26] Preparing to walk out of adjacent doors, however, the two men encounter quite different weather conditions. The man on the left of the ad exits the club to rain, while the man on the right side heads out into what appears to be a clear, sunny day. Although their coats look different from one another, the ad declares in bold print: "One article of clothing = two coats." The two men, in fact, are wearing the same type of reversible coat that can be adjusted based on the weather.[27] The highlighting of this useful feature is typical of those ads directed at men that emphasize the practicality of men's fashions. Such ads defined men as intrinsically rational and calculating about their clothing purchases, interested in clothes for their quality, practicality, and durability.

In contrast, fashion ads portraying female subjects placed much less emphasis on these features, focusing instead on issues considered more "naturally" feminine, such as taste and beauty. For example, a 1921 advertisement from France for H. J. Nicoll that depicts two female figures has as its focal point the bold-printed words "PERFECT ELEGANCE" printed entirely in capital letters. The text of the ad focuses centrally on the fact that the advertised clothes are "more aesthetic" and have a "distinguished style."[28] A Burberrys ad from 1938 that pictures a woman strongly stresses the "absolute comfort" of an advertised coat, and assures the reader that it is not only "ELEGANT AND COMFORTABLE," but also "SOFT AND LIGHT." The ad also promotes the aesthetic values of the coat, describing its "silky appearance" and "pleasant colors."[29]

Contemporary sources from the French *grands magasins* also make this point quite unmistakably. As an example, the Galeries Lafayette *agenda* for 1924 contains an illustration of a woman in the foreground holding a hatbox in each arm, while in the background two other women stand before a few hip-high piles of hatboxes. The women are all wearing hats. Discussing the "pretty cardboard boxes," the illustration's accompanying text states that "inimitable Parisian taste" continues "manifesting itself in all domains dedicated to feminine grace." The boxes and original packaging of products that can be bought at the Galeries Lafayette, such as hats, need not be thrown out; instead, the ad declares that the store's "elegant clients" can use them to add a "refined style" to their homes.[30] Indeed, the term "elegant" appeared quite frequently with respect to women in interwar catalogs as well, particularly those of the store Printemps, which developed a slogan geared toward this connection between femininity and elegance: "Every elegant woman is a customer of Printemps." This motto appeared in Printemps' publicity materials throughout the 1920s and 1930s.[31]

German advertisements for women's fashions displayed much the same preoccupation with issues of elegance, attractiveness, and good taste in clothing. As with French ads, the term "elegant" constantly appeared in discussions of women's fashions, thus focusing on perceived feminine abilities with respect to taste and style, but not necessarily quality.[32] Other German ads incorporate the term "beauty" or "beautiful" into their descriptions of advertised items of clothing.[33] One ad from 1926 for the store C&A portrays a smiling woman in a dress and hat; the text of the ad exclaims: "The dress of which you have dreamed!" explaining that this piece of clothing is beautiful, elegant, charming, and available in "tasteful colors."[34]

A couple of examples neatly capture much of this discourse by contrasting masculine and feminine traits within a single ad. A French advertisement for

Burberrys from 1927, under the header "The weather is uncertain," promotes Burberrys coats. The text of the ad explicitly states the different reasons that men and women acquire and use such coats, saying that a "sportsman" needs a coat that can be exposed to long periods of rain, while "the elegant woman desires only to protect an attractive outfit."[35] Thus a man requires a coat that performs on a practical basis for extended outdoor activity, while a woman simply wants to preserve the pretty clothes that she wears beneath the coat. In the German case, a 1921 ad for Wertheim department store contains no images of people, but rather consists solely of two boxes of text—one dealing with men's clothes, the other with women's clothing. The men's clothing box highlights the "distinguished manufacture" of the products, while the women's side describes the products foremost as "elegant."[36]

The wider effect of this dichotomous ideology of quality-driven masculinity and elegance-centered femininity was to reinforce prevailing, traditional conceptions of sexual difference, thereby undercutting the reality of changing gender roles. Presentations of men as calculating and rational, concerned with a product's manufacture, quality, and durability—that is, with questions of practical import to the life of the consumer good—existed in opposition to constructions of women in fashion advertising as irrationally emotional and impulsive, concerned only with traditionally feminine matters.[37] Opposing masculine rationality to feminine emotiveness served to undermine any feminine agency with respect to public life, further solidifying men's position as the masters of public spaces and roles. Feminine emotion and irrationality is suggested in a couple of department store ads from France and Germany. In the French case, an advertisement for Galeries Lafayette consists solely of an outline of a woman's head and neck, viewed from the side. Written repeatedly across this outline—thus literally inscribed on the feminine figure—are the words "Galeries Lafayette." Beneath this image is the message: ". . . in the head of every Woman . . ."[38] While obviously not directly stating as much, the thrust of this ad is to undermine any notion of feminine rationality with respect to shopping, instead presenting women as consumed by thoughts of the *magasin* to the exclusion of all else. This is certainly not a portrait of calculating, rational consumption, but one of emotion and impulse. A German ad for the C&A store chain makes a similar point. In the ad, a huge throng of mostly women is pictured outside a C&A store, anxiously awaiting entry into the shop. A giant hand in the illustration seems to hold back the tide of these women, and the ad's header orders: "Don't shove!"[39] The implication is that the crowd is potentially an unruly mob desperately and impatiently awaiting the opportunity to get into the shop. Thus in this instance as well, women are shown as totally devoted to shopping and consumption in a way that strongly suggests that impulse and emotion, not rationality, are the basis of their actions.

THE CULT OF FEMININE BEAUTY

In both France and Germany, the first half of the twentieth century witnessed an increased emphasis on the imperative of physical beauty for women. Studying the United States, Kathy Peiss traces the existence of a "beauty culture" from the late nineteenth century onward. Analyzing the increased cultural acceptance of cosmetics use in conjunction with shifting gender roles and social upheaval after the Great War, she detects a connection between beauty culture, specifically cosmetics, and modernity.[40] The use of such products and the importance of feminine physical appearance were tied ever more closely to "proper" womanhood. As Mary Lynn Stewart argues for France, beauty advertisers "correlated cleanliness, comeliness, and ultimately femininity with the consumption of health and beauty products."[41] Thus striving for a beautiful appearance came to be defined as an intrinsic part of being a woman. Indeed, French and German advertising materials in the 1920s and 1930s illustrated the desirability, even necessity, of feminine beauty, associating an attractive appearance with a woman's character, health, and acceptance of male authority.

Beauty and Character

One's external physical form purportedly made a statement about one's internal character. As Kathy Peiss notes with reference to the United States, "the face was a window into the soul, and complexion problems were indicative of a life that was disordered, out of balance."[42] This is a vitally important point: in an age wherein cultural fears and anxieties about feminine independence and sexuality, particularly as represented in the concept of the "modern woman," were at perhaps unprecedented levels, one means by which women could exert their independence was in their physical appearance, especially their hairstyles. The refusal of the "modern woman" to live according to social dictates regarding "proper" femininity was embodied most visibly in her visage, and it is thus no accident that feminists and "modern women" were frequently labeled as ugly.[43] This appellation thus represented not just a subjective assessment about the agreeability of one's physical appearance, but a value judgment of a woman's lifestyle. Beautiful women were those who lived according to social dictates regarding "proper" femininity, while unattractiveness was a signal of a woman's refusal to obey such cultural imperatives. Discussing discursive beliefs in Wilhelmine Germany, Michael Hau notes: "Deviance from behavioral norms had its expression in a deviation from aesthetic norms. . . . [W]omen could only hope to approach the ideal of perfect beauty if they complied with the traditional gender norms of the Bürgertum, which relegated women to motherhood and a place within the home."[44] Thus the advertisements discussed below, in their unanimous insistence on beauty and the means to achieve or maintain it, were at the same time exhorting women to live according to culturally defined norms of femininity emphasizing home, hearth, and children.

Advertisements from the French popular press repeatedly addressed questions relating to feminine beauty. Perhaps most common were ads that simply offered advice about the general improvement or maintenance of one's physical appearance. A 1928 ad for Palmolive soap, for instance, pictures a man and woman at a formal affair, as evidenced by her elaborate dress and his tuxedo. The ad's header, "Years pass, beauty remains," introduces the text of the advertisement, which focuses on ways in which Palmolive helps "women of a 'certain age'" to maintain their youthful appearance.[45] A 1932 ad for Dulmin crème, moreover, pictures a woman in a bathing suit playing with a beach ball. The ad's header declares: "It is necessary to fight in order to be beautiful!"[46] Such ads were typical of French beauty advertising.[47]

Such advertisements were just as prominent in the German press. One example is a 1933 ad for Steckenpferd soap, which consists simply of the name of the product, an image of a woman, and the words, "The secret of my beauty," an obvious reference to the advertised soap (fig. 14).[48] As in the French case, many ads cautioned that the maintenance of beauty required considerable work and care.[49] In addition, as in French advertisements, German discourse asserted that it was possible and desirable to maintain one's beauty at an advanced age. Perhaps the best example of this comes from a 1926 ad that features an image of a middle-aged woman above the header: "What a marvelous appearance at 40 years old!"[50]

German advertisements were sometimes explicit about the perceived importance of personal beauty to a woman's well-being and self-worth. A 1926 ad, for example, depicts a woman above the header "Beauty." The ad states:

FIG. 14. Ad for Steckenpferd soap, *Illustrirte Zeitung* (5 October 1933)

"Beauty is the crown of a woman's life."[51] Even more blunt is a 1938 ad for Laun cream products. Above a drawing of a woman's face, the ad's header reads: "The greatest fortune in life is health, but the matter of greatest importance is *beauty!*"[52] This ad and others like it suggested that beauty represented the very apex of femininity and a woman's life. Thus the cultural importance attached to notions of feminine physical appearance cannot be overlooked.

Beauty and Health

In addition to these advertisements that promised beauty in a general sense, a number of other ads, often for more specialized beauty products, dealt with particular aspects of feminine beauty, and these advertisements are also noteworthy. Ads for skin- and hair-care products deserve attention in this regard. Ads for these types of products not only made claims as to the achievement and maintenance of beauty, but also promised in many cases to help ensure good health. The subject of health and its gendered implications will be explored in the final section of this chapter, but its links to beauty must also be raised here. Michael Hau's examination of German ideals of health and beauty reveals that beauty was regarded as a sign of good health and normal physiological functioning, while unattractiveness was read as an expression of an unhealthy, even diseased, body.[53]

The implication that cleanliness, health, and beauty were all linked was made in several ads. A 1927 ad for Leodor cream from Germany highlights the supposed connection between such products and feminine beauty: "The secret of the beautiful woman lies in the correct selection and correct application of skin-care materials."[54] Indeed, such products often claimed both to heal and to care for the skin while adding to a woman's overall beauty. Most notable in this regard was a series of German ads for Kaloderma soap in the 1930s. One such ad points out that "skin care is more than beauty care alone." Containing an image of an apparently freshly showered woman—she has a towel wrapped around her—the ad states: "Not only the beauty of the complexion, but also in large part our good health depends on the correctly functioning 'breathing of the skin.' When this breathing of the skin is hindered by the gradual blocking of skin pores, not only does the skin become ashen and dirty, but the health of the body itself suffers." Indeed, the ad continues, Kaloderma cleans these pores, allowing for the perpetuation of health and beauty.[55]

In France, there was less emphasis on such skin-care products, and a greater focus instead on hair care.[56] In advertisements for these hair-care products, the most common theme is the importance of maintaining or recapturing a youthful appearance in one's later years. A 1937 ad, for example, pictures a young girl, but the ad is directed at older women who are encouraged to attempt to get rid of their gray hair.[57] Even more visually striking is a 1928 advertisement that shows a distressed-looking woman apparently removing an offending hair from her head. The ad's header refers to "white hair" as a "sign of old age."[58] This is not to suggest that there were no such ads for similar products in Germany; indeed, a number of ads addressed the issue of aging and graying of the hair. A 1938 ad for Sebalds (a hair-coloring product) shows the back of a woman's head. An arrow points to what are apparently gray hairs. The ad states that streaks of gray "always impair the gracefulness of the hairstyle," and thus the ad encourages the reader to use Sebalds.[59] Another Sebalds ad, showing a woman pouring from a kettle in the kitchen, states: "The woman in the household . . . must especially be anxious about the care and preservation of the health of her hair. Steam from cooking and dust make the hair unsightly and impair the recovered growth of hair. A few drops of 'Sebalds Haartinktur' clean and stimulate the scalp and preserve the hair."[60]

These ads, taken together, represent another layer in the cult of feminine beauty in France and Germany. Beauty could be appealed to and invoked at a number of levels, all of which were designed to preserve an idealized gender order through the continued emphasis on notions of "proper" and attractive femininity.

A few advertisements launched appeals to women on more unique bases than hair or skin care. For example, several ads address the issue of retaining a youthful- and full-looking bust. A 1934 ad for Pilules Orientales declares in its header that "a beautiful chest is essential to the woman," and explains that the advertised pills can assist women in restoring a desirable bust.[61] A 1939 ad for Kala-Busta, a breast-enhancement product, depicts a distraught woman looking down before a mirror with her head in her hands. The ad's header states: "It is in the CHEST that one ages most rapidly." The ad explains that the firmness of women's breasts declines with age, but that Kala-Busta can restore youthful vigor to a woman's chest, having "immediate and beneficial repercussions on the intimate life of the woman."[62] In the German case, there were a couple of references to maintaining a "beautiful figure," but little information as blunt as that appearing in the French press regarding women's chests.[63] Nonetheless, German advertisements, too, offered singular perspectives on feminine beauty. One advertisement from 1923, which depicts a woman's face looking back at the reader, poses the question: "Are your eyebrows and eyelashes as beautiful as mine?"[64]

All of the above evidence suggests a pervasive and powerful cult of beauty for French and German women throughout the 1920s and 1930s. From attractive faces and complexions to firm busts and alluring eyelashes, French and German discourse delineated to a considerable degree the necessary steps toward beautification for women. This attractive appearance was meant to mirror one's good health and acceptable behavior and lifestyle vis-à-vis social norms and mores relating to gender.

this is nothing new

Beauty and Masculine Authority

One final aspect of this beauty cult deserves attention. Mary Lynn Stewart points out that, in the end, the scientific authority so often invoked in beauty advertising may have been used simply to advance a patriarchal agenda. The primary purpose of feminine beauty ideals in France and elsewhere in Europe was largely to camouflage as "natural" a pursuit that was designed in reality mainly for the pleasure of men.[65] Invocations of feminine beauty thus allowed for the cultural perpetuation of ideals of masculine authority and dominance over women, in this case along with the objectification of women under the guise of "natural" physical appearance. Some advertising images indeed suggest that beauty culture was to a significant extent an exercise in patriarchal control designed to fulfill male pleasures and subordinate women discursively to masculine authority.

This discursive subordination of women to male authority can be seen in a couple of advertisements that depict or discuss masculine figures. A German ad from 1935 for Palmolive, for instance, contains an image of a male doctor instructing an attentive woman in the proper care of her skin.[66] The suggestion is that even though health and beauty care is a subject that greatly interests women, they need to have a male expert instruct them in the proper method of such efforts. Thus women are not given independent agency in regard to beautification of their own bodies; in this endeavor, as in so many others, cultural ideology dictated that a male expert serve as intermediary.

A 1929 ad from France for Bertimay cosmetic powder makes a similar point. The ad pictures a woman sitting in front of a vanity mirror, apparently applying makeup and grooming herself for an unspecified occasion. In the illustration, she is looking up in evident surprise at her husband, who stands to her right. The ad's header reads: "How Bertimay powder was born." The ad explains that one day Monsieur Bertimay happened to enter the boudoir of his wife while she was using multiple powders to achieve a desired tint in her complexion. Monsieur Bertimay asked her why she needed so many different powders, expressing concern at the presumed expense of these various products. His wife responded that, even more annoying than the number of powders required, was that those products lost their effectiveness after several weeks. The ad explains what happened next: "Bertimay is a man of action. He thought about the question, understood that there was something to do, put the most famous expert chemists in charge of finding an entirely new formula of powder. It was after only thirty-nine weeks of persistent labor that Frenchwomen were equipped with Bertimay powder."[67] Thus in this advertisement as well, women are given no cultural agency with respect to their own beauty. It takes a "man of action," not an apparently passive woman, to take care of those issues relating to health and beauty care. Once again, even in the pursuit of feminine beauty, men were placed squarely in a dominant position over women.

The very fact that this pursuit of beauty was confined to women and did not extend to men is also a subject that merits consideration. After all, given that notions of beauty were tied to health, it might have been logical that men would also be concerned with maintaining their physical appearance. Yet very few such indications appeared in the French and German press, further illustrating the point that the scientific basis of beauty culture was simply a façade. Even the rare ads that do address men in relation to physical appearance demonstrate key differences from ads featuring women. One example is a French ad for Silvifix hair cream. It depicts a man tipping his hat, thus revealing his "always well coiffed" hair. The text of the ad states that it is "[p]ointless to tell a good representative, a serious worker, a man of the world, that it is always necessary to be impeccably coiffed. They employ Silvifix. Instinctually."[68] The subtext of this advertisement is quite the opposite of ads directed at women. The notion that men use this hair cream based on natural instinct contrasts sharply with suggestions that women must be educated about the benefits of health and beauty products. In addition, the implication of the ad is not that a man should use this product simply to improve his physical looks (although there is, it should be noted, a mention of health in the ad); rather, the allusions to workers, men of the world, and representatives suggest that the cream is effective at giving men an appropriate look for professional purposes—a suggestion completely absent in ads directed at women, which almost unanimously avoid references to paid labor or employment.

An ad from Germany makes a similar suggestion, albeit in a different manner. This ad about hair care features the silhouetted images of two women's heads. However, the text of the ad appeals to a male reader, stating that "your wife and your daughter" should use the advertised hair-care product.[69] Thus in this case, even though a male reader is presumed, there is no indication that he should be worried about hair care for his own sake, but rather simply for the females in his family. Along analogous lines, a 1935 ad for Kaloderma shaving cream and soap addresses a male audience, and even pictures a male figure. The ad's focus, however, is simply on the maintenance of a beard— there is no mention of issues of health or physical attractiveness.[70] Thus even when a male subject is shown and addressed in an ad, there is no indication that he must worry about the same problems that women were constantly exhorted to monitor.

A final set of examples illustrates the related point that the cult of beauty was ultimately geared toward the pleasures of men. A 1929 advertisement from France, for instance, features a profile of a woman's face; the header is simply: "Men prefer blondes."[71] There is no extended discussion of any alleged health benefits of coloring one's hair, nor any rationale offered that would explain how this proposed action would make one more beautiful. Instead, the message is simply that blond hair will prove pleasing to men. A final example comes from Germany. This ad, for Pixavon shampoo, depicts a man and woman standing together. He stands slightly behind her and is bending down slightly, apparently to smell her hair. The ad states that the pictured woman is "much older than her friends, but she has an irresistible attraction and a fresh appearance," all thanks to Pixavon. Most revealing, though, is the ad's header: "Why do men adore her?" The answer, of course, is that Pixavon shampoo is the "secret" to her allure.[72] By focusing attention on attracting men, the ad's message becomes that women's use of this product is designed not so much for its ability to beautify or keep one healthy, but simply to attract and please men.

MEDICAL PRODUCTS AND THE GENDERING OF HEALTH

The notion of masculine dominance was a thread that continued into the realm of medical and health discourse in French and German publicity materials. Indeed, the massive quantity of advertising materials for health-related products marks these as a key site of advertising discourse. As Marc Martin has shown in the case of France, by the late 1930s ads for pharmaceutical products accounted for almost 30 percent of all spending on advertising.[73] The subject of health and hygiene, at the personal and public levels, was an increasing concern in European societies from the turn of the century onward.[74] The overarching theme uniting much of the publicity materials relating to medicine and health was that men were naturally strong, active beings while women were inherently frail and weak. The suggestion of much of the materials to be discussed below was that women could never really achieve good health, but rather that they were so intrinsically susceptible to ill health that the best they could hope for was some relief from innate and seemingly unalterable general poor health. As will be shown, such messages ultimately served to reinforce the notion that the public sphere was men's realm, while women were consigned to the private sphere.

Frail Femininity

An illustration entitled "Exaggeration" from the 1928 *agenda* of the Bon Marché shows a woman talking to a male doctor. The text accompanying the image consists of an exchange between doctor and patient in which the latter describes her symptoms.

> Sick woman. —10 minutes of terrible anguish, many dreadful pains, many intolerable suffocations, 10 more minutes of sharp pains, then finally calmness until the next crisis.
> Doctor. —That happens to you often?
> Sick woman. —Every quarter of an hour.[75]

The intended comical aspects of this portrayal notwithstanding, the most common publicity materials relating to medical products depicted women who, like the one portrayed in the illustration above, were trying to cope with various and seemingly ever-present medical ailments. Taken together, these sources suggest that femininity was unavoidably accompanied by health problems.

A few such ads from Germany can be seen in relation to the cult of beauty. A 1936 ad, for example, focuses on caring for the healthiness of one's skin. The ad features a woman apparently looking into a mirror and refers to an unclear complexion as evidence of "sick skin."[76] An ad from 1926 that also features an image of a woman encourages her to take the advertised product, Biomalz, for it will allegedly cure a variety of ailments, leading not only to improved health but also to "a good, blossoming look."[77] Most visually striking, however, is a 1922 ad for a "forming" device that pictures a woman sitting with no apparent fear, pain, or apprehension as a pair of male arms inserts the device into her breast (fig. 15). The ad explains that the procedure will assist a woman's circulation and help the development of breast tissue cells, with the result that an "underdeveloped" breast "becomes voluptuous and buxom."[78] Thus a number of ads in the German press emphasized a correlation between health and physical attractiveness.

In the French context, a 1922 Pilules Pink ad featuring an image of a woman is instructive. The main text of the ad takes the form of a poem, which claims that women need to spend as much time attending to their health as they do to their physical appearance, for by increasing the attention given to their health, their beauty will be augmented as well. The ad assures the reader that Pilules Pink ensures the well-being of one's blood, nerves, and overall health.[79] Moreover, a 1934 ad for a weight-loss product shows a formally clad man and woman dancing. The ad's text specifically addresses the woman, saying that "what a woman wants is youthfulness, is thinness." Such traits can be

Eta-Formenprickler
(gesetzl. geschützt)

Eine neue medizinische Erfindung.

Wirkung: Ein tiefes angenehmes Prickeln erfolgt, kräftigt u. festigt durch neu angeregte Blutzirkulation intensiv die Brustgewebszellen. Die unentwickelte oder welkgewordene Brust wird üppig und drall. Für Erfolg verbürgt sich die Firma. — Preis komplett M. 24.—mit Garantieschein.

Laboratorium „ETA", Berlin 243, Potsdamerstr. 32.

FIG. 15. Ad for a "forming" device for the breast, *Simplicissimus* (1 March 1922)

gained by losing weight safely, according to the ad, which will also contribute to one's good health.[80]

Just as these ads suggested that women required treatment or products for the improvement of their health, other medical ads unrelated to beauty culture likewise made evident the perceived frailty and ill health of women. In some cases, these ads even pictured happy or healthy-looking women, but the textual descriptions of ill health contained within the ads belied the contented appearance of the illustrated subjects. A 1934 ad from Germany, for instance, contains an illustration of a smiling, happy woman who obviously feels better after having used Biocitin, the advertised product. The ad suggests that one's quality of life can be improved by using Biocitin, particularly with respect to the increased health and strength of one's nerves.[81] Similarly, a contented-looking woman is shown in an ad for Besankura, which promises to protect against a variety of maladies.[82] Moreover, a series of ads for Melabon capsules from the mid-1930s shows happy, smiling women; the ads invariably vow that the product will help with common aches and pains, such as backaches, headaches, and the like.[83] While none of these ads depicts an ill-looking woman, the textual references to numerous illnesses leave the unmistakable impression that women are destined to be beleaguered by an array of health problems.

A number of French advertisements also recounted feminine ailments despite picturing apparently happy women. A 1936 ad for a tonic, Cocarsine, shows a smiling woman, from whose happy face emanate beams of light. The ad's header, in large bold print, is: "Health!" Immediately underneath this term, however, the words "depressed and anemic" appear also in bold print, undermining any notion that the woman's health is complete or assured. The ad's text advises the use of Cocarsine in order to avoid a "deficient state," which according to the ad can lead to illness.[84] An ad for Nestlé baby cereal, moreover, shows a woman sitting and eating the advertised product; her young toddlers see her doing so, and comment with surprise that she "is eating *our* baby cereal!" The ad explains that the product is a healthy food not only for infants, but also for pregnant women, the elderly, and convalescents.[85] Since the woman shows no signs of pregnancy and is obviously neither elderly nor an invalid, the reader is left to wonder why she needs to be consuming this product. The implication is that there are unseen health problems beneath the woman's exterior that demand the ingestion of the baby cereal.

Other ads from both nations make similar claims about curing various maladies, but in doing so show women in far less contented postures. A fruit industry ad from Germany from 1926, for example, shows two women and a man sitting and reading together. The ad promises that eating fruit will help one to sleep better. The demeanor of the pictured subjects is revealing, for the man in the ad is smiling, showing no signs of health or sleeping problems, while the two women look downtrodden.[86] The message, then, seems to be directed at the female figures in the ad, and does not appear to apply to the healthy, happy male who is with them. Further, in a 1921 ad, a nude woman covers her face with her hands; she is clearly extremely distraught. The ad's opening lines are: "No shame, but it is unfortunate." The ad goes on to reveal that the woman is suffering from venereal disease.[87] This suggestion is all the more powerful given the social context surrounding the "modern woman," who was threatening precisely because of her independence in both matters of labor and sexuality. The ad, in fact, can almost be read as a cautionary note for such women—the end result of this promiscuous sexuality could be the "unfortunate" situation that has befallen the woman in the ad.

French advertisements likewise showed women in varying states of discomfort or unhappiness due to ill health, further revealing the underlying nature of these medical ads. Ads for medical products claiming to solve a range of problems including rheumatism, digestive disorders, blood deficiencies, and ulcers, among many others, depicted women as victims of poor health not just in the text of the ads, but in accompanying illustrations as well.[88] A brochure distributed in 1936 by the Fluxine-Villefranche laboratories, a manufacturer

FIG. 16. Ad for Globéol, a cure-all tonic, *L'Action Française* (3 March 1921)

of medical goods, contains a number of images relating to the promotion of the labs' products. One such image, in promoting the laxative Evonyl, shows a husband and wife eating at the table. A box of Evonyl is visible on the table between them, slightly to the wife's side. The text of the ad does not explicitly address either the male or female figure, but the picture of the man and woman is instructive—the husband is smiling and happy, while the wife has a very apprehensive look that clearly indicates that she is the one having the problem requiring Evonyl's intervention.[89]

Other ailments were depicted as affecting women in French publicity materials. One purported source of problems was varicose veins. A March 1923 advertising flyer for Velpeau bandages, for instance, shows a woman looking sadly at her leg. Among the merits of the bandages, according to the ad, is the "indisputable" success and "constant relief" they provide in dealing with varicose veins.[90] A 1938 advertisement for Vertex stockings claims that they were designed to help with varicose veins and shows an image of a sitting woman who is obviously wearing the product in question. The ad states that "56% of women suffer from varicose veins."[91] The suggestion is that not just individual women, but women in general, tend to be afflicted with problems of ill health and are enfeebled by their very nature.

A final set of examples of these types of advertisements from France depicts women who are not just downtrodden or uncomfortable, but who are in fact made to appear helpless, lifeless, or desperate in their search for better health. A 1921 ad for Pilules Pink, a widely advertised cure-all, shows a woman desperately fleeing a giant hand, symbolic of illness broadly defined, that is poised to grab her. The text of the ad describes the numerous health problems that women may face, counseling that "it is pointless to run" in the face of such problems, and that a woman would be well-advised to take Pilules Pink to cure her ills.[92] Even more striking is a 1921 ad for Globéol, another cure-all product (fig. 16). Dominating the ad is an image of a virtually lifeless woman being carried by a Globéol bottle with arms and legs. The caption underneath declares that she has been "saved from anemia by Globéol."[93] Such ads characterized women as frail, weak, and helpless in the face of health problems; the curative powers of a wondrous tonic or drug was needed to help them.

Women's Illnesses, Men's Cures

The healing power of such medicinal products was paralleled in French and German discourse by a masculine authority over those curative goods. Just as beauty culture was ultimately an avenue for the perpetuation of masculine dominance over women, so too did popular medical discourse establish a similar authority for men in the realm of treating and solving women's ills.

Most commonly, this was accomplished by the involvement in advertisements of a male expert, often a doctor, who recommended and explained the virtues of a particular medical good to a woman in need of such help. Such incorporation of expert male figures served to undermine any female agency with respect to the independent understanding of such products.[94] One such example from Germany is actually an advertisement for Palmin vegetable oil. In the ad, a woman is being given the advertised product by a professional man in a lab or pharmaceutical coat. Asking her if she has a weak stomach, he recommends Palmin as safe for frail digestive systems.[95] In the French case, a 1935 ad for Quintonine tonic speaks at length of the merits of the product for the restoration and reinvigoration of one's health. The ad depicts a line of women waiting to be given a dose of the product, standing in line as a man at the front pours Quintonine to the women in turn.[96] More dramatic is a 1921 ad for cure-all product Urodonal. It shows a woman lying in bed; her facial expression and contorted posture make it clear that she is in great pain. At the head of the bed, two other women stand consoling her. These two function passively in the scene, while the only active participants are two men in the ad. An older man, apparently a doctor, is holding the afflicted woman's hand and beckoning with his free hand to an assistant. The assistant is running across the room with a bottle of Urodonal, which the doctor will administer to the sick woman in hopes of healing her.[97]

A couple of advertisements are even more fantastical. One, a 1928 ad for yet another health tonic, shows a woman standing in a bathing suit (she is vacationing, the ad reveals) outside of a car driven by a man. In front of her is a man with a head, arms, and legs, but whose body and neck are actually a bottle of the advertised tonic. This figure explains to the woman that this product can restore her spirit, reinvigorate her, and prevent health problems.[98] Another example is an advertising postcard printed by Chantereau medical laboratories to promote its product Sympathyl. The postcard is preaddressed to be returned to Chantereau, and contains a space where different medical products made at its laboratories can be ordered. The illustration on the card shows an older gentleman—symbolic of Chantereau and its scientists—winding up a young woman from behind as though she were a wind-up toy.[99] The implication is that the woman's continued physical functioning is dependent on the products and (male) scientists at Chantereau labs. Just as such a toy can only operate with sustained impetus from an external force, the woman in this case also must be metaphorically wound on a relatively frequent basis whenever she ceases proper functioning.

Such advertising materials from both France and Germany may seem innocuous or merely comical in intent, yet they perpetuated a discursive masculine dominance over expert medical knowledge and treatment, thereby denying women agency with respect to solving their own health problems. Without the intervention of wise, expert men, the advertisements imply, women would be stricken with irreversibly poor health and untreatable maladies. Indeed, closely linked to this discourse privileging male expertise in health problems was an insistence that virtually all women, simply by virtue of being women, were likely to be afflicted with relatively significant health problems at some point in their lives. Femininity, according to such reasoning, meant an inescapable vulnerability to illness—it was, according to popular thinking, a "natural" aspect of womanhood.

The best evidence of this ideology comes from France.[100] One example is a 1921 ad for Charbon de Belloc, a medicine designed to cure stomach ailments such as indigestion. The ad's illustration is striking: a bottle of Charbon de Belloc has grown arms and legs, with which it is choking the life out of two humanized health problems, labeled "stomach pains" and "enteritis," and stomping on a third, constipation. Each of these three stomach-related troubles is personified in the ad as a female figure.[101] The significance of this fact should not simply be brushed aside; the representation of these problems as female asserts by extension not only that women were prone to such problems, but also that women themselves were equated with weakness and frailty.

Even more commonly, products in many cases directly cited *maladies de la femme,* or illnesses of the woman, in their advertisements. Such materials asserted that women were prone by nature to health problems, and that many health-related maladies were in fact largely isolated to women; men, in a sense, were immune from them. One such ad for Fandorine tablets shows a woman literally in chains, imprisoned by illness, looking upward helplessly as a bottle of Fandorine tablets, itself having arms and legs, tries to break the chains. The ball at the end of the chain reads simply: "MALADIES DE LA FEMME." That same phrase appears also in the ad's header. The ad states that "80% of Women are not satisfied with their health!" and lists a variety of illnesses to which women are allegedly vulnerable.[102]

A 1922 advertising booklet for herbal tea discusses various illnesses as well. Included along with "illnesses of the stomach," "illnesses of skin," and others is the category "illnesses of the woman." The booklet states that women are constantly bombarded with health problems from their youngest to their oldest days. An average woman, according to the text, "often feels backaches, dizzy spells, migraines, dizziness, ringing of the ears, sometimes heaviness in the side." The advertised herbal tea, the text claims, can help to cure these problems.[103] The point made in this example about women's health problems regardless of age—that is, that they must deal with health problems from youth into old age—is an important one; the text did not imply that woman's health simply declined with age, but rather that women were stricken with various maladies from a young age, and continued to struggle against them as long as they lived. The obvious suggestion was that health problems were an inherent aspect of femininity. This message was further articulated in a 1922 ad for Pilules Pink tablets, which describes the story of a woman who purportedly would have been overrun by her health problems were it not for these pills; she has had to take them, according to the ad, for eleven years, since she was just eighteen years old.[104] Another ad for the same pills from a few months earlier linked health problems not simply to women in general, but to *all* women: "There is certainly not a woman who, at some moment in her existence, has not suffered from anemia."[105]

FIG. 17. Ad for Jouvence de l'Abbé Soury, another cure-all, *Paris-Soir* (26 November 1935)

Such images reached their most sustained expression in countless advertisements from the interwar years for the product known as Jouvence de l'Abbé Soury. Frequently headlined with the familiar phrase "Maladies de la femme," these ads relentlessly promoted the rejuvenating and healing powers of this product (fig. 17). Claiming its ability to cure everything from menstrual cramps to poor circulation to migraine headaches, these ads strongly suggested that a woman's regular functioning was dependent on the use of a product such as this one; without it, she would be condemned to an uncomfortable life of ill health.[106] One of these ads went so far as to assert that ninety out of every one hundred women suffer from some type of health problem.[107]

Strong Masculinity and the Public Sphere

In contrast to such depictions, images of men in medical ads (when not as medical experts for the benefit of women) emphasized not that men were intrinsically unhealthy or vulnerable to illness, as was the case with women, but instead that men were by nature healthy beings. They were instead merely momentarily slowed by an occasional illness, from which they could quickly recover. In both French and German advertisements, often colorful imagery suggested that men could play an active role in maintaining or reclaiming their own health, quite the opposite of the discursive situation with respect to women.[108]

Most obviously, such ads do not suggest that men's health problems in-here in their very nature as men, as was often the discursive message regarding women. Instead, men's afflictions were presented as occasional, temporary, and rather easily reparable. A German ad for Spalt tablets from 1939 illus-trates this (fig. 18). The ad shows a man's face from the nose up; his expres-sion suggests pain or discomfort. Superimposed on his forehead is a smaller image of two men preparing to take drinks from wine glasses. The ad's header reads: "Yesterday one glass too many—and today a headache?"[109] Thus unlike virtually all ads directed at women that cite headaches (as well as backaches and body aches, common types of ailments in ads featuring women), this ad depicting a man describes his health problem as a temporary one caused by drinking too much alcohol the previous night. The problem is not inherent to masculinity, but rather has both a clear cause and a simple solution: the taking of Spalt tablets. Meanwhile, a 1935 ad for the skin-care product D.D.D. also features a man. He is visibly uncomfortable and is scratching his left arm with his right hand. The ad discusses the problems of skin afflictions such as ec-zema, but the ad's header is the most instructive part of the ad: "Why struggle with skin diseases?"[110] The message here, although subtle, is that despite the man's obvious discomfort and suffering, he can choose to improve his health and easily do so. This is a clear departure from ads featuring women, which virtually never empower them to solve a health problem, but instead assure them that such problems, while perhaps controllable, are routine and normal for women to endure.

One final advertisement from Germany is worthy of mention in this re-gard. It is a 1922 ad for a prosthetic leg device that depicts a male figure, and that specifically notes that the product is recommended by "amputees."[111] Thus this ad also cites a medical problem experienced by men that does not originate in the very nature of masculinity. Instead, the reference to amputees in this advertisement, particularly occurring as it did in the early 1920s, when memories of the Great War were still very fresh, implies that the wound was a result of war injuries. Thus not only does the man in this ad avoid any conno-

FIG. 18. Ad for Spalt tablets, *Völkischer Beobachter* (21 February 1939)

tations of naturally ill health as part and parcel of masculinity, but his health problems are in some sense a badge of national service and self-sacrifice.

Although in most cases starkly different in form and execution, French advertisements also suggested, like their German counterparts, that men's health problems were not intrinsic to manhood and were temporary problems only. The theme of the soldier is once again at issue in a 1934 advertisement for Autoplasme Vaillant. The ad's image shows soldiers standing in formation; the military leader, standing in front of the formation, asks one of the soldiers why he is present, since he was supposed to go to the infirmary. The soldier responds that he has already recovered, for he has taken the advertised product.[112] A Quintonine tonic ad from 1935, moreover, shows a man dressed in a suit smiling at himself in a mirror. The ad's header states: "No depression can resist QUINTONINE." The ad explains that the tonic is effective at overcoming "a moment of" depression or fatigue. In this case, then, it is explicitly specified that the pictured man is not dealing with a long-term, serious problem that is an inescapable part of masculinity, but rather is simply undergoing "a moment" of difficulties, which Quintonine can quickly and easily solve in order to restore him to "perfect health."[113]

In fact, this flawless state of masculine health was seen to last until old age, when health might then begin to decline. Whereas women were told that their health problems would last their entire lives, a number of ads directed at men claimed that, if men did experience health problems, it was simply due to old age and the passage of time.[114] Even then, it was sometimes specified that male health only gradually deteriorated in old age. For example, in a 1935 ad, an older man is pictured who is described as a grandfather. The ad states that he is becoming disabled "little by little."[115] Thus even at an advanced age, men could remain largely healthy, only incrementally losing control of their life-long good health. Some ads actually proclaimed that by taking the advertised products, a man could even avoid having health problems in his later years, or at least slow down the aging process.[116]

Other medical ads directed at men in the French and German press invoked the world of work, a connection largely absent in medical ads dealing with women. In the French case, a common way to raise this issue was through testimonials, reputedly by actual customers, that were frequently printed in advertisements for health products.[117] One example is the ad recently cited for Quintonine tonic that features a smiling man looking into a mirror. Part of the ad's text consists of a testimonial from a man who discusses how the product helped him to recover when he became depressed due to overwork.[118] In addition, a 1935 ad for Tisane des Chartreux depicts the face of a worried man who appears to have a lot on his mind. The ad states that one cannot afford to allow health concerns to be compounded with business concerns. One should take the advertised product to ensure good health, thereupon by implication being able to devote one's full energies to one's job.[119] Along similar lines, a 1937 advertisement for Vittel shows a man sitting at a desk in his workplace; this ad also focuses on the need for one's health to be in order so that one can work with maximum efficiency. The ad states: "Without health, intellectual life is compromised. It is a harmonious game of all of the organs that gives the body its full flowering, indispensable foundation of healthy mental activity."[120]

In the German case, an almost identical tone was sounded in a fruit industry advertisement from 1926. It shows a man with a studied expression on his face. The ad's header declares, "Our career lives demand nourishment of the nerves: fresh fruit!"[121] Moreover, a 1926 ad for Wrigley candies, headlined "During work," shows a man working with an industrial machine in a factory setting. The ad suggests that the advertised product helps the man to perform his work effectively during the day, noting that the candies soothe the nerves and quench one's thirst.[122] Such ads from both France and Germany proclaiming that the product would allow men to work effectively connected men with the public sphere and paid labor in marked contrast to most ads dealing with women's health. These examples begin to illustrate the male appropriation of the public sphere.

As we have seen, several images of women depicted them as lifeless, helpless creatures who must be rescued or saved by men or by the medical products men have created. An incredibly striking contrast to such images is evident in French and German advertisements, which often depict male figures as actively engaged in the maintenance or recapturing of their health. For example, a 1935 ad for Okasa tablets from Germany pictures a man steering the wheel of a boat in a storm. The ad states: "A true helmsman feels in his element, when the force of a storm and the surging of the sea demand a whole man."[123] Thus this ad constructs the man in question as the master of his own fate, who is at his best in complete health and can endure rough conditions. Likewise, a 1927 ad shows an older man with a mallet raised above his head, about to strike a nail on a surface below him. The ad states that the man has "hit the nail on the head" by using Stuvkamp healing salts, which treat such afflictions as nervous and metabolic problems.[124] The physical act of striking a nail stands as a metaphor for the man's ability to recognize and solve his own health problems—once again, a marked contrast to ads depicting women.

Examples from France were similar in tone. In one ad, a man happily walks through a raining downpour of flu (the raindrops are labeled as such), protected by his umbrella and the bottle of Pilules Afluquine tucked under his arm.[125] A 1926 ad for Pilules Pink shows a knightly figure dressed in a suit of armor and holding a sword. A castle is visible in the background. The knight is also holding a shield, which bears a picture of a Pilules Pink bottle. The ad's header states that by using the product, he can be "invulnerable" to health problems.[126] The message was clear: this warrior was not a victim of an intrinsically unhealthy or frail nature, destined to be plagued by health problems. Instead, he could fight off any potential ailment with the help of these pills. Another Pilules Pink ad shows a man standing in a small boat, rowing it through rough waters on a dark night toward a bottle of Pilules Pink, which doubles as a lighthouse (fig. 19).[127]

One final and quite unique example from France must be mentioned here,

FIG. 19. Ad for Pilules Pink, *L'Action Française* (15 June 1923)

for it connects the strong, healthy, virile male to the strength, well-being, and even survival of the nation. The 1939 ad, for the Dynam Institute, depicts a man standing with arms crossed; behind either shoulder in the background is the head of, on one side, Hitler, and on the other, Mussolini. Underneath the ad's header, "A Strong France," is the word "invincible." Below that, written across the chest of the man representing France, is the response to the assertion of a strong, invincible France: "Yes, if all French are strong." The ad states: "More than its armaments and its fortifications, it is the 'HUMAN MATERIEL' of a country that gives it its strength." Under the bold, large-printed phrase "Alert to all French," the ad claims:

The strength of France depends on your strength.
Its physical health depends on your physical health.
Its moral health depends on your moral health.
The solidity of its nerves depends on your equilibrium.[128]

The Institute, as the "National Institute of Physical Perfection," according to the ad, can provide this necessary health and strength to French men, and in turn to the French nation.[129] Thus this ad depicts masculine strength and health not just as a possibility, but as a national imperative upon which the entire well-being of the nation depended.

The broader implications of such ads hold important ramifications for constructions of masculinity and femininity in the public and private worlds. By constructing women as helplessly weak, medical ads both insisted on female reliance on men and consigned them to the private realm, at least by inference. Scholars working on discourses of commemoration, such as Daniel Sherman and Mariatte Denman, have shown that women have been marginalized in commemorative sites such as war memorials, assigned a role as mourning and grieving in contrast to constructions of men as heroic and aggressive. Sherman in particular notes the implications that such ideologies held for the exclusion of women from public and political life.[130] The medical ads discussed here performed the same discursive task: by relegating women to roles in which they are weak, frail, and dependent on strong, expert, and working men, cultural ideology identified the public sphere as an exclusively masculine realm.

Between the world wars, French and German publicity materials demonstrated a powerful gendering of the public and private spheres through images related to fashion, beauty, and health. Fashion ads showed men in public spaces and settings quite frequently, whereas women were most commonly shown without a contextual backdrop or in a domestic scene. A veritable cult of beauty existed in both French and German discourse as well, objectifying feminine visage in order to perpetuate patriarchal control and the primacy of masculine pleasure in women's appearance. Moreover, notions of beauty were tied closely not only to women's health, but also to their character. Women were exhorted to strive for personal beauty due in part to beauty's alleged demonstration of a culturally "acceptable" character—one that did not subscribe to the hairstyles, behaviors, and transgressions of "modern women." Finally, cultural conceptions of health asserted that men were active and healthy, while women were frail, passive, weak, and reliant on masculine expertise in order to recover virtually any semblance of healthiness. In so doing, cultural ideology further demarcated the public sphere as solely a masculine realm, for participation in it purportedly demanded the physical attributes that only men possessed.

CHAPTER FOUR

EVE'S CONQUEST OF THE STEERING WHEEL

Gender and Automobiles

One aspect of European life in which change was especially evident in the interwar years—and that provoked many questions about gender roles—was the proliferation of automobiles. As an article from the 1933 *agenda* of the Galeries Lafayette put it, the greatest contributing factor to "feminine emancipation" in the interwar period was "the automobile in the hands of women" or, more bluntly, "the steering wheel conquered by Eve."[1] The cultural emphasis on reconciling women's perceived liberated roles with those of age-old tradition—a process that we have already seen at work in various forms—also extended to automobiles. This cultural task was accomplished by emphasizing women's domestic roles as wives and mothers in order to offset the worrisome potential of females operating cars in unfettered independence in the public sphere; by establishing a male monopoly over technological knowledge; and by excluding women from the crucial process of maintaining and redefining a distinctive national identity, particularly in light of the perceived threat to the foundations of national culture posed by "Americanization."

Viewing gender ideology through the lens of automotive discourse can bring larger cultural issues into clear focus. As Nicholas Zurbrugg has noted, the car was a major preoccupation in popular culture throughout the twentieth century, providing "a fascinating index of successive dominant social, intellectual, and cultural concerns."[2] In the words of Wolfgang Sachs, "the automobile is much more than a mere means of transportation; rather, it is wholly imbued with feelings and desires that raise it to the level of a cultural symbol."[3] These cultural symbols in turn can and do send messages about those who use them. A car is in many ways "a mobile signifier, something which says something about you and which comes 'wrapped' in a web of meanings and values."[4] Indeed, during the 1920s and 1930s, cars were discussed in the wider context of what they portended for European society and culture writ large—within which the specific issue of gender was a central theme. Before exploring the gendered elements of automotive discourse in the interwar period, however, a brief overview of the history of the automobile in France and Germany between the world wars is in order.

THE AUTOMOBILE IN INTERWAR FRANCE AND GERMANY

Cars burst onto the European landscape in significant numbers only following World War I. Prior to the war, vehicle ownership across Europe had been limited to a small group of elites and adventurers, and many people looked upon automobiles as mere playthings for the rich.[5] World War I changed this widespread perception dramatically. With their service to the war effort—carrying food to civilians and soldiers, supplying front-line troops with necessary equipment, and ferrying rank-and-file soldiers to and from the battlefront, automobiles favorably impressed average Europeans and were thenceforward seen in a much more positive light.[6] In addition, the lessons industrialists learned during the conflict were pivotal to the history of the automobile. During the war years, most European automotive works were given over to military production, establishing industrial conditions that allowed cars to be produced after the war on a larger scale than had previously been feasible.[7] This greater production, coupled with the increasing receptivity of the general public to motorized vehicles, suggested that the 1920s could well be a decade of unprecedented growth for the automobile industry.

The 1920s: French Growth, German Struggles

Indeed, the 1920s proved to be a time of striking expansion in automobile production. In France, the decade witnessed a fairly steady upward climb, from a yearly output of 18,000 vehicles in 1919 to more than a quarter million in 1929.[8] France had led the world in automobile production in the late nineteenth and early twentieth centuries, and although it remained in the 1920s the leading European automobile producer, by the outbreak of the Great War the United States far outstripped it and all other European manufacturers in production levels.[9] Viewed within the European context, however, the French automotive industry proved successful in the first postwar decade. There were several reasons for this period of prosperity in automobile manufacturing. One key factor was the greater efficiency and scale of Fordist-style production, which allowed for the production of many cars at relatively low prices.[10] Citroën exemplified the prosperity of the industry in France, producing more than 100,000 vehicles annually by 1929—more than any other European automaker.[11] A second critical element in the success of French auto manufacturing in the 1920s was protection—through high tariffs—from an influx of foreign-made cars.[12] Even the American automotive powerhouse Ford enjoyed only modest returns and comparatively slim sales in France.[13]

In Germany, by contrast, domestic automobile manufacturers struggled through the 1920s, and production of motorized vehicles fluctuated wildly. In 1929, overall automobile output stood at approximately 150,000.[14] The economic difficulties and social dislocations experienced by the nation had severe ramifications for car producers. Just when auto manufacturing was beginning to show signs of significant expansion, the Great Depression crippled the industry in the 1930s.[15] This is not to say that the financial difficulties of German citizens represented the sole problem faced by German auto manufacturers. The Weimar government maintained high taxes on automobiles and gasoline, making car ownership too costly for many Germans, and invested more heavily in the maintenance and extension of the state railway network than in auto subsidies or road improvements.[16] Moreover, Weimar leaders lowered tariffs during the 1920s, helping foreign firms to flood the German automotive scene; by 1928, General Motors became the second-largest producer of automobiles in Germany.[17] GM even purchased the largest German automotive company, Opel, buying 80 percent of the corporation in 1929 and the remaining 20 percent in 1931.[18]

The 1930s: Reversal of Fortunes

With the onset of the Great Depression, German auto production plummeted 60 percent from 1929 to 1932.[19] Then, on 30 January 1933, Adolf Hitler became chancellor of Germany, and the fortunes of the German motor industry changed virtually overnight. Production figures more than tripled between 1933 and 1938.[20] Virtually all of the reasons for the dramatic turnaround in the German car industry in the 1930s have their roots in the auto-friendly policies of the Third Reich, as Hitler's regime actively sought to encourage wider dissemination of cars throughout Germany. Richard J. Overy has argued convincingly that automobile policy, not rearmament, provided the catalyst for the swift German economic recovery of the 1930s.[21] The Nazi regime eliminated taxes on new car purchases, and developed ambitious plans for a vast national highway system, the Autobahn.[22]

While overall automobile production increased startlingly during the Nazi years, the relative share of foreign companies in the market declined considerably.[23] Certainly the Depression played a role, but to a significant degree, this drop was the result of companies like Ford switching completely over to German parts and assembly or the integration of foreign firms with domestic producers—such as GM's purchase of Opel—as much as a withdrawal of foreign companies from the German automotive landscape.[24] Still, companies like Ford remained frustrated by the perceived obstacles to their growth as foreign-based corporations—such as exclusion from lucrative government projects—imposed by the Nazi regime.[25]

National considerations entered into Nazi automotive policy in other arenas as well, not least of which were plans for a "people's car" in Nazi Germany. As early as 1934, Hitler began planning for the mass production of a small, efficient, and affordable German-made car, the acquisition of which would be within the economic means of most Germans. Originally intended for private investment, the Volkswagen project became publicly funded after major German auto producers proved unable and unwilling to undertake the financially risky venture. The plan for the creation of a "people's car" that was ultimately announced under the auspices of the German Labor Front involved ordinary citizens collecting savings stamps each week in order to acquire a car in several years.[26]

In France as in Germany, the first years of the 1930s were difficult for the automobile industry as well as the entire economy.[27] Recovery remained elusive throughout the decade. Whereas Germany exceeded its 1929 automobile production levels in 1934, France would not match its 1929 output until 1950.[28] In part, this can be attributed to the clash between state policy and auto industry interests. To the chagrin of car manufacturers, for instance, the French government heaped an increasing amount of taxes on auto-related products, especially gasoline, in an attempt to make up for fiscal shortcomings.[29] Citroën found itself on the cusp of bankruptcy by mid-decade, and though it managed to avoid that fate, the company's production levels by the end of the 1930s still were lower than they had been before the Depression.[30]

Consumer Realities and Mentalities

Even in the best interwar economic years, the number of vehicles purchased by French and German consumers between the world wars did not nearly approach American consumption levels.[31] Nonetheless, the important point is the mentality rather than the reality of consumption. In the German context, Wolfgang Sachs argues that while a relative few acquired a car in the immediate aftermath of World War I, an image of mass motoring was rapidly manifesting itself in the popular imagination. Germans at all levels of society aspired to own a car, even if their economic circumstances precluded such a purchase.[32] "The automobile indeed conquered the people's imagination," Sachs writes, "but it far outstripped the realities of the purse. It had taken twenty-five years for the car to become, at least in fantasy, a commodity for mass consumption: from 'sporting pleasure of the rich' to 'cars for everyone.' In the 1920s the automobile won a permanent place in desire."[33]

The conclusion of the tale of Hitler's "people's car" effectively illustrates the adoption of such a consumer mentality. Lacking the means to buy a car but desiring desperately to be consumers of automobiles, thousands of Germans in the late 1930s engaged in what Hartmut Berghoff has dubbed "virtual" consumption of them.[34] Even before the Volkswagen assembly plant was built, ordinary Germans dutifully began to save their weekly stamps in the hope of someday acquiring one of these vehicles. From the middle of 1938 to the middle of 1939, more than a quarter million Germans contributed payments for the scheme.[35] Even after the outbreak of World War II, when the assembly plant was given over to military production upon its completion and economic conditions tightened considerably, more and more people invested in the plan. By the end of the war, some 336,000 Germans had entrusted a sum total in excess of 267 million Reichsmarks to Nazi coffers in anticipation of receiving their much-awaited "people's car," all without a single vehicle ever being produced for private consumption.[36]

THE AUTOMOBILE AS EMANCIPATOR

Europeans clearly aspired to be consumers, and in particular to be consumers of automobiles. Cars, in many ways the very embodiment of modernity, seemed to hold a promise of emancipation and "unchained mobility" in the modern industrial age.[37] As Wolfgang Sachs explains, before the dawn of the automobile, modern forms of transportation had been psychologically problematic, especially for males of some social status. Traveling by rail, for instance, meant acceding to unwanted constraints and limitations, such as abiding strictly by a transit schedule. As Sachs puts it, riding the train involved subjugating one's autonomy and becoming a veritable prisoner to the rail system.[38] The automobile offered the tantalizing prospect of an escape from such limitations, presenting instead an empowering image of pleasure, freedom, and self-determined mobility.[39]

Whereas the emancipating and liberating nature of automobile travel was lauded with respect to men, placing women in the same conceptual position yielded less celebratory discursive results. Notions of "proper" feminine virtue dictated that women's lives center upon the household and be subordinated to masculine authority, and cars threatened this traditional, idealized gender order through the immediate, individualized, and emancipating access they offered to the public world. The images of mobility and independence that were closely associated with the automobile, therefore, were much less palatable in interwar culture in regard to women.[40] As such, French and German discourse devoted considerable effort to extolling the boundaries of the masculine and feminine as they related to the automobile.

Home and Family

As far as the automobile was concerned, the preponderance of discursive efforts to construct a gender ideology in interwar Europe involved determining acceptable limits for women's use of this new technology. The car was particularly unsettling as it related to women, for it offered instant, unfettered access to the public sphere—at a time when French and German cultural commentary repeatedly emphasized a "proper" feminine focus on home and hearth, as opposed to the independent lifestyle of the "modern woman." As a result, images of women with automobiles were carefully constructed so as to remain consonant with women's marital and maternal responsibilities. A French advertisement for Ford clearly demonstrates such a link to the familial in French marketing materials depicting women (fig. 20). In the ad, a woman is seated behind the wheel of a car; two older figures, perhaps the driver's parents, are seated in the back. Standing beside the car, apparently about to climb on board, is a child. The text of the ad, rather than expounding on the car's various technological features, focuses on its elegance and luxury. Even more notable is the ad's header: "The Car of the Family."[41] Thus the threatening po-

FIG. 20. Ford ad featuring "The Car of the Family," *L'Oeuvre* (15 March 1925)

tential of a liberated female driver was defused by a focus on the familial; she obviously was not a "modern woman" headed off to a workplace, but rather was apparently embarking on a family outing of some sort.

Other advertisements performed a similar ideological function. Two ads from the summer of 1930 for Citroën, for example, also raise the issue of family when picturing women together with automobiles. In the first, a woman stands outside the car holding the door as numerous family members (the ad's thrust was to demonstrate how many people could fit into the car; six people were shown sitting inside it) await their departure for a "happy excursion."[42] In the other ad, the car sits in the background, having already transported a large extended family (seven people in total, plus the family dog) to a park for a picnic.[43] Finally, in a short story published in *L'Illustration* in 1930 entitled "Madame Conduit . . . ," a young woman obtains a driver's license only after verbally jousting with her skeptical husband to convince him that it would not be pointless for her to have one. After experiencing a few unpleasant adventures behind the wheel when she drives for her own personal pleasure, Madame at the end of the story comes around to the value of using her newfound driving ability to chauffeur for her children.[44]

In some cases, images of men moving within the public sphere were counterpoised with women remaining tied to the private realm. An advertisement for Ocleir polish, for instance, contains two different images. On the left side of the ad, a man applies the polish to an automobile; on the right, a woman makes use of the polish inside the house to maintain the appearance of her furniture.[45] Such a dichotomy was evident also in a pair of advertisements for Monet & Goyon motorized bikes. The first ad features a man riding one of these machines. An industrial setting serves as the backdrop for the ad, and the text specifically mentions using the bike to go to work.[46] The second ad, however, which shows a woman standing alongside a bike, has a decidedly residential setting; a house is clearly visible behind her.[47]

In Germany, two advertisements for Adler automobiles from the spring of 1930 provide a parallel set of examples to the Monet & Goyon ads. The ads are virtually identical in their spatial arrangements and illustrative imagery—both feature a face, one of a man and the other of a woman, behind and beside which is a drawing of an Adler car. The advertisement with a male figure notes that he "uses his car not only for Sunday drives, but above all for his profession."[48] By contrast, the ad picturing a female subject says nothing of work, instead simply listing a few features of the car in question.[49]

German motorcycle advertisements exhibited a similar set of ideas. In a 1939 ad for Ardie motorcycles, for example, a man drives a motorcycle while behind him is pictured the skyline of a city, presumably Nuremberg (where the Ardie manufacturing plant was located).[50] Meanwhile, an ad for NSU motorcycles from December 1936 shows a woman walking home from a store carrying two armfuls of goods. She is looking enviously at another *Hausfrau* (a term explicitly invoked in the ad) in the distance who has loaded her purchases onto her motorcycle and is quickly speeding away. The text of the ad claims that, given all of the work with which a housewife is occupied leading up to Christmas, an NSU motorcycle can help her to get her (domestically related) work done more quickly and easily.[51] Thus here, too, women are associated with the domestic realm.

The focus on the familial was also evident in the German press in the 1920s and 1930s. In a 1934 advertisement for Victoria insurance, a man drives alone in a car, smiling as his thoughts (revealed in a circle above him) turn to his wife and children. In the circle, his wife is serving the kids from a large pot at the table.[52] A 1926 Ford ad, moreover, shows a woman holding the hand of a child and approaching a car parked in the background of the ad. While this woman and her child are the obvious focus of the ad—and thus the woman is the one to whom the ad is directed—there is in the background a man sitting at the steering wheel of the car while another child is climbing inside. The ad discusses the fun and traditional nature of excursions, particularly on holidays—days on which, not accidentally, an entire family would be taking a trip, not just a woman.[53]

Overall, however, German imagery portrayed women drivers in their roles as mothers less often than was the case in France. This disparity became even more pronounced after the middle of the 1930s. From 1936 onward, women were more commonly depicted in advertisements driving to a spa or speaking to a man standing outside the vehicle within which a woman was sitting.[54] Such images had been present before the middle of the 1930s, but not with the same regularity. The reason for this shift in imagery seems to rest in changing Nazi priorities from the mid-1930s onward. As the economy recovered and remilitarization was undertaken in earnest, the Nazi regime needed more women to enter the workforce in order to continue economic expansion. Once this was the case, Nazi ideology deemphasized women's domestic roles.[55] Henceforward the German government actually encouraged women to become part of the labor force, and thus their entry into the public sphere in cars was less often tempered in popular discourse by an association with the familial.[56]

THE MASCULINE TECHNOLOGICAL MONOPOLY
Technological Men, Elegant Women

One prevalent feature of both French and German discourse throughout the interwar years—in fact, it was the most frequent and significant way in which masculinity and femininity were defined vis-à-vis automobiles in this period—was the delineation of technological knowledge as an exclusively masculine domain. Building on preexisting ideas of sexual difference, French and German commentary linked masculine involvement with automobiles to issues of practical and technical interest. Women's association with cars, on the other hand, was discursively much more closely related to traditional feminine aptitudes regarding taste, style, and judgment of beauty.[57] A line was drawn, as Virginia Scharff notes in the case of the United States, between masculine function and feminine form, the latter of which was considered "cosmetic or superfluous."[58]

Auto advertisements in Germany that featured male figures tended to explore cars' technological and mechanical values at great length; indeed, technological features were the centerpiece for many ads directed at men. The engine, chassis construction, hydraulic system, and suspension are all discussed in detail in a full-page advertisement for the Opel Kadett from 1936. The car's high-quality, modern construction, sturdiness, and durability are all highlighted in turn in this text-rich ad that also includes an image of an Opel being driven by a man.[59] Likewise, an ad for the Ford Taunus that depicts a man driving hypes its powerful engine, high-speed capabilities, maneuverability, steel construction, hydraulics, and its long-lasting durability and reliability.[60]

Other advertisements made mention of such technical characteristics while giving even greater primacy to the awards and achievements claimed by particular vehicles. An ad for the Auto Union, a partnership of several German car manufacturers, shows several cars and motorcycles being driven by male figures. The text of the ad explains that the Auto Union's vehicles are subjected to rigorous tests, and must be equal to the "unbelievably difficult demands" placed upon them as their construction and materials are "strained to the most extreme limits." Due to this strenuous process, the ad proudly proclaims, the Auto Union's cars have been so expertly produced that they have been awarded "the absolute best score in four ratings categories."[61] An ad for Sachs-Motor from 1934, moreover, pictures a man riding a motorcycle. The ad boasts of the company's achievement in winning a French motorcycle race competing against the best French motorcycles, breaking world records in the process.[62]

French images that depicted masculine subjects evinced closely related themes regarding vehicles' technological merits. In a 1933 article from L'Illustration detailing current automotive technology, various images refer at least implicitly to men. Illustrations accompanying the article are revelatory for their masculine associations (and absence of feminine presence); hands that point to car parts under the hood as well as pour motor oil into a car are identified as unmistakably male by their coarseness and rough nails. More explicitly, two men appear with a car pictured in the article, one behind the wheel and another standing alongside it.[63] Further, a 1937 advertisement for Simca cars closely resembles many of the German ads explored above: two men are shown in a car, and the surrounding text focuses on the automobile's steel bodywork, hydraulics, and transmission.[64] The same is true of an ad for Sizaire from the middle of the 1920s that shows two men in the front seat of the car, with their two female companions relegated to the back seat. The ad discusses issues such as the car's fuel mileage, suspension system, and speed capabilities.[65]

Meanwhile, advertisements and articles that dealt with women in relation to automobiles often centered upon wholly different issues considered more appropriately feminine, especially a vehicle's appearance and comfort, while downplaying or completely ignoring technical issues. A number of German advertisements illustrate this phenomenon. One such ad for the Opel Regent convertible makes special note of the car's elegance as a selling point.[66] A Hanomag ad from 1936 that features a woman driver makes virtually no mention of the car's technical merits. Instead, the ad relies on the main point that the new "charming" Hanomag convertibles are "truly more beautiful" cars.[67] A 1935 advertisement for Ford is similar in tone. The ad shows a man loading baggage into the trunk with the help of two porters. The focus of the ad, however, is the woman climbing into the front passenger seat. The text of the advertisement speaks of the "beautiful design" and "comfortable furnishings" of the car. This is not to say that there was never any overlap between the discursive poles of technology and elegance; certainly, at least some of the discourse directed at men did touch upon issues considered more womanly, and vice versa. By and large, however, those issues were relegated to a minor role in terms of amount of content and their relative spatial arrangement within the discussion.

French sources sent the same types of messages as their German counterparts. Of particular note is the 1933 *agenda* of the Galeries Lafayette, which contains an article whose very title, "The Woman Driver or Elegance in the Automobile," demonstrates this ideology. The article even comments on women's ability to bring elegance to a vehicle, claiming that the "presence of a woman driver clarifies, emphasizes, perfects the elegance of an automobile."[68] In an ad for Lincoln automobiles, two women are shown sitting inside a very spacious interior. Arching across the top left side of the ad is the word "comfortable" in large print. A text box within the advertisement declares: "As comfortable as a *boudoir,* the LINCOLN offers all the refinements that an elegant woman can wish for," including spaciousness, soft seats, and good lighting. There is no mention at all of the car's technological features.[69] In a series of ads for Peugeot cars from 1936, photos of women in or standing astride automobiles appear, and the ads' focus is on the elegance and beauty of the vehicles.[70]

A 1925 advertisement for Renault goes a step further. Below an image of a woman seated behind the wheel and another woman standing next to the car, the text of the ad declares that, for the French woman, taste is of utmost importance in an automobile. The ad goes on to affirm that the car indeed is the most elegant and comfortable car she will find.[71] In a 1934 Berliet advertisement, a man and woman, presumably husband and wife, stand beside an image of the car; the husband appears to be showing it (perhaps even presenting it as a gift) to his wife, and the text of the ad is directed to her, proclaiming that she is "pleased by its simple elegance and by its agreeable proportions."[72] An article from the 1921 *agenda* of the Grands Magasins du Louvre does invoke the term "practical" with respect to women and automobiles, but it has nothing to do with the operation or performance of a car. Instead, it is in the context of women's fashions; the article instructs women to be both elegant and practical in considering what to wear for a car ride, citing as an example a hat that will prevent one's hair from becoming unkempt and will not obstruct the view of the road.[73]

A series of articles and pictures recounting the events at an annual French auto show from the late 1930s shows a further distinction between the technological domain of men and the feminine realm of comfort, beauty, and luxury. The auto show in question was a Grand Prix (or simply Competition, depending on the year) of Automobile Elegance. The text of the articles focused primarily on the issues of elegance on which each car was judged (although in some cases a cursory mention of the technological merits of the cars was made near the end of the articles). Given that the competition involved a test of elegance rather than technological merit, it is not surprising that these pictures almost always featured women with the competing cars, standing beside them or driving them as part of a procession during the event. At the same time, however, the captions for these photographs were always careful to identify the (invariably male) designers of the cars.[74] As such, the women shown with the automobiles became mere passive instruments of male technological authority.

Lastly in this regard, an article dealing with an all-female driving event is illuminating. The 1925 article from *L'Illustration* recounts the first-ever all-women's touring trip across France. In describing several of the cars and drivers that took part in the event, the article's author, Jean Clair-Guyot, states that the vehicles were all "comfortable and more or less luxurious," noting specifically the elegance of the entries. Moreover, Clair-Guyot highlights the fact that the women taking part became "a little emotional" when it came time to begin the excursion.[75] This association of women with emotionality was no coincidence; instead, it fits with a pattern of gender ideology, particularly evident in marketing strategies, that defined females as emotional and impulsive as opposed to calculating, rational men, thereby further undermining female agency in regard to technical abilities.[76] Clair-Guyot's article reinforced traditional gender notions as it nonetheless—and as a means of negating the extraordinary nature of this first-ever event—described a powerful new manifestation of feminine appropriation of the automobile.

Child's Play

A number of other ideas were deployed in French and German discourse to blunt the potentially transgressive impact of female utilization of the automobile. In addition to depicting women in domestic settings or focusing on their perceived talents for judgment of taste and beauty as opposed to a masculine inclination for the technical, examples from French and German sources also reveal a construction of women as childlike, able to operate a vehicle only due to its superior masculine conception, design, and construction.

A couple of German examples illustrate this aspect of gender discourse surrounding vehicles. An advertisement for Mercedes-Benz from 1928 pictures a woman alone in a car, seated behind the wheel (fig. 21). The text of the ad declares that driving the car is Kinderspiel (child's play) due to "the ease of its operation and the clear, well thought-out arrangement" of its controls.[77] Similarly, a 1939 advertisement for the Opel Admiral states that the car has become the choice of "elegant women" because it is "so easy to drive."[78] In a 1926 Ford ad, moreover, in which a woman and child are the central visual focus, the car is described in the following manner: "It is quite maneuverable, easy to steer and its operation quickly learnable."[79] In the French case, a good example is provided by a Citroën advertisement from 1929 that shows a woman driving alone in a car. The ad announces that the car is "easy to handle" due to its excellent design and construction[80]—and it is crucial to recognize here, as with the German examples above, the implication that this design was conceived and the construction done by men.

As another example, two sets of advertisements alluded to previously are

FIG. 21. Mercedes-Benz ad declaring that driving the car is "child's play,"
Simplicissimus (9 January 1928)

instructive. The first ads are those from France for Monet & Goyon motorized
bikes. The Monet & Goyon ad featuring a man boasts that the subject in the
ad will reach his destinations quickly and without any mechanical failures.[81] In
contrast, the ad that shows a woman preparing to use a bike, rather than emphasizing its efficiency, focuses on the vehicle's ease of use. The header of the
ad reads: "In order for you to travel easily." The text of the ad further states:
"Of a remarkable simplicity, this device does not require any special knowledge and can be driven by a child."[82] The second set of examples comes from
spring 1930 ads for Adler automobiles. The ad depicting a man focuses on typi-
cally technical issues, mentioning, for instance, that the car is "powerful and
reliable, built from good material, precisely manufactured."[83] The Adler ad
with a woman's image, though, while it does indeed mention the car's power
and safety, also devotes considerable attention to establishing both the car's
beauty of form and its "easy manageability" and "simpler steering control."[84]

These images clearly illustrate a gendering of technological knowledge, an
issue that Arwen Palmer Mohun has studied in relation to British and American laundry machine businesses in the nineteenth and twentieth centuries.

Mohun argues that laundrymen constructed an ideology that, while conceding that women were capable of using a technological product such as a laundry machine, insisted that "laundries as technological systems were essentially masculine; that they required masculine ways of thinking about and organizing technology in order to function properly."[85] It was, as Janet Lungstrum maintains with respect to German ideologies of technology, "the ultimate Pygmalionesque fantasy of control."[86] Women, it was viewed, mindlessly utilized technologies created by men, and over which men still held an intellectual monopoly. A virtually identical process is at work in French and German automotive discourse. These articles and advertisements never claimed that women were incapable of driving a vehicle; they could drive, but only because an inherently technology-oriented male designed the product so expertly that it was easy enough for anyone, even a child, to use. As Lungstrum explains, women were depicted as merely "technologized carrier[s] of modernity." They were passive objects in whom modern technology might be present, but who were not full-fledged appropriators of that technology.[87] By employing this kind of ideology, French and German discourse limited women's access to modernity—as embodied in automobiles—to culturally acceptable levels.

Masculine Dominance, Feminine Incompetence

A French auto advertisement for Hotchkiss from 1932 makes this masculine mastery over technology even more explicit. In the ad, a man is shown driving a car. The ad's text asserts that "a good car must always be ready to obey" and be "submissive to all the demands of its masters."[88] Thus the man in the ad controls and dominates the technology embedded in the car. It is significant to note that there is no parallel for this kind of advertisement with respect to women; a language of dominance and authority over the vehicle was never invoked in advertisements or articles portraying female figures.

Rather than being masters of technology, women were constructed as helpless and incompetent in terms of automotive skill and knowledge.[89] This can be clearly seen by returning to the story "Madame Conduit . . ." from *L'Illustration* in 1930, in which Madame has to convince her incredulous husband that it is worthwhile for her to have a driver's license. In one of the story's illustrations, Madame, with a look of trepidation and uncertainty on her face, is shown trying to remove the spare tire from the back of her car (fig. 22). She

« *Tout au plus estime-t-elle qu'il convient mieux à un homme de changer un pneu... »*

FIG. 22. Illustration from the short story "Madame Conduit . . .," *L'Illustration*
(4 October 1930)

is looking behind her, as though hoping for someone (a man, no doubt) to help her. The caption of the illustration says as much, declaring that she feels it more suitable for a man to change a tire. The story itself, moreover, suggests Madame's incompetence as a driver. Soon after obtaining her license, Madame goes driving alone around Paris. Not long thereafter, despite the fact that she took driving lessons before acquiring her license, Madame causes an accident, damaging her car so thoroughly that it must be towed away. Virtually every part of the car was affected—"Madame alone was unscathed." An accompanying illustration shows the car being towed in the background; in the foreground of the illustration, Monsieur, her husband (neither of them is given a name in the story), literally and figuratively looks down on her as she cowers, her face downcast, from his contemptuous glare.[90]

Other images from the French press make similar suggestions. An illustration from the 1926 *agenda* of the Grands Magasins du Louvre, contained within an article about women and automobiles, shows the incompetence of women in relation to driving and, in particular, directions. The image depicts a uniformed man, evidently a chauffeur of some sort, alone in a car and seated behind the wheel. He looks frazzled by the women who stand pointing on each side of the car. One of these women is pointing toward the front of the car, while the other gestures in the direction behind it.[91] It seems that this professional driver has inquired for directions, and the women cannot agree on which way he needs to go. In addition, in a cartoon from 1938 satirically depicting a number of "public enemies," a woman is shown seated behind the wheel of a car applying cosmetics to her face (fig. 23). Behind her, a short line of stopped cars with flustered men inside make it evident that the woman has halted traffic in order to care for her personal appearance. The sole words attached are: "Public Enemy No. 3: Lipstick."[92] This cartoon also demonstrates a phenomenon noted by Erving Goffman, whose study of gender in advertising contends that, in order to neutralize or trivialize the potentially disconcerting impact of an image or idea—in this case, a woman driving independently on her own, without any connections to family or household—an advertisement may portray the action in question as "a lark or a dare," something not to be taken seriously.[93]

This masculine appropriation of technical knowledge and the establishment of men as the masters of technology and women as mere passive receivers of it were also made clear in a number of German advertisements. One ex-

FIG. 23. Cartoon depicting "Public Enemy No. 3: Lipstick," *Gringoire* (20 May 1938)

FIG. 24. Ad for the Opel Admiral, *Völkischer Beobachter* (25 March 1939)

ample is a 1939 ad for the Opel Admiral (fig. 24). The text of the ad describes the merits of the car as a vehicle for travel, citing its combination of quickness, comfort, and elegant furnishings. The accompanying picture, however, is the most revealing aspect of the advertisement; in it, a male driver sits in the car, as do a man and woman in the back seat, while another man, apparently a servant, loads baggage into the trunk. Meanwhile, a woman in the front passenger seat is giving a standing ovation to an apron-clad man standing outside the vehicle, possibly the car's mechanic but certainly symbolic of the entire masculine technological know-how that has made the car a reality—a technical aptitude for which the woman can do nothing more than applaud in appreciation.[94]

Other German advertisements accomplish a congruent discursive function, albeit in an often more subtle manner. Particularly instructive in this case are a myriad of advertisements for German cars that address the issue of test driving a vehicle—a point that is raised almost exclusively in ads featuring men.[95] A typical example is an Opel advertisement from 1936, in which two men watching an Opel drive past discuss the price of the car. In addition to its reasonable price, the ad's text centers upon various technological issues that, as has been shown, were consistently highlighted in ads depicting male figures. Below a list of the vehicle's selling points are the bold-printed words: "A test drive is its most powerful argument."[96] Further, a 1936 ad for the Auto Union that features a male driver states: "A test drive will convince you!"[97] The suggestion in these advertisements that men test drive a vehicle implies that they have the ability to judge the technical qualities of the automobile for themselves— all men, not just automotive engineers and designers, are in a sense technological experts, and can evaluate an automobile's merits by driving it.[98]

By contrast, advertisements featuring women virtually never referred to the possibility of taking a test drive, something routinely mentioned in German ads directed at men. A good example is another 1936 ad for Opel that shows a woman driver waving out the window to the reader. The ad's primary emphasis is on price and quality, and it even goes into a considerable amount of technological discussion for an ad depicting a woman (although it is still not nearly as much as in previous examples where men are the subjects). Whereas many ads, after describing a car's features and price, directed men to take a test drive, this ad depicting a female subject instead encourages her to "now say 'yes'!" to buying the car.[99] The woman in this advertisement is not permitted the discursive possibility of judging the car's quality and merits herself by test driving, but rather is expected already to be persuaded by the sales pitch. By implication, she has no technological authority or ability; she is instead to rely on the (once again, masculine) expertise of the car's conception and construction, unquestioningly accept that as evidence of the vehicle's worth, and on that basis simply go out and buy the car. Such ideology also recalls the previously mentioned prevailing conceptions of men as calculating and rational, with women conversely constructed as emotional and impulsive.[100]

Of further note are advertisements for cleaning products that tout their capabilities in relation to cars. In the French case, a good example is an advertising flyer from May 1923 for a liquid antiseptic, *Le Savolin,* that, according to the flyer, allows people to wash their hands without water. The flyer concentrates on the applicability of this product to an automotive context. According to the advertisement, if one becomes stranded by a car problem and must tinker with the automobile while on the road, one's hands could become dirty and require cleaning, but water may not be immediately available in such a situation. In that case, the ad states, *Savolin* can get one's hands clean. All three people depicted in the flyer are male; there is no sign of a woman anywhere in the ad.[101] The suggestion was that only men were to work at repairing automobiles.

This point is made even more explicit in an advertisement from Germany from 1939 for a cleaning product called ATA. The ad takes the form of a five-frame cartoon detailing the tribulations of "Fräulein Kläre," whose car, as the reader learns in the first frame of the ad, has suffered a breakdown, leaving the engine in need of repair. In the second frame, Fräulein Kläre spends "a few hours" attempting to fix the car. Unsuccessful, she is left "desperate" and, even worse, her hands have been "blackened" by her efforts under the hood. Luckily for her, a man comes along in the third frame of the ad and "quickly repairs the damage." In the final two frames, he introduces Fräulein Kläre to the wonders of ATA, which gets her hands perfectly clean.[102] This ad recalls the story "Madame Conduit . . ."; both Madame and Fräulein Kläre are completely frazzled by their inability to resolve their automotive troubles, and look to the expertise of a man to save them.

A couple of final pieces of evidence in regard to the masculine dominance over technology come from the German press; they concern the construction process of German automobiles. The first example is a 1926 advertisement for Ford. Its header refers to the "precision labor" that goes into the construction of a Ford automobile. In addition to an image of a car, the ad also shows a man wearing an apron, hat, and gloves working on an industrial machine, apparently in a factory. Presumably, this man is part of the precision manufacturing process of Ford automobiles.[103] Second, there is an article by Arno Wölke in *Westermanns Monatshefte* in 1937, "Deutscher Kraftwagenbau," that details the production of German cars. The text of the article is highly technical and tightly focused on issues of construction and engineering; while it does make a few references to topics like the "American invasion" of automobiles onto the German market, the article generally does not comment on larger social questions. At the same time, however, specific references are made to the quality work done by men in German auto factories. Moreover, the illustrations that accompanied the article can be seen as further evidence of the exclusion of women from positions of cultural authority vis-à-vis automotive technology. The illustrations, drawn by Carl Grossberg, dramatize various aspects of the plant floor and assembly process. In six of the nine drawings, male figures are visible, sometimes performing manual labor but in many cases appearing to review (though the captions are unclear as to their precise roles) the work that has already been done—thus exercising their technological and industrial expertise to evaluate the quality of work indeed being accomplished. In light of this, it is instructive that there is neither any mention of women in the article nor any depiction of them, as either workers or engineers, in the illustrations.[104]

Automotive Maintenance

One final discursive arena wherein the masculine mastery over technology and feminine ignorance of it was highlighted can be seen in advertisements for products related to automotive maintenance. As Deborah Simonton argues with respect to gender ideologies and technology in the workplace, men were to be the ones to repair and maintain machinery; women "were not supposed to understand machines and were only to tend and operate them."[105] Utilizing a product such as motor oil necessitated a wider understanding of the workings of an automobile, not simply passive and mindless operation of a vehicle, and thus women were very rarely depicted in advertisements for these types of goods. Even in the infrequent instances in which women did appear in such situations, their subjugation to the technological expertise of men was usually directly and unabashedly articulated.

In the German press, ads for automotive maintenance products portrayed men quite often, usually either driving a car or holding a can of the product being advertised. The text of the ads generally dealt with the product's ability to make one's car function optimally and smoothly.[106] In addition, a male expert figure was occasionally pictured extolling the merits of a given oil to another figure in the ad or the reader.[107] French publicity materials showing men were quite similar in tone, though their execution frequently differed from their German counterparts. Some ads did employ the predominant German imagery of a man either driving a vehicle or holding the product,[108] but more commonly in the French case, men display a more explicit mastery over or knowledge of the product. This variously involved picturing a man who provided a testimonial about the quality of the product based on his own experience and knowledge,[109] showing male figures working on their cars with the products in question,[110] or, in one case, male engineers working in a laboratory to "perfect" the product.[111] A rather singular example in the French case is an advertising flyer for an automotive service station from the early 1930s. It depicts a bustling scene as two cars, both driven by men, are being serviced at the station. Various masculine figures are shown working with either of the cars—under the hood, under the car, bringing in a tire. The reverse side of the flyer discusses in technical detail some of the services performed by the station, among them oil changes and brake adjustments.[112]

Even in those comparatively rare instances that women were connected to auto maintenance, this was presented as occurring strictly under masculine supervision. For instance, a 1937 Solex advertisement shows two women riding together in a car. The ad cautions "not to wait until the moment you depart" on a trip to have the car's engine checked. The text of the ad makes clear that the intent is not that either of the women pictured will perform this check on their own; instead, the ad instructs them to consult a Solex specialist or their

mechanic.[113] An ad for Esso motor oil from 1937 makes this masculine expertise visually evident, as a man hands a woman a can of the oil at what appears
to be a service station, informing her of its high quality and reliability.[114]

A set of images within an article from the Grands Magasins du Louvre
agenda from 1926 presents further evidence along these lines. Entitled "The
Automobile and the Woman," the article discusses the increasing use of cars
by women. The article comments that women were driving frequently enough
that they were beginning to try to fix cars if breakdowns occurred while driving. The article's illustrations, however, tend to undermine this assertion. Only
one illustration shows a woman performing any maintenance-related work—
in that image, a woman is changing a tire. In the article's other drawings, it is
men who are working on or driving cars, including two in which men are performing repairs on vehicles while women stand by idly. In the first of these, a
man is working on a car by the side of the road; meanwhile, several feet away,
a woman rests under the shade of a tree while reading a book. The other such
illustration shows a standing woman applying lipstick while nearby a man toils
underneath a car.[115]

One final example of the gendering of auto maintenance knowledge can
be found in an article from 1929 in *L'Illustration* entitled "Express Diagnosis
of the Automobile for a Young Woman Troubled on the Road." The article
details several potential automotive problems that a woman might encounter on a trip (although the article reassuringly asserts that a serious problem
is unlikely), offers troubleshooting tips for those problems, and also suggests
various items to be sure to bring in the car, such as extra spark plugs and a
spare gasoline can. While some of the possible problems outlined were strictly
mechanical—for example, a headlight going out—the problems given primacy of place in the article, and which were described as the most common
difficulties besetting the female traveler, were troubles that resulted from the
ineptness of the car's operator. For instance, the second-most common cause
of a general breakdown, "remarkable for its *naïveté*," is that the driver, having neglected to replenish the gasoline tank, runs out of gas.[116] This article reveals multiple aspects of the discourse about automotive technologies. Its very
title suggests that women are the only group that needs to be made aware of
what these problems are and how they can be fixed; men, by implication, already know this information. Further, the article contributes to notions of
feminine ignorance of proper maintenance of an automobile; the most common breakdowns, according to the article, are likewise "the most ridiculous"

ones in terms of the low level of automotive sophistication needed to prevent them in the first place. Finally, the article presents another situation in which such technical knowledge is handed down to a woman by an expert masculine figure, for the article's author was French automotive guru Baudry de Saunier. Thus this article encapsulates a number of common themes in French (as well as German) discourse, illustrating yet again the gendering of technological agency that constructed automotive—and larger technological—expertise as a solely masculine affair.

THE AUTOMOBILE AND NATIONAL IDENTITY

In both countries in question, discourse surrounding motor vehicles was linked to issues of national welfare, pride, and identity, particularly in the 1930s. As the ultimate embodiment of modernity, cars occupied a privileged place in thinking about the relationship of the modern to the future of the nation-state. For interwar Europeans, modernity represented a threat of international homogeneity at the expense of national identity and distinctiveness. Modernity was associated in the 1920s and 1930s above all with the United States, and widespread fears of "Americanization" claimed an inordinate amount of attention from both French and German commentators. The most visible aspect of this threat was the automobile.

Although envious of America's economic success, European observers were concerned about the larger consequences of adopting a U.S.-based economic and industrial model. The concern commonly expressed invariably equated adopting American economic methods with accepting an encroaching American social and cultural hegemony as well. As Richard Kuisel explains with respect to France, there were concerns that, "once equipped with automobiles and electric kitchens, the French would no longer be French."[117] Similarly, Marjorie Beale maintains that French elites despaired of the possibility of "the wholesale adoption of American cultural values and the concomitant destruction of everything French."[118] Confronting the modern, according to Beale, was above all an exercise in the preservation of French identity in the face of a myriad of outside influences.[119] Kuisel argues that the French throughout much of the twentieth century have jealously guarded and reasserted their sense of national identity—their "Frenchness"—against the perceived infiltration of American culture: "America served as the other that helped the French to imagine, construct, and refine their collective sense of self."[120] Yet ardent objection to Americanization did not mean that the French stood in complete opposition to modernity. Rather, they sought to co-opt it into a more acceptably and distinctively French form as a means of enjoying its economic benefits without simultaneously accepting the cultural hazards with which it was associated. Thus a "peculiarly French solution" was sought to the question of modernization.[121] The French attempted to twist foreign notions of modernity into a form that was more compatible with preexisting ideals about "Frenchness."[122]

In Germany as well, the prospect of "Americanization" caused uneasiness. Just as in France, prevailing concerns revolved around the intrinsic acceptance of American culture as a corollary of borrowing from American economic examples. For the Germans as for the French, America was the symbol of modernity, and for economic reasons, if no other, modernity had to be reckoned with. At the same time, Germans resisted taking on this modernity wholesale, lest they risk the loss of their unique cultural identity.[123] In describing this widespread sentiment, Erik Eckermann refers to the interwar German expression "the American Peril" to demonstrate the powerful currency of such fears.[124]

As the French were doing at the same time, Germans sought to contain the social and cultural effects of modernity by reconciling its elements with national tradition.[125] Mary Nolan aptly discusses the German incorporation of the term "rationalization" into the lexicon of modernity as a means of "Germanizing" it. Avoiding more foreign terms such as "Fordism," she argues, was an attempt to create a distinctly German spin on modernization.[126] In his work dealing with what he refers to as reactionary modernists, Jeffrey Herf shows how these German thinkers sought to transform technology into a viable part of German *Kultur* and remove it from the realm of internationalist, materialist, and foreign *Zivilisation,* seen as devoid of history and tradition. In Herf's words, these reactionary modernists "incorporated modern technology into the cultural system of modern German nationalism."[127] Their ultimate goal, according to Herf, was to reconcile technology with "the German soul," to make the modern consonant with German national identity.[128] Wolfgang Sachs argues that Hitler's very conception of the nation under Nazi rule was inextricably linked with the automobile, commenting that "Hitler saw National Socialism as arising from the *Volksgemeinschaft* plus motorization."[129]

German commentators explored a plethora of issues under the rubric of modernity or technology, one of which was automobiles. Technological items, including cars, were brought under the purview of traditional "Germanness" in German discourse. For example, one reactionary modernist, Joseph Bader, referred to the motor as the greatest symbol of German technological prowess, tracing the origins of the invention to the very "Nordic soul."[130] Moreover, delivering a speech at the Berlin Auto Show in February 1939, Nazi Minister of Propaganda Joseph Goebbels proclaimed that the Nazi regime had "filled [technology] inwardly with soul," and in doing so had "place[d] it in the service of our people."[131]

Given the powerful ties between technology, particularly the automobile, and the concept of the nation in both countries, it was logical that evidence from the popular press in this regard would appear as well. References to the nation began creeping into French and German advertisements particularly in the 1930s. This was, perhaps not surprisingly, especially true in the case of Germany, where a virulently nationalist government concerned almost obsessively with the "purity" of the Reich held sway from 1933. While the nation was unquestionably invoked in the French press, national concerns tended to be dealt with more subtly and with less regularity there than was the case in 1930s Germany.

Made in France, Made in Germany

At the simplest level, invoking the nation in the press often meant exhibiting a "made in France" or "made in Germany" tenor.[132] Renault, for example, proclaimed itself "L'Automobile de France" in many of its advertisements.[133] Likewise, Citroën frequently invoked its French manufacture in advertisements, calling itself the "original" (mass-produced) French automobile.[134] A 1930 advertising flyer for an exposition of Peugeot motorcycles by dealer C. Bourdon is colored unmistakably in imitation of the French tricolor.[135] Highly similar themes were evident in German auto advertisements. A Brennabor ad from 1927, for instance, in its header encourages the reader to "favor the German car!"[136] A full-page Daimler-Benz ad from 1937 consists solely of the company logo and a box of text that proclaims: "Further Ahead for the German Automobile!"[137] A series of ads for the Auto Union provides other examples of this; one from 1934 refers to its cars as a "masterpiece of German technology and German quality work."[138]

Domesticating Modernity

In some instances, rhetoric from both countries built upon this pride in national work and technology in order to promote the worth of French or German automobiles on the worldwide stage. Most notable in the French case is an article from *L'Illustration* summing up an annual auto show in 1936 at which Hispano-Suiza was accorded top honors. Although the article only mentions the mechanical merits of the car in its last paragraph, the last sentence of the article states that the Hispano-Suiza automobile, by virtue of its French construction, attains a quality almost unequaled on the globe.[139]

Invocations of the worldwide ramifications of the domestic auto industry appeared more often, however, in Germany. In a 1939 advertisement for German car producer Hanomag, an image of the globe dominates the scene as, slightly in the foreground, a Hanomag car and truck drive along a road. Hanomag declares proudly in the ad the "worldwide reputation" enjoyed by the company, thanks to German quality work (fig. 25).[140] An image of the globe is likewise utilized in a Mercedes-Benz ad from 1936, in which the company logo dwarfs the earth. The ad's header refers to the automaker as "a star known throughout the world."[141] Speaking specifically of its automobiles for commercial use, a 1938 Mercedes-Benz ad declares that these vehicles "have distinguished themselves in the home country and abroad," adding that the autos' "absolute dependability and high economy is recognized throughout the whole world."[142]

The above examples drawing on a language of global reputation and competitiveness indicate how French and German society attempted to respond to the challenge of modernity by, in a sense, domesticating it. The references to international reputation go beyond the earlier examples where the theme was simply something akin to "made in France" or "made in Germany." That pride in native production is still present, of course, but added to it is an emphasis on the exportable potential of the domestic product. In other words, rather than modernity threatening to impose foreign values on the nation, the above images suggest that the flow of modernity could be reversed; French or German automotive accomplishment was such that it could now set the worldwide standard for the modern. Modernity, then, was now not just being reconciled to national identity from outside sources, but was being home-grown as well.

Foreign Companies

Even with this new domestically concocted modernity, technology from foreign-based producers continued to be available in France and Germany. As the 1930s progressed, such foreign auto-related companies became increas-

FIG. 25. Ad for German car producer Hanomag, *Völkischer Beobachter* (18 February 1939)

ingly concerned with promoting their ties to the nations in which they were doing business, incorporating the same kind of "made in France" or "made in Germany" language that domestic manufacturers were utilizing. In French advertisements, this process came through most clearly in the case of the Shell Oil Company. A series of ads by this company in 1938, regardless of their other content, invariably ended with the same proclamation: "The new SHELL oil *is refined in France.*"[143] The emphasis is in the original ads; Shell was highlighting explicitly its ties to the French nation, printing it in distinctive type designed to grab the reader's attention. In Germany, oil companies employed the same type of thematic tactic. An ad for Mobil oil, for instance, claims that the product is derived "exclusively from German crude oil."[144]

The most dynamic evidence in this regard, however, is to be found in German advertisements for Ford automobiles, which strongly emphasized the company's close ties to the German nation.[145] One ad from 1934, for instance, refers to Ford cars as a "further contribution to German motorization," and describes Ford automobiles as a "German product."[146] Other advertisements reminded German readers of the company's production plant in Cologne.

FIG. 26. German ad for Ford, *Völkischer Beobachter* (30 January 1936)

One such ad, with the header "The Three from Cologne," features three different Ford models parked in a row alongside each other, with the Cologne skyline sketched in as the background image.[147] Perhaps more striking is an ad from 1936 in which there are no cars pictured at all (fig. 26). Instead, the only image is of a building—presumably the Ford plant in Cologne, although this is not specified in the ad—and a Ford logo at the bottom of the advertisement. The core of the ad is a paragraph of text, under the title "Our Way in Germany." The text exudes Ford's pride in being a part of the German automobile landscape, and is laced with references to German production, workmanship, and the automotive industry. The ad claims that Ford is "integrated into the working and business community of the nation." At the bottom of the ad, written through the Ford logo, are the words "10 Years in Germany."[148]

The "People's Car"

Another example for which French sources present no parallel is the Volkswagen. The "people's car" was unique to Germany, of course, as a domestically produced vehicle for all Germans sponsored by the ruling government. The evidence suggests, not surprisingly, a strong connection between this particular type of car and the German nation. Indeed, Simon Reich mentions that the Nazi regime, despite its seemingly blanket appeals to automakers to produce a "people's car," excluded all foreign-owned firms, including Ford and the GM-owned German powerhouse Opel, from consultation and involvement in the Volkswagen project.[149] An ad from March 1939, as an example, is fairly simple in conception—it merely contains a few words about production and a drawing of a Volkswagen. Above and behind the car, however, is the ad's focal point: a swastika from which beams of light emanate in a circular arrangement, thus linking the car to the Nazi regime and, by extension, the nation.[150] Moreover, another 1939 ad depicts a line of Volkswagens driving down a street. The ad's header declares that Hitler's Four-Year Plan for German economic development has pointed the way to a "new road for German motorization."[151]

Gender and the Nation

The preceding analysis, however, does little to advance the role of gender in this process of negotiating modernity on behalf of the nation. In large part, this is due to the fact that gender was almost never explicitly raised in relation to this issue. In most such ads, a car was simply pictured in a still setting without a driver, or being driven along a road with a male figure inside. Even in this latter case, however, the text of the ads never explicitly addressed men as opposed to women. Still, it is inescapable that such advertisements virtually never showed a female driver—nor even a female passenger, for that matter. The implication is that women were left out of the process of reconciling the modern with national identity, unable discursively to participate in this important cultural task during the interwar period. They were, yet again, merely to be passive receivers of the technologies and messages produced by men.

The scholarly work of Stephen Harp and Mary Nolan can shed light on this issue, particularly as it relates to fears of Americanization. Both of these historians—one analyzing France, the other Germany—have explored the ways in which concerns about the impact of American culture intruding onto the European continent were intimately tied to perceived gender roles in the United States. With respect to France, Harp discusses the unease with which the French viewed American gender relations, especially the seemingly unending number of women in America who cast off their roles as wives and mothers in order to live independently, exemplified by such issues as their hairstyles, clothing, and the fact that they drove automobiles. Harp notes that "a woman behind the wheel of a car was the worst of what modern America had to offer France, constituting a threat to the very foundation of what many considered to be 'traditional' French society."[152] Thus women were part of the problem rather than any solution to the modernist quandary. For women to be privileged in this discourse would have been self-defeating, for their very use of cars was dangerous and destructive to the nation if undertaken outside of the bounds of their traditional household roles. Thus the discourse surrounding car and nation was, virtually by default, an exclusively masculine affair.

Mary Nolan's description of German perceptions of American women resonates closely with Harp. Germans were aghast, according to Nolan, at American women's alleged dominance of American culture. The American woman, Nolan says, "was absolutely central to *Kultur*, or what passed for it in America."[153] Germans' attempts to incorporate modernism into their national polity were grounded in attempts to preserve their *Kultur* and indeed their very soul, but most Germans viewed American women as having effected a soullessness in American society. Men had given over control of the realm of culture to women in the United States, it was viewed, with results that would have been mortifying if they were repeated in Germany.[154] Thus women's influence in the realm of culture had had precisely the opposite impact in the United States from what was necessary in order for modernity to gain greater acceptance among Germans. As in France, women were seen as antithetical to the project of transforming modernity in order to make it consonant with the nation.

"As the cathedral is not merely a shelter, so the automobile is more than a means of transport; automobiles are, indeed, the material representation of a culture. Although both creations contain considerable engineering artistry, under the technical design lies a cultural plan in which the assumptions of an epoch find expression."[155] This statement by Wolfgang Sachs was never more applicable than in the 1920s and 1930s, when cars were the most immediately visible emblems of modernity (and all of the cultural baggage that accompanied it) in European society. Indeed, motorized vehicles were used as a discursive tool to establish cultural boundaries of masculinity and femininity. Cars were a visible expression of women's newfound liberation in the interwar years, providing instant, unfettered access to an unending array of public spaces. As a result, gender discourse in French and German publicity materials emphasized traditional, backward-looking notions of sexual difference as a means of confining feminine utilization of automotive technology within acceptable limits. Women were depicted as using cars in association with their duties as housewives and mothers, portrayed as only interested in and cognizant of automobiles' aesthetic features, and shown as laughably ignorant of the upkeep and repair of vehicles. French and German popular discourse constructed men, by contrast, as the exclusive bearers of technological knowledge and mastery. Finally, in the task of reasserting the primacy and heritage of the nation in the face of an internationalizing modernity, women were defined as inherently counterproductive to the effort to maintain a distinct national identity. Thus this critical discursive task was yielded de facto to men, who solely would create a conceptual space for the integration of a unique national culture with Americanized modernity. Eve's conquest of the steering wheel, therefore, was far from complete, as French and German cultural ideology sought to preclude any feminine agency in the realm of automotive discourse, national identity, and modernity by casting women's interactions with cars as conforming to long-standing sexual conventions and traditional gender roles, not as the actions of independent, modern women.

CHAPTER FIVE

AT WORK AND AT PLAY
Labor and Leisure

Two final aspects of popular discourse between the world wars merit consideration: leisure activities, such as sports and vacations; and employment outside the home. Leisure pursuits were becoming more prevalent and socially significant in the interwar years. Meanwhile, despite wider discursive strictures regarding traditional roles for women, in some cases females were depicted in employment-related settings. Yet these images were crafted so as to reinforce gendered divisions of labor, and to suggest that such work was undertaken only with the approval and guidance of a male supervisory figure.

WOMEN'S WORK IN INTERWAR FRANCE AND GERMANY

In France, demographic realities following World War I dictated that many women would have to forgo a life centered exclusively upon the household in favor of earning livelihoods in waged labor. Largely as a result of the carnage of the Great War, there were in 1921 nearly two million more Frenchwomen than Frenchmen.[1] In this environment, it was recognized that numerous women unable to find a marriage partner to be the presumed breadwinner for the family would have little choice but to support themselves financially, whether or not they wanted to do so.[2] Yet in actuality the number of women employed (as a percentage of the labor force overall) remained relatively steady well into the 1920s (in the range of 37 to 39 percent of the workforce).[3] In Weimar Germany, there was also a "surplus of women" following World War I, meaning that many women would have little choice but to remain single.[4]

Still, Marilyn Boxer and Jean Quataert contend that during the Weimar Republic, most women lived largely upon the earnings of their husbands or even their adult male children rather than working themselves.[5] The percentage of women who had been employed in 1907, 34.9 percent, was nearly identical to the 35.6 percent who worked in 1925.[6] Nonetheless, a common belief persisted that women were achieving increasing financial success and independence at the expense of male labor.[7]

In 1933, when Adolf Hitler became chancellor of Germany, the number of working women in Germany was approximately 11.5 million, the same as it had been in 1925.[8] Echoing numerous voices from throughout the tumultuous years of the Weimar Republic, the Nazis portrayed Germany's economic problems as in part the fault of working women, who, they contended, were taking jobs away from deserving men. The Nazis claimed that eliminating women from the workplace was crucial to lowering male unemployment and promoting economic recovery.[9] As had been the case in the Weimar Republic, such campaigns especially targeted married women. In the summer of 1933, Hitler's regime began offering newlyweds interest-free marriage loans, with the stipulation that the bride not engage in waged labor.[10]

As the German economy quickly recovered under Hitler's program of militarization and public works, the Nazi regime by the second half of the 1930s faced a quandary with regard to its gender and labor policies. Although at the height of the Great Depression the Nazi government had encouraged women to avoid waged work in favor of running the household, by 1936 the German economy's turnaround portended a possible shortage of workers, especially in heavy industry.[11] As with so many other facets of Nazi ideology, Nazi attitudes toward women, at least as far as waged labor were concerned, proved to be malleable in the face of changing political exigencies.[12] In the latter half of the decade, the German government began more actively promoting women's entry into the workforce, and women joined the ranks of laborers in increasing (if still only modestly larger) numbers.[13]

The Nazi reversal of policy on women's waged work is noteworthy for other reasons as well. As Jill Stephenson points out, the government now even encouraged women to take jobs heretofore singled out as masculine.[14] In 1937, the government made a wholesale change in the prerequisites for obtaining an interest-free marriage loan. Previously obtainable only when the wife agreed not to work, the 1937 alteration in the program made the loans available only if the bride engaged in waged labor.[15] At the same time, it is important to note that the government's imploring of women to act as housewives did not end in the latter part of the 1930s; an ideology of domesticity continued to exist, though the drive to support the burgeoning economy increasingly coexisted with it, as women were expected both to work and to maintain the home.

Even though the numbers of working women did not accelerate dramatically during the interwar years, a notable shift had taken place in the nature of female labor—namely, increasing employment in white-collar positions. Only a small number of women were able to gain access to more high-paying professions such as medicine and law, and as Ute Frevert suggests, their miniscule numbers were not enough to make them the target of socially projected anxieties about working women. Instead, she argues, "the hotly-disputed prototypes of female emancipation were in fact the young clerical workers."[16] The number of working women engaged in clerical occupations in 1925 was more than three times the number of 1907.[17] As they moved from the agricultural fields and domestic service into the factory and office, women at work (especially married women) became more visible and an object of male anxieties, but in reality they did not encroach greatly on traditionally masculine occupations.[18] It was similar in the French case: whereas during the war years women were most visibly present as workers in the industrial sector, by the middle of the 1920s they were more frequently employed in white-collar occupations, such as secretaries and primary school teachers.[19] Most of these jobs were already gendered feminine, were not well compensated financially, and held little opportunity for advancement.[20]

While considerable anxiety regarding women's white-collar work remained in Germany, these fears were less pronounced in France, where such jobs were already largely viewed as feminine domains. This gendering of labor in the French case is evident in a 1929 ad for Pigier schools that touts the benefits of its informational brochure in helping people to choose a particular occupation. Numerous images of different jobs are pictured with masculine figures—accountant, cashier, salesman, and director or manager—while only the pictures for secretaries and typists depict a woman worker.[21] By assigning women to tasks that were gendered feminine and thus connected to women's "proper" roles, the cultural impact of working women on society could be better neutralized, and women could be discursively assigned to roles that were consonant with larger cultural prescriptions.

A 1930 ad for the Society of Art Workshops makes this clear. The ad pictures a woman within her home painting a ceramic figure. Other, finished pieces sit in front of her. The header reads: "Earn money during your leisure time by painting these pretty objects yourself."[22] Thus the header itself, by invoking traditional associations of femininity with taste and beauty, implicitly declares that such work is not masculinizing, but rather reaffirms one's femininity. Moreover, the reference to the woman's leisure time is informative as well, for it suggests that this work will not interfere with her other duties within the household; painting these objects will not become her sole avocation, but rather can simply be a hobby she takes up in her spare time. The text of the ad also recalls the gendering of technical knowledge discussed earlier in relation to automobiles. The ad specifically states: "Do not think that special talent is essential in order to paint these artistic works. You only have to follow the instructions provided by the society."[23] Although painting is not a technological task, it certainly is a specialized skill, and thus Arwen Palmer Mohun's argument that women were deemed capable of performing tasks, while men asserted a monopoly over the technological mastery of them—in this case, the instructions as to how to perform the work—applies here as well. The society, the ad suggests, has taken care of the technical or specialized knowledge necessary to understand the precise nature of this artistic medium and style; the woman is merely performing a relatively mundane task that requires neither broader understanding nor, in the words of the ad, talent.

This gendering of technical knowledge is further illustrated by ads for Royal typewriters. A 1932 Royal ad contains two separate windows, each depicting a different scene. In the first, a female secretary is typing, while her male boss works busily behind her at his own desk. In the other, a man is catching a train to depart on a business trip; he carries a typewriter with him in its case.[24] Thus in the first picture, a woman is connected to what was an acceptable outlet for female labor: secretarial work. However, the second frame constructs the discursive limits of her involvement with this modern machinery. She does not take it outside the office, but rather it is the man who appropriates it if it is to be taken outside the normal office setting.

Interestingly, in Germany, due to the stronger discursive proscriptions against female clerical work, imagery of women's labor was much less in evidence, and a disproportionate number of ads for products such as typewriters remained entirely gender neutral, with no images of men or women, and no textual references to either sex.[25] One exception to this was the portrayal of male figures in situations that highlighted their unique mastery over items such as typewriters. The text of a 1935 ad for Mercedes typewriters from Germany, for instance, discusses the proud history of quality handicrafts at the Mercedes works. An accompanying image shows a male figure putting together a typewriter.[26] Here as well technological knowledge regarding the conception, creation, and construction of machinery is rendered exclusively masculine. In the French case, the text of another Royal typewriter ad is completely devoted to urging potential buyers to call Royal, so that the company can send an employee to demonstrate personally the product's numerous features. While gender is not specifically mentioned in the ad, the two images in it are revealing. On one side of the ad, there is a typewriter, and on the other, a telephone. While no people are visible, each item is being grasped by male hands (the style of the sleeves quite obviously connotes a man's business suit).[27] Thus it is only men who are calling for and providing demonstrations, implying not just that only a male could explain the technological features of the typewriter, but also that only another man—namely, the one reaching to make the phone call—will be able to understand it. Once more, Mohun's argument applies here, as women are completely ignored in discursive discussions of a modern item's technological aspects.

Just as the gendering of particular occupations was an important factor in women's work between the wars, so too was marital status. Given this fact, French discourse paid attention to married women and their connection to the working world—after all, these were not women who could not find husbands to support them in the midst of demographic upheaval.[28] The extraordinary infrequency of images of obviously married women in relation to work demonstrates the relative cultural discomfort with this reality. When they did occur, images of such married working women evinced a pronounced emphasis on married working women's domestic and maternal roles; discursively, such women were viewed as still dedicated foremost to their duties as wives and mothers. According to common cultural assumptions, such married working women were simply forced to work out of economic necessity or to help their families in a time of extraordinary need, but did not choose to work for basic personal satisfaction or fulfillment. Thus married women's work could be ascribed to "acceptable" reasons.[29]

That assurance was reinforced in publicity materials by images that explicitly suggested that married women would engage in employment only under the supervision of their husbands. This is illustrated by figure 27, one of a series of French ads for Pigier schools that market a brochure detailing how to obtain desired positions. In these ads, a woman sits in a chair reading, while standing

FIG. 27. Ad for Pigier schools, *L'Oeuvre* (29 September 1927)

above her, looking over her shoulder, a husband lovingly looms.[30] Thus the message in each ad is that the woman is undertaking this endeavor only with her husband's endorsement—his happy gaze underlines his acceptance—and under his supervision. When women were safely subordinated to a masculine figure, their foray into feminized jobs could be more readily accepted; certainly this male authority figure would ensure that his wife would not fall prey to the vices of the "modern woman," but rather would remain focused on her wifely duties while holding a job.

Almost never did an ad from either nation explicitly depict a woman working outside the home. In a German ad from 1934 for Ihagee photo enlarging, however, a woman stands working with the enlarger. It is unclear from the ad whether she is performing this task at home—with the implication being that she is merely handling family photos—or in a professional setting, where she would be employed developing such enlargements. Moreover, wherever she is supposed to be, the woman is small in comparison to the long shadow cast by the male figure in the ad who embodies Ihagee. To be sure, his purpose is partly to highlight the impressiveness of enlargements, yet he also provides another image representing the seemingly ever-present male supervisory figure.[31]

In the 1920s and 1930s, leisure culture assumed an importance hitherto unseen across much of Europe, including France and Germany. Arguably the most important and popular aspects of interwar leisure were sports and travel. Both were intimately tied to larger contemporary cultural issues and provide insight into the wider workings of French and German popular discourse. In many parts of Europe, pursuits such as sports and tourism or vacationing were being adopted by an ever-expanding number of citizens and becoming more closely linked with consumption.[32] Reflective of a process that in many places began in the late nineteenth century, the spread of sport and travel to wider swaths of society accelerated in the first half of the twentieth century. The shortening of the average workday and the increasing adoption of paid time off for workers removed previously stifling time constraints for many in the working classes and provided increased leisure time.[33]

This is not to say that a democratization of travel came to fruition overnight.[34] For instance, most of the tourists taking advantage of the Nazi leisure program Kraft durch Freude (Strength through Joy), or KdF, came from more white-collar occupations, as had the majority of tourists during the Weimar era.[35] Still, the KdF did cater to a lower-income demographic, offering quite affordable packages, and many manual laborers did go on KdF-sponsored outings, even if these were usually shorter excursions than those taken by their middle-class counterparts.[36] Mass tourism was certainly on the horizon, with the period from the World War I until the 1950s in Germany witnessing a trend of rising tourist travel, notwithstanding the economic and political upheavals that characterized German society in those decades.[37] Tourism was likewise being enjoyed by more and more French citizens in the 1920s and 1930s. Even if a clear democratization of vacationing did not occur until the era of the Popular Front, as Douglas Mackaman contends, travel had long since become more commonplace among members of lower socioeconomic groups.[38] Vacations were increasingly viewed as a veritable entitlement owed to all citizens, culminating with the Popular Front's policies on paid vacations. As in Germany, although not all workers could yet afford a tourist endeavor, more took part in such programs than ever before.[39] In the realm of sports participation, democratization was more rapid.[40] Citing as one example the existence of more than five thousand football (soccer) clubs in France in the 1930s,[41] Richard Holt argues that sport became an item of mass consumption for the French in the interwar years.[42] The same point about the onset of mass consumption of sport has likewise been made with respect to interwar Germany.[43]

Leisure culture was also an inextricable part of the modern in French and German society, and the interwar years were pivotal in the development of modern forms of sport and tourism. Modern sport began emerging in France and Germany at the beginning of the twentieth century. Richard Holt explains in the French case how traditional village games, characterized by their casual and communal nature, were overshadowed or replaced by more urban sports, such as football, that were uniform across regions, were organized, and, most importantly, placed central emphasis not simply on participation in and enjoyment of physical activity, but on results of a contest—namely, victory or defeat.[44] Likewise, a pronounced emphasis on competition, records, and uniform rules marked modern sport in Germany starting in the 1920s, often driven by newly formed sporting clubs and associations.[45] During the Weimar years, many thinkers even formulated notions about the sportsman as a prototype for the modern man.[46] Conceptions of modernity were just as bound up with tourism. The centrality of tourism to modern society in general has been noted by several scholars. Dean MacCannell, for instance, argues that "the empirical and ideological expansion of modern society [is] intimately linked in diverse ways to modern mass leisure."[47] Moreover, MacCannell claims that "'the tourist' is one of the best models available for modern-man-in-general."[48] Such ideas highlight what other scholars have pointed out: the crucial role of tourism in shaping the progress of modernity and the very nature of modern society.[49]

As such ideas suggest, the importance of tourism in helping to shape modern culture cannot be overlooked. Tourism—indeed, the concept of leisure as a whole—has been "truly centrifugal" in influencing the course of modern history.[50] Shelley Baranowski and Ellen Furlough claim that "tourism and vacations can be interpreted as laboratories of modern life in the industrialized world."[51] Some scholars have described tourism as a means of negotiating the upheavals and dislocations often associated with modernity, noting that sightseeing can be interpreted as "a way of attempting to overcome the discontinuity of modernity, of incorporating its fragments into unified experience."[52]

Both sport and tourism played significant roles, moreover, in the cultural construction of gender. Wider gender orders in society play a key role in gendering the various activities and meanings of sport and tourism, and both of these elements of leisure culture serve as conduits through which gender roles and conceptions are reproduced and legitimated.[53] In this chapter, I explore those gendered meanings. French and German publicity materials demonstrated a clear gendering of sport along competitive lines. Performance-oriented, competition-centered sporting games and events were gendered masculine; in contrast, popular discourse emphasized the easygoing, carefree, distinctly noncompetitive nature of women's participation in sports. In the realm of tourism, popular ideology emphasized travel's ability to rejuvenate and seemingly to slow or reverse the perceived disappearance of tradition. Given this situation, it was women rather than men who were most frequently at the center of travel images, associated with the familial and the traditional, and presented as the bearers of age-old, historic culture. In both cases, popular leisure discourse sought to utilize feminine participation in leisure as a means of negotiating the disconcerting effects, real or imagined, of modernity.

GENDER AND MODERN SPORT

Socially prescribed norms regarding innate gender difference have historically served as a basis for excluding women from some sporting activities.[54] Traditionally associated with masculinity, much sporting activity, such as football and track and field, was deemed inappropriate for women, as the prospect of women's participation was equated with a challenge to an idealized gender hierarchy.[55] It was felt that men's involvement in sport should instill values tied to military training and combat—that is, to prepare a man for a potential career as a fighting soldier.[56] Meanwhile, medical theories about the ill effects of "inappropriate" sports for women, especially those that demanded strength or endurance, flowered in the interwar period, almost always centered on the alleged hazards posed by "masculine" sporting activities to women's ability to bear children.[57] A related concern, reflecting wider fears circulating in interwar Europe about the transgressively masculine behavior and appearance of "modern women," was that women's participation in masculine sports would lead to a masculinization of their appearance and bodies.[58] Above all, what these discursive restrictions had in common was their insistence that women not take part in sports that required the allegedly masculine attributes of strength or endurance, or that were based foremost on competition, record-breaking, and performance—that is, sports that were quintessentially modern. Women who tried to take part in such activities could become the objects of scorn and ridicule, as happened to those who organized and played on a women's football club created in 1930 in Frankfurt. The public outcry against this endeavor was so powerful that many players quit the team, and the club was disbanded in 1931.[59] Women as well as men accepted and even actively helped to construct the prevailing gender hierarchy of sport (and of society more generally).[60]

Thus women's participation in sporting activities should not be viewed simply as a frivolous pastime or meaningless set of games.[61] Wider cultural issues of the interwar era were also at stake, among them the prestige of the nation. Political regimes of the interwar era sought to utilize sport as a means of demonstrating national greatness on the international stage. In Nazi Germany, for instance, Hitler's regime paid close attention to the role of sport in national prestige and power.[62] Nazi ideology originally opposed modern sports because their internationalized nature meant that they could not be "extolled rhapsodically as a unique expression of the German *Volk*."[63] Soon after seizing power in 1933, however, the Nazis' realization of the potential propagandistic benefits of sport for German national prestige prompted a shift in ideology, as Hitler's regime was able to define international sporting performance by German competitors as an expression of the new Nazi national community.[64] While such politicization of sport is often associated with the fascist governments of Hitler's Germany and Mussolini's Italy, scholars such as Pierre Arnaud and Richard Holt argue persuasively that it was in fact liberal-democratic regimes—France being a prime example—that first attempted to use sport for such propagandistic ends.[65] Powerful evidence of the manipulation of sport for national prestige can be found in France's (and Britain's) exclusion of Germany from international sporting competition during the first half of the 1920s.[66] In part, this exclusion was due to unresolved bitterness and resentment from the war. At the same time, however, a more culturally significant process was at work: Germany was excluded because of the severe blow that its triumph in an international sporting venue would have delivered to French national pride and prestige.[67]

Women's Sports

French and German advertising materials tended to present images of women taking part only in sports gendered "acceptably" feminine. In France, the sport most commonly associated with femininity was tennis. Advertisements for everything from vacation resorts to department stores incorporated images linking women with this sport. In such images, women were most often depicted simply standing and holding a tennis racket; only occasionally did advertisements picture them actually playing tennis. Additionally, even those latter images tended to show merely a woman swinging a tennis racket without any other pictorial context, not even a net or court.[68] This point will prove germane in contrast to depictions of men's sports.

By contrast, a sport in which German portrayals of women were more common was skiing (in France, a more popular winter sport was ice skating).[69] As with French tennis ads, in German advertisements that featured images of skiing, women were almost never shown actually skiing, but rather simply standing with their skis.[70] Both French and German advertising materials presented ample evidence of women's involvement in swimming. German advertisements in this case are quite instructive. Almost none of these actually show women swimming; rather, ads for products such as swimsuits and skin creams usually merely make some textual reference to swimming. The women featured in such ads are simply shown standing or sitting next to a body of water, or they are pictured in a swimsuit without any background context.[71] Another summer sport deemed suitable for women that occasionally appeared in French and German publicity materials—and one women were sometimes shown actually playing—was golf.[72]

The most notable national difference among these varied images was the greater prevalence of tennis imagery in French publicity materials as opposed to German ones, a situation that can largely be accounted for by the stature of French tennis professional Suzanne Lenglen. A six-time Wimbledon singles champion in the 1920s (including doubles, she won a total of fifteen titles there), Lenglen was well known not just for her playing ability, but for her brashness and bold fashions on the court, and it was in large part her celebrity and accomplishments that helped to catapult tennis to the great popularity it enjoyed among her fellow Frenchwomen in the interwar years.[73] Although her temperament and dress often seemed at odds with traditional notions of femininity, the French press demonstrated considerable admiration for her. Despite the widespread discursive exclusion of women from national prestige with respect to sport, when a woman like Lenglen competed against a non-French player, it could indeed stir feelings as powerful as those inspired by other international sporting events.[74] Lenglen's victories served, as other sporting triumphs did, to rekindle feelings of French reinvigoration and national strength.

Lenglen's stature as a heroine of French sport was amply evident in the French popular press between the world wars. Referred to frequently as "our" Suzanne Lenglen, the tennis star was described (and revealed in such paeans) as a beloved national figure.[75] In a retrospective on her career, an article from *Paris-Midi* on 12 October 1935 calls Lenglen "our still great Suzanne" and "the greatest champion of all time."[76] The national merits of a French tennis champion were expressed unmistakably in an article from *Excelsior* on 3 July 1937. The article, which for the most part recaps the men's singles victory of the American Don Budge at Wimbledon, also addresses the mixed doubles tournament, wherein a French duo has advanced to the final. The article states that, although "American tennis triumphed, French tennis was brought back to public attention" by the semifinal victory of French mixed doubles team Madame Mathieu and Monsieur Petra. Having already won the French title, according to the article, Mathieu and Petra will now try to capture the Wimbledon championship in order to "inscribe their names on the renowned list of winners."[77] The article shows how closely the performance of individuals at such international competitions was tied to national achievement, as the triumphs of the players are described as victories for their countries. Only in such rare cases in which women's sporting achievements could serve such nationalist ends was female involvement in professionalized, modern sports met with anything less than widespread cultural condemnation.[78]

Men's Sports

An analysis of advertisements featuring male athletes reveals sharp distinctions between men's and women's images in sport-related publicity materials. Most visibly, men are depicted as taking part in a wider range of sports and games, including boxing, football, and track and field, sports with which women were almost never associated due to their gendering as solely masculine endeavors.[79] Perhaps even more noteworthy, though, was the context of men's sports on display in such images. These routinely pictured men not only performing the sporting events in question, but doing so in an unabashedly competitive, even professional, environment. Two French ads for Bessa cameras from 1937 are typical in this regard. In the first ad, a man is shown riding a horse in the lead of what is apparently, given the other riders visible behind him, a

FIG. 28. Ad for Bessa cameras, *Gringoire* (13 August 1937)

competitive horse racing event (fig. 28).[80] Similarly, in the second ad, a male track-and-field athlete is jumping over a hurdle. Although no other competitors are visible, discernible behind him in the background are spectators in a grandstand, thus leaving no doubt that this is indeed a man in the midst of a competitive race.[81] In a final example, an illustration in the 1928 *agenda* of the Bon Marché, two men are boxing in a boxing ring while a crowd (itself made up almost exclusively of men) watches the bout.[82]

German images employed similar strategies with respect to male sporting involvement, most often in ads for cigarettes. A 1930 ad for Josetti Juno cigarettes, for instance, shows men engaged in various track-and-field events, among them throwing the javelin and the shot put, and a hurdles race. As was the case with many French ads featuring men, there is a grandstand of spectators in the ad, making it clear that these men are involved in a public, competitive set of events. The text of the ad, moreover, draws comparisons to the

FIG. 29. Ad for Muratti cigarettes, *Völkischer Beobachter* (14 July 1935)

"intense competition" involved in both the athletics pictured in the ad and in the industrial realm, namely competition between cigarette manufacturers.[83] Two ads from 1935 for Muratti cigarettes are not unlike this previous ad. In the first, a man leaps over a hurdle in a track-and-field race (fig. 29), while in the second, men are shown playing rugby, another masculine-gendered sport. In both advertisements, a packed stadium of onlookers is visible in the background.[84]

These French and German publicity materials featuring men are crucial to the wider meanings and boundaries attached to masculinity and femininity vis-à-vis sport in the interwar period. A woman like Suzanne Lenglen turns out to be the proverbial exception that proves the rule. Only in a very exceptional case could a woman enjoy the kind of stature she did from athletic accomplishment. Instead, as the advertising images discussed above strongly suggest, it was men, not women, who were associated in the popular imagination with competitive sport and public sporting achievement. As a rule, women's involvement with sports was still discursively treated as little more than a hobby or passing recreation, not as a professional, achievement-oriented competition.

Recreation versus Competition

As the preceding discussion suggests, advertising images portrayed women's participation in sport as a mere hobby taken up for private recreation, not the public, competitive sport depicted in publicity materials featuring male athletes. This aspect of popular discourse, though present in both French and German ideology, took somewhat different forms in each country. In Germany, two 1922 ads centered upon skiing help to illustrate this point. The first, an ad for a liqueur, shows a man and woman sitting on a snowy slope; their skis rest on the ground around them. They seem to have taken a break during their skiing (or perhaps before starting it) to have a drink, as the man holds a bottle of the advertised product in his hand.[85] The second ad, this one for Engelhardt cigarettes, similarly shows a man and woman with skis—he on his skis, she holding hers. Already smoking himself, the man is lighting a cigarette for the woman.[86] These ads clearly demonstrate that skiing is not, in these cases, a competitive pursuit. Once again, the women pictured in the ads are not even skiing or actually wearing their skis. Such images do not depict an achievement-oriented sport for women or men, suggesting instead the milieu of a mere pastime.

A 1921 advertisement depicts a more competitive masculinity, while at the same time showing women who are decidedly not engaged in competitive sport. The ad shows several men and women swimming, along with others resting on a beach nearby. The overall mood of the ad is convivial, even jovial—an apparently carefree woman frolics in the water, while elsewhere a man is wading into the water and kissing the hand of another woman. Thus, in this example as well, recreation and fun are suggested, not competition. However, a couple of the swimming men—with looks of determined concentration on their faces—do seem take their efforts more seriously than their female counterparts. Both of them are swimming intently, as can be seen by the water they are exhaling as they come up for another stroke.[87] Thus while some of the men, and all of the women, in this advertisement are depicted as swimming for their personal enjoyment, a couple of male figures suggest a more competitive spirit. Finally, a 1937 advertisement, headlined "Household Gymnastics," includes an illustration of a woman mopping a floor while performing a handstand, resting her hands on her mop and bucket, respectively.[88] Obviously, this woman does have considerable athletic skill; this is obviously not a maneuver that anyone can perform without practice. Yet the ad undercuts any sense of competition by portraying her athletic efforts within the domestic sphere. She is not taking part in any competition, and she is certainly not performing for an audience. Instead, though she certainly is skilled at what she is doing, she seems to lack any competitive impulse, and is instead happy to perform her gymnastics in the home as something of a hobby.

In the French case, a typical example is provided by an Alpes & Jura advertisement from 1932 that shows a contented-looking woman skiing down a snowy slope (fig. 30). The ad's scant text associates "winter sports" with "joy" and "health."[89] While seemingly innocuous, an advertisement like this holds potentially significant meanings for the gendering of sport. The ad's upbeat, carefree tenor suggests a complete lack of concern with achievement and per-

FIG. 30. Alpes & Jura ad, *Notre Temps* (18 December 1932)

formance. The woman is certainly not skiing as part of any competition, and there is not the slightest hint of the intensity suggested in some ads picturing male athletics. Instead, the entire tone of the ad is one of healthy joyfulness; this is a lighthearted trip down the ski slopes for simple recreational purposes. An illustration from the 1928 *agenda* of the Bon Marché makes a similar point. It depicts a woman riding a horse, while nearby a man behind the wheel of a car looks at her going past. Text accompanying the image states that horseback riding has always been an aristocratic sport in France.[90] As with the previous example, this seemingly innocuous image suggests that this sport is a mere recreational activity rather than a serious sporting pursuit. Moreover, although the description of horseback riding as an aristocratic pursuit may seem intended to empower the pictured woman as having significant social status, in fact that reference actually returns her to the realm of the past and tradition, a time when a true aristocracy held sway in France. In that sense, the man's presence is again important, for in an automobile he represents the coming of modernity in opposition to the feminine embodiment of tradition encapsulated by the horse-riding woman. Just as modern sports were gendered masculine, in this case modernity as a whole is given a male identity, from which the female realm of the past and tradition is unequivocally differentiated.

Elegance, Appearance, and Traditional Femininity

This notion that women's and men's sports are fundamentally different was also made evident in a number of advertising materials suggesting that women's interest in sport was primarily linked to concerns of fashion—that is, that women were more preoccupied with what to wear when taking part in a sporting activity than with participating in the sport itself. In France, a series of images and text from the late 1930s from "Pour Vous, Madame . . .," the women's page of *Gringoire,* demonstrates this notion. One of the issues occasionally dealt with on this page, in addition to housework, personal hygiene, and child rearing, was sports. However, sport was virtually never discussed on its own merits or in terms of women's abilities or desires to compete in a sporting event. Instead, images and text about sport from "Pour Vous, Madame . . ." repeatedly emphasized simply what women should wear during their sport outings. Clothing selected for sports, women were reminded in these pages, should be not only fashionable, but also comfortable, practical, and charming or elegant.[91] As was the case with advertisements, images from "Pour Vous,

Madame. . ." almost never showed women engaging in the sports in question, but rather simply standing and holding the sporting equipment.[92]

Another item revelatory of such ideas is an article from the 1921 *agenda* of the Grands Magasins du Louvre entitled "The Fashions of Dancing and Sports." Given the title of the article, it is not surprising that the text should deal with fashion issues in relation to sport. What is noteworthy is the implication of these descriptions for broader ideologies of gender, particularly the place of traditional feminine roles in helping to assign "acceptability" to certain sports. The article notes that women's increased participation in sporting activities since the end of the Great War has not hindered women's elegance or prevented them from wearing "charming costumes" during the playing of these sports. The end of the article then moves on to deal with the purported sport of the future for women: aviation. The article envisions that, in a relatively short time, a number of women will want to possess and fly a plane. Yet women will have to figure out something different to wear when flying, the article contends, as previous and contemporary aviatrixes have hardly demonstrated elegance.[93] The implication is that women's participation and cultural acceptance in sport is dependent on maintaining their natural feminine elegance. A traditional emphasis on elegance and charm as a vital part of femininity helped to dictate the types of sport that would prove acceptable to society at large. A lack of elegance and charm in a sport (and its fashions) adversely affected one's femininity and bordered too closely on masculinization to be acceptable.

That point is also made in the 1924 *agenda* of the Galeries Lafayette, which in a paragraph dealing with women's sports makes mention of the maintenance of feminine attributes as part of women's sporting involvement. Naming sports such as tennis as those in which women were increasingly taking part, the text claims that "swarms of young girls indulge themselves, every morning, in these graceful sports, which add the flexibility of movement to the grace of feminine attitudes."[94] A similar line of commentary can be gleaned from two May 1926 articles in *Figaro,* both entitled "Golf at the Galeries Lafayette." These articles reported on the course of a weeklong publicity event at that department store in which women were invited to golf in the store's lounges and on its terrace. The first article, written while this event was still in progress, describes golf as a "charming, elegant" sport that provides perfect exercise for a woman, since it "cultivates vigor, health, grace."[95] The second article, appearing after the conclusion of the event, similarly describes golf as a "healthy, graceful, harmonious sport."[96] Once again, the importance of sport being consonant with traditional aspects of femininity was evident.

Some materials focused on other traditional roles for women. For instance, an article in *Minerva* from 17 January 1937 entitled simply "Women's Sports" provides "advice for sportswomen." The advice is that women should not give up sporting activities altogether, since these can be helpful to one's health and personal beauty. However, the article, suggesting a continued uneasiness with women's competitive and professional sport, warns that "specialization in sport is always harmful," and leads to women becoming "overworked" and physiologically imbalanced. Such a condition is dangerous for women, "whose essential function, it is necessary not to forget, is being a mother, a creator of life."[97] This concern remained central even for those women who did engage in professional athletics. A 1938 article from *La Française,* declaring that sports should always have a place in women's lives, lists and briefly describes several successful female athletes. Many of these women, however, were described in terms that associated them with more traditional feminine realms, such as noting that they were married or had children, rather than focusing on their sporting achievements.[98] Finally, an article in *L'Intransigeant* from June 1922, entitled "Woman and Sport," lists some responses from a recent reader survey dealing with women's participation in sports. While opinions were printed from both supporters and opponents of women's participation in sports, both sides used similar justifications for their often quite disparate positions on the subject. Virtually all respondents situated their arguments in the realm of women's traditional roles, especially maternity, arguing that women's participation in sports would either enhance or detract from their ability to bear children, depending on which side of the argument was being put forward.[99] Thus in a variety of ways, women's involvement in sport was, at the cultural level, related discursively to such activities' resonance with traditional notions of femininity and women's roles.

Along similar lines, some advertisements linked women's sporting activity with their physical appearance and care, again suggesting that women's foremost concern with respect to sport was not competition or achievement, but rather the maintenance of essential elements of femininity. For instance, a perfume ad from Germany from 1926 shows a woman driving, accompanied by her golf clubs. The ad declares that the fragrance will endure reliably through the woman's sportive outing, and even promises to invigorate her "body and spirit." Unlike virtually all other ads of its kind, this one actually contains a reference to achievement in sporting activity, as the ad further declares that the perfume can improve one's performance and thus the likelihood of victory.[100] Given the nature of the product in question, however, this promise seems facetious. No elaboration is given to explain how a perfume can make one a better golfer. Scholars such as Gertrud Pfister and Paul Willis comment on humor being used as a means of negating any potential transgressive overtones or gender-blurring consequences of women's participation in sports, a plausible interpretation of this description of a perfume as a performance-enhancing agent.[101] French advertisements also emphasized women's concern for the care of their bodies when taking part in sports. In particular, this was a message sent by ads for depilatory creams. One such ad for Sulthine from 1927, accompanied by an image of a tennis-playing woman, discusses the capabilities of the cream in light of a woman's tennis wardrobe, in particular the sleeveless shirts of women tennis players.[102] An ad for Ozoin lotion from 1927 that also features a female tennis player urges upon women the importance of using the lotion on one's skin after having played a game of tennis. The ad states: "You always need to refresh your face after a good game of tennis played sometimes under a blazing sun."[103]

Like ads emphasizing elegance, charm, and other aspects of traditional femininity, these French and German advertisements that focus on personal care and appearance likewise avoid most suggestions of competitiveness in women's sport, choosing instead to depict women's greatest concern with regard to their sporting endeavors as their bodily appearance. Gertrud Pfister notes in the case of pre-1914 female sport that the physical activities considered suitable for women, such as tennis and figure skating, were acceptable to society because, at least to an extent, they adhered to customary visions of women as essentially decorative (even erotic) objects.[104] Paul Willis also raises the issue of the objectification of women in sport—in an explicitly sexualized context—as a means of ensuring that women's participation in sport remained discursively foremost an object of masculine pleasure.[105] Such objectification of women can be seen as contributing significantly to interwar French and German depictions of bodily care in relation to feminine sport; women were maintaining their pleasant appearance and fragrance, presumably, for the pleasure of men.

GENDER AND TOURISM

Mirroring the growing participation in sports, vacations were increasingly common in interwar France and Germany, as more socioeconomic groups took such trips and went to more kinds of destinations, from spas and seasides to mountain and provincial locales.[106] Yet tourist imagery remained widely consistent in France and Germany throughout the interwar decades. In part, this situation can be explained by Rudy Koshar's idea of "normality," which suggests that both tourists and the government relied conceptually on pre-existing conventions and practices of cultures of travel.[107] European governments, as they did with sports, increasingly looked to the political potential of the nature and meanings of tourism, and took great interest in holidays for their citizens.[108] In France, for example, the antifascist coalition known as the Popular Front had an impressive leisure program, and is perhaps best remembered for its establishment of paid vacations (congés payés) and a forty-hour work week for French citizens in 1936.[109] Not unlike the Nazi regime, the Popular Front sought to use vacations as a means of effecting solidarity and social harmony among French citizens, even going so far as to organize inexpensive trips within the means of the working classes.[110] While Hitler's government did not codify mandatory paid vacations for all workers, its leisure program, Kraft durch Freude (Strength through Joy), or KdF, still sought to ensure that working Germans would have an opportunity to take a holiday, even if just a short one. The KdF program became the largest travel agency in Germany, building a fleet of cruise ships, planning the construction of massive resorts geared toward workers, and promoting organized package tours for vacationing Germans.[111]

The motives and desires of the tourists themselves have been scrutinized as well. Above all, scholars emphasize that tourists are not simply mindless, hedonistic wanderers, but rather that tourism centrally involves a search for meaning, frequently a quest for a sense of authenticity and tradition.[112] Tourists often seek out what is different or unique, and in the context of a modern, urban existence that often translates into a search for traces of an idealized, nostalgized past: "For moderns, reality and authenticity are thought to be elsewhere: in other historical periods and other cultures, in purer, simpler lifestyles."[113] Amidst the turbulence of modernization, an important cultural facet of tourism was an attempt to discover a sense of cultural heritage.[114] It was from there a short conceptual step to the nation and national identity within ideologies of leisure travel. Rudy Koshar asserts that tourism is more powerful than many other forms of consumption in establishing a sense of national belonging, as "tourists learned not only about the sites they visited but also about their origins in a national collectivity."[115] Shelley Baranowski and Ellen Furlough also point out the increasing importance of tourism as a conduit for enhancing such a sense of national belonging, identity, and even loyalty.[116]

This building of attachments to the nation was pursued by both French and German officials. In the German case, the Nazi KdF program once again provides perhaps the best example. The leaders of the organization, as Shelley Baranowski notes, recognized the tendency of many Germans to adhere more closely to local or regional loyalties than national ones, and set about deliberately to cast the KdF as an organization that could help to create a new national community loyal to Hitler's regime and its ideology.[117] Traveling across different parts of the country, the Nazis hoped, would introduce Germans to their fellow countrymen and to their Fatherland, thus building loyalty and solidarity among Germans on a national level, not to mention buoying support for the Nazi regime.[118] This theme could even be found in the travel culture of the Weimar Republic, as its government was also concerned with promoting national heritage and culture as part of tourism.[119] In the French context, the work of Stephen Harp on French gastronomy and tourism is particularly instructive. Harp notes, as was the case in Germany, a strong identification with regions (specifically with respect to French cuisine), and demonstrates the ways in which the differences among France's various regions were actually used as a means of reinforcing a unified national conception of France.[120] Along similar lines, Patrick Young's examination of the Touring Club de France reveals an emphasis on a singular "Frenchness" amidst the country's regional diversity, as Touring Club organizers sought to use tourism to familiarize French citizens with their varied national landscape—particularly as embodied in the "old France" still allegedly apparent in the provinces—as a means of strengthening national identity and discovering a national essence.[121] Thus in both France and Germany, the value of tourist culture in helping to forge national identity and loyalty was a powerful and widespread trope.

The Countryside

Given the importance of tourism in popular discourse, it is understandable that vacations were referred to rather frequently in French and German publicity materials. General images of idyllic travel destinations, from tropical getaways to mountainside resorts (and much else in between), abound in advertisements, although their images often are exclusively focused on the specified locations and thus sometimes do not depict any human figures.[122] One of the most common destinations was the countryside, an area removed from the hustles and pressures of urban life. Images of rural, country settings were ample in both French and German publicity materials in the 1920s and 1930s. Overwhelmingly, the people depicted in such advertisements were women, sometimes accompanied by children or a male figure designated as a husband and father. Still, the central focus of the ads remained female figures in the vast majority of instances. A French radio ad from 1929, for example, shows two women and a man enjoying a relaxed, leisurely picnic in a country setting of greenery and trees (a radio is on the ground next to them), and the ad notes that the radio can be brought on vacation.[123] A 1922 ad for Kodak cameras, meanwhile, lacks any adult male figures. Instead, the ad pictures a woman watching four children playing in a scenic, rural, nature setting, complete with a church steeple visible in the background. The ad reminds the reader to bring a camera on vacation in order to preserve memories of the trip.[124] One final French example comes from a 1927 Nestlé baby cereal ad. It shows a woman and two children in a train compartment, while out the window the French countryside passes by (the ad states that the advertised product can be brought on such a journey and quickly prepared just as at home).[125]

German advertisements were often similar in tone and intent. A 1938 ad for a resort shows a woman in a nature setting, carrying flowers that she has apparently just picked from the ground around her.[126] In addition, a 1934 ad for the Nazi organization Hilfswerk Mutter and Kind shows four female figures taking a hayride among farm fields.[127] These numerous images of vacations and excursions in the countryside were intimately tied to the process analyzed above in which images of the past and tradition represented the unifying power of the nation against a seemingly inherently destabilizing modernity. The inclusion of pristine, country locales in this light is thus an important aspect of popular leisure discourse. Such places were seen as bastions of tradition, as settings in which an idealized prewar social order, romanticized in opposition to the urban-oriented, fast-paced modern world, still endured.[128]

The place of gender in this process is important, as suggested by the fact that most of these ads centered upon female figures. In part, the very nature of women's images in these advertisements is noteworthy, for they are almost never pictured alone. Such an image would suggest the possibility that a single female traveler was a "modern woman." Instead, women were consistently depicted with their children or, on occasion, husbands, ensuring associations with "proper" femininity as embodied in family relations. Depicting women in these idyllic locations also tied them to the realm of tradition, further undermining the dislocations and upheavals consequent with the onset of modernity. Indeed, Patrick Young argues in the French case that such settings with respect to French regions were strongly gendered female—that the customs and the very spirit of such areas were allegedly embodied quintessentially in women, who were seen as "the archetypes of cultural constancy."[129] As was the case with sports, men were associated with modernity, while women were consigned to the realm of tradition. Although women could serve as a conduit through which modernity was negotiated, they were not fully a part of that modernity themselves, instead remaining traditional beings.

Rejuvenation and Regeneration

Not only did images of the countryside operate as a unifier at the national level, but they also reflected a strong belief in the rejuvenating abilities of such vacation locales. As Shelley Baranowski and Ellen Furlough point out, vacation spots have often been represented as places wherein one can seek an escape from daily stresses and find greater freedom of time and energy.[130] The perceived restorative powers of the vacation, at the personal and the national level, were evident in ads from interwar France and Germany, and in this case as well, women were the focal points of most advertisements.

A German ad from 1933 for the Ullstein travel agency, which actually focuses on cruises, shows a man and woman smiling and looking quite happy, apparently on the deck of a boat (fig. 31). The ad promises that sea travel can bring travelers both relaxation and a good temperament.[131] Another Ullstein ad from 1933, this one promoting a trip to the Bavarian mountains, is similar. It shows a man and woman in traditional Bavarian dress. They are dancing with each other; the visual focus is the woman who faces the reader, rather than the man who has his back turned. An accompanying image shows grazing livestock in the foreground while mountains dominate the background. The ad's header is, "Happy Relaxation."[132] A final example pitches a trip to the springs of Baden-Baden. The ad shows a woman driving a car, looking down happily at the town she is approaching. The image of the town is again one of rural serenity and natural beauty, and it is clear from the visual image that the woman feels reinvigorated just by looking at Baden-Baden as she drives toward it.[133]

FIG. 31. Ad for the Ullstein travel agency, *Vossische Zeitung* (23 July 1933)

French examples explored similar themes, though at times were more explicit than their German counterparts about the rejuvenating powers of holiday destinations. A 1938 ad encouraging travel to St. Moritz demonstrates this. It shows a man and woman driving, with a mountainous background visible behind them. The man is lifting his arm to show the woman the scene, as though she is the one in need of the vacation. The ad declares that the "secret of St. Moritz lies in the atmosphere of the place." "Surrounded by scenery of a unique beauty," at St. Moritz one can enjoy, among other things, "the peaceful joys of nature," as well as the powers of a healing spa.[134] A 1928 ad, moreover, for the bottled water of St. Galmier-Badoit, shows a woman in a bathing suit, obviously at or on her way to a seaside locale. The ad's header reads: "Time for vacation." The ad cites the "beneficial relaxation" that one obtains "for your spirit" on vacation, and insists that one provide the same treatment for one's physical being by purchasing and using the advertised product.[135] A final example comes from a short article from 1939 entitled "Pour le weekend." Although the article seems geared less toward a vacationer per se than a wealthier audience with a country home for weekend use (its main focus is on the accommodations of such a residence), its message is still very much that of a leisured getaway. The article begins by noting: "*Le week-end* has become a necessity." The article points out that, during the weekend, one can enjoy two full days of "silence in the garden," as well as other relaxing pursuits, all of which serve to make one forget about daily troubles and worries.[136]

This discursive emphasis on rejuvenation and reinvigoration as an important facet of travel culture bears significant meaning for wider gender ideology during the interwar period. These images of rejuvenation, usually focused on a female figure, represent in a key sense a microcosm of the wider national rejuvenation that was such a focal point for French and German officials and commentators. The rejuvenation and even regeneration of the nation, according to interwar ideology, was a vital step toward the recovery of national glory and prestige. Just as sport played a role in this recovery, so too did tourist culture, for the reinvigoration that one could find on vacation embodied a larger project of revivifying the national body politic. The fact that women were the visual focus of such discourse reveals a more important cultural ideology at work, for in the political discourse of national renewal and regeneration, it was women who were expected to bear that responsibility, most importantly by providing and raising happy and healthy children who could ensure the future power and stability of the national entity. Thus women's presence in tourist advertising represented in an important manner the centrality of women to national recovery in the interwar years.

The Beach

Such an ideology of rejuvenation was also implicit in French and German publicity materials that depicted one of the most popular vacation sites: the beach. Seaside resorts and locales were immensely popular in both countries, and this was reflected in tourist imagery. Like the images discussed above, these seaside vacations were also thought to provide an opportunity for spiritual reinvigoration. Scholars such as Shelley Baranowski and Orvar Löfgren, who separately have explored the cultural meanings assigned to beaches, particularly with respect to the Strength through Joy (KdF) program, emphasize seaside resorts as yet another place to escape from the worst aspects of the urban landscape and to find good health and relaxation.[137]

In French advertisements relating to beach or seaside vacations, women were overwhelmingly depicted in familial scenes. Most frequently exemplified in ads for Kodak cameras, which were urged upon readers as a way to preserve the happy memories of one's vacation, a wide variety of images showed women at a beach or wading into a body of water with their children and sometimes their husbands.[138] For instance, a 1931 Kodak ad shows a smiling woman with two smiling children; wading in the water, she holds the hand of a walking youngster while carrying a younger child in her other arm (fig. 32). Meanwhile, the ad's header reminds the potential vacationer about a camera, which is referred to in the first person: "Don't leave without me!!!"[139] Similar imagery is to be found in the 1928 *agenda* of the Bon Marché, which includes an illustration and accompanying text dealing with taking a trip to the beach. The image yet again depicts a mother and child together. The text notes that, although there are many things to do at the beach, "the beaches of France are above all familial."[140]

In German advertisements, by contrast, it was more common for a woman to be depicted without a husband or children in ads for products such as suntan lotions, cameras, and film manufacturers.[141] A set of virtually identical ads from the first half of the 1930s for the tourist destination Swinemünde provides evidence of this (fig. 33). In these ads, a woman is usually depicted sitting alone on a beach holding an umbrella to shield her complexion from the sun; other tourists are only barely visible (and certainly not identifiable) in the distant background. The ads declare that this location contains "the most beautiful beach in the world."[142] Another series of examples can be found in ads for Nivea skin cream and suntan lotion from the latter half of the 1930s. In these ads, women are generally shown relaxing alone or with other women on the beach, sometimes in the midst of applying the advertised product to their skin.[143] In some cases, women were pictured with male companions, though even then usually not with children. For instance, a 1939 ad for a haircare product discusses the problems that can beset one's hair due to exposure to the sun and wind when on the beach. The ad features a photograph of a woman applying the product to her hair, as well as an illustration showing two couples. The first couple stands on the beach waving to the other man and woman, who are enjoying a ride aboard a sailboat. Yet again in this case, though, the woman pictured applying the product to her hair remains the visual focal point of the ad.[144]

Although often not as explicit as advertisements depicting peaceful rural settings, beach scenes in publicity materials likewise were designed to send a

FIG. 32. Kodak camera ad, *Le Matin* (24 July 1931)

message of rejuvenation and relaxation. Seaside locales appeared as yet another place where one escaped the hassles of daily urban existence, emerging with a reinvigorated spirit. Women were the primary focus of such advertising materials, which portrayed them as the standard bearers for national renewal and regeneration.

Automobile Tourism

One final aspect of tourist discourse that must be examined is automotive tourism. A couple of examples dealing with cars in relation to vacations have already been cited, and indeed automobiles were central to tourist culture in the interwar era.[145] In many ways, cars represented the fullest expression of the irony of modern leisure: traditional, historical locales rooted in an idealized past age of simplicity were pursued thanks to the technological prowess of modern machines such as trains and cars, which facilitated the relatively quick

FIG. 33. Ad for the tourist destination Swinemünde, *Vossische Zeitung* (12 July 1933)

and efficient systems of travel necessary for the mass consumption of tourist sites.[146] As Rudy Koshar shows, cars in the interwar decades were viewed foremost not with respect to a daily commute to work, but for their ability to be vehicles of tourist discovery.[147]

A couple of German advertisements demonstrate the association in popular discourse of the automobile with tourist travel. A 1933 ad for the KaDeWe (Kaufhaus des Westens) department store advertises various goods for sale at the store, among them items to keep in mind "for the weekend," such as photographic film, folding chairs, and sunglasses. An image in the ad depicts a woman behind the wheel of a car in a nature setting; a man stands next to the vehicle.[148] An ad for maps from 1937 shows a car driving along a stretch of highway in a regional scene; mountains and a forested area are visible in the background. The ad's header is: "Through beautiful Germany."[149] This ad in particular bears significant meaning in the context of German automotive tourism between the world wars, especially with respect to the construction of the Autobahn. The thrust of such ads was to emphasize that automobiles would not sully the natural, wondrous landscape of Germany (a theme that will be seen in slightly altered form in the French case). Indeed, the previous ad's illustration is focused on the visual harmony between the road and the scenery; the car's image is small and barely visible, and no people can be discerned inside the vehicle. The implication was that the precious national patrimony of Germany—its beautiful regions, pristine and idyllic—was not adversely affected by the utilization of a car to reach these destinations. The Autobahn project itself was steeped in an ideology that emphasized maintaining the romantic aura and natural beauty of the German countryside in spite of the building of massive highways for automotive travel. As such, highways and automobiles were made consonant with the German *Volk* ideal. As Jeffrey Herf suggests, in this light the Autobahn itself became not a modernist, technological intrusion into nature, but instead, in an important sense, another natural element in the landscape and potential source of national unity.[150]

French publicity materials often provide analogous examples, though one aspect of automotive tourism depicted in French ads—the place of the family—is rarely featured in German advertisements. A 1930 ad that pictures a woman standing outside a car notes that the vehicle is "essential for familial tourism," especially longer trips, because it has a luggage rack atop it, a veritable "trunk on the roof," that will permit the reliable transport of a great deal of baggage.[151] In a 1930 Citroën ad, moreover, seven people are pictured sitting comfortably in a Citroën model designed for family use. The ad states that the car can carry the entire family on a drive to its vacation destination.[152]

As their German counterparts did, French ads emphasized the compatibility of cars with the natural landscape of the nation. Once again, women—still regarded as emblems of tradition amidst modern upheaval and invention—were usually at the center of such imagery in publicity materials. A March 1934 ad for Goodrich tires shows two women and a man standing outside a parked car on a hill overlooking an idyllic-appearing village. The ad, which wishes the reader a happy Easter vacation, emphasizes that rather than intruding upon the traditions of the past, the automobile blends with them, promising in fact not to devalue them. This last point is highlighted by the only other text in the ad besides the name of the product and the Easter reference: "The tire that does not skid." Indeed, the image in the ad includes enough of the stretch of road on which the car has driven before being parked to illustrate that point.[153] Thus this ad does not promise a long-lasting tire, or one that will not deflate during an outing in the countryside; instead, its focus is on the avoidance of skidding—that is, on not defacing the environment that is to be admired. Thus the harmony of technological vehicle and traditional France is assured. Even more visually striking is an advertisement from 1931 for the Shell Oil Company (fig. 34). In it, a car carrying both men and women is driving away from an attractive French village, presumably returning to the city after a holiday. The dominant image in the ad, however, is a large advertising billboard for Shell Oil that has been marked with an *X* over it. The ad states that Shell, "concerned about respecting this national wealth that are the landscapes of France," is adhering to public opinion by removing obtrusive signs from French roadsides.[154] This powerful advertisement is a dramatic expression of the discursive efforts to reconcile the aesthetic of the natural landscape with automobile-related tourism.

A final example from France turns slightly away from this message of environmental preservation, but evinces a similar overall tone. It is an illustration from the 1928 *agenda* of the Bon Marché that shows a man driving with a woman passenger. They are out in the countryside, and a few buildings are visible in the distance. Accompanying text takes the form of a dialogue between the man and woman. Entitled "The Madness of Speed" and prefaced with the backdrop "A pretty village dominated by the ruins of an old keep; the auto flies by," the dialogue is as follows:

Her: —What is this village, this mansion, I wonder?
Him: —Who cares, in five seconds we'll be somewhere else.[155]

Thus the woman, representative of the countryside and tradition itself, wishes to stop to admire and learn about this charming village and its historic ruins, but the man, the embodiment of surging modernity, has no interest in such historic or traditional matters; all that matters to him is the speed with which he will travel to the next part of the landscape. This example encapsulates a considerable portion of the popular travel discourse of interwar France and Germany. A feminine figure, intimately linked to tradition, national patrimony, and an idealized social order, is the staunch advocate not just of tradition, but of an entire national renewal, reinvigoration, and rejuvenation—a project for which responsibility falls squarely on her shoulders. She must negotiate the treacherous path to modernity without allowing it to compromise this sacred and stabilizing historical order of things.

As with other aspects of popular discourse in the interwar years, French and German ideologies of labor and leisure were imbued with gendered meanings that focused on a continuing connection between women and tradition in

FIG. 34. Ad for Shell Oil, stating that the company is adhering to public opinion by removing obtrusive signs from French roadsides, *L'Illustration* (4 April 1931)

order to mitigate the unsettling effects of a veritable onslaught of modernity in the 1920s and 1930s. In the realm of employment, advertising imagery suggested again women's subordination to masculine authority and control, as well as the compatibility of certain types of work with "proper" femininity, as a means of containing the potentially transgressive aspects of female participation in the labor force. With respect to leisure discourse, the process of linking women and tradition can be seen clearly through the examples of sports and tourism. In the former case, modern sports were defined as intrinsically masculine, requiring as they did the allegedly male attributes of strength and endurance and focused as they were on competitiveness and achievement. The only sports popularly associated with femininity were those that did not require such traits, and that could be portrayed as simply hobbies or recreational pastimes, unlike the public, professional, and competitive sports of men. In addition, cultural acceptance of women's sporting involvement also was tied

to highlighting the ways in which such activities were consonant with traditional notions of womanhood, such as feminine elegance, grace, and charm.
In the tourist realm, women were the main focus of promotional imagery, as
they were seen as the bearers of an idealized, unbroken cultural heritage and
tradition in opposition to the speed and uncertainties of modern life. As such,
tourist images located women in the countryside and on the beach, highlighting the rejuvenating powers of the vacation that represented the reinvigoration
of the nation as a whole in the aftermath of the Great War. Even images associating women on vacation with that most modern of inventions, the automobile, were constructed so as to emphasize the ways in which automotive
tourism likewise meshed with the natural landscape and could still be compatible with notions of authenticity and historicity. In these ways, French and
German leisure discourse between the world wars cast women as the arbiters
of the traditional, confirming long-standing cultural conceptions of gender
as a means of negotiating the modern.

CONCLUSION

The concern in cultural discourse regarding "appropriate" gender roles in France and Germany reached what may have been its greatest expression in the two decades separating the world wars. In an age when old-fashioned ways of thinking about and organizing categories of gender seemed to many to be blurred beyond recognition, the cultural imperative for a clearly defined, traditional gender order attained arguably unsurpassed heights. The perceived rush of modernity into French and German culture appeared to contemporaries as one of the prime causes of many of the unsettling changes in gender roles. Indeed, the archetypal image of transgressive, "improper" womanhood was given the appellation "modern woman." However, even though the prewar days were idealized after the fact as a time of stable, harmonious, and firmly differentiated gender roles, social realities had altered so dramatically that popular ideology was forced to incorporate at least some aspects of modernity in its presentation of appropriate gender roles.

The interwar years likewise witnessed the ascending importance of consumer culture in popular discourse. Although no part of Europe could be unequivocally classified as a mass consumer economy before World War II, consumerism was vital to the ways in which interwar French and German identities were formulated. People were coming to define themselves and were being defined by their societies primarily as consumer citizens, and thus consumption-related goods, services, and materials played an inordinately powerful role in establishing the bounds of personal and national identities. For this reason, I have focused in this work on sources drawn from the realm

of consumer culture—mainly, advertisements from the popular press and department store publicity materials—in order to delineate the connections in
popular discourse between consumption, gender, and modernity.

In the interwar years, French and German cultural ideology, utilizing consumer goods as its point of entry, put forward a definition of womanhood that,
while associating women with modernity, was primarily intended to reassert
a conservative, traditional image of femininity that did not raise the haunt-
ing specter of independent, liberated, "modern women." This cultural task
took a number of different forms, all of them pointing back toward the same
allegedly universal, seemingly timeless "truth": women were to stay devoted
to home and hearth, leaving the public world largely to men. In perhaps its
most subtle form, this frequently meant balancing (or outright superseding)
the more liberated aspects of women's discursive roles with an emphasis on the
duties and obligations to which they had to adhere at all costs. These duties
involved submission to masculine authority as well as ensuring the strength
and perpetuation of the nation. For housewives, this entailed recognizing that
the joys and empowering facets of modern housewifery, such as the easy operation of modern appliances and increased leisure time, were outweighed by
obligations to satisfy husbands' desires and to manage household finances as
a microcosm of the national economy. As mothers, meanwhile, women were
told that their greatest joys in life were to be found in having and raising children. Being a mother brought with it immense responsibilities as well, however, for the mother was exhorted to submit to paternal authority in the home,
and in addition was held ultimately responsible for the health and well-being
of her hearth and her children, and as such for the health of the nation and
the maintenance (or better yet, increase) of its population, without which the
nation might not survive. Even in the realm of beauty culture, despite the
promoted health benefits to be derived from caring for one's physical appearance, in the final analysis women's beauty was above all significant as a signal
of their acceptance of their "proper" social roles and masculine authority.

In addition to these responsibilities, and in fact closely tied to their duties to the nation, women had to be wary of the perils of Americanization. Although the economic potential of Americanism was undeniable, the social and
cultural risks of adopting its methods were to be carefully avoided. Only men
were allowed discursive space to negotiate the modern with the national polity.
Maintaining national distinctiveness was imperative, and deemed too crucial
and delicate a task to entrust to women. Women were not even granted discur-

sive access to modern sports, in part because these were too internationalized in nature. More importantly, however, women were seen as the root cause of the soullessness of American life that French and German ideology perceived as a threat to their distinct national cultures. As was most apparent in the case of automobiles, that most visible symbol of modernity, women were not associated in popular ideology with questions involving the treacherous path to Americanization. Men, and men alone, were qualified to handle this immeasurably significant process, according to popular thinking. While women could play a role in rediscovering distinctive national heritage and tradition, as exemplified in tourist discourse, men were the sole bearers of an integration of Americanism with the national body politic.

This exclusion of women from the discourse of reconciling Americanism with the nation is instructive also in its reflection of beliefs of "natural" sexual differences. Such purported differences were highlighted in various arenas of French and German cultural ideology as a further means of undermining feminine agency with respect to public, independent life. Repeatedly, men were defined as inherently rational, logical, and analytical beings who, in selecting items ranging from coats to automobiles, relied on their powers of reasoned thought to determine what types of purchases were best in terms of practical value or technological prowess. Women, by contrast, were constructed as emotional, impulsive creatures whose decisions were based not on questions of reliability or quality, but instead on aesthetic factors. Women were allegedly concerned above all with a product's appearance, elegance, or comfort. With women portrayed in advertising imagery as almost completely unfamiliar with the inner workings of technological wonders, it usually took a male expert to explain to a feminine audience the merits of a particular technological good like a car or a vacuum cleaner. Once again, women's subordination to and dependence upon men was made quite explicit. Although women were depicted as capable of using and operating a modern technological product, they were given no discursive authority over building, maintaining, or repairing them—such skills were assigned only to male figures.

The assertion of intrinsic sexual difference likewise continued the justification in popular ideology of a gendering of public and private along masculine and feminine lines, respectively, even if this "separate spheres" arrangement did not adequately reflect social reality. The promulgation of a masculine rationality in juxtaposition to feminine emotionality was one aspect of this process. Cultural definitions of femininity relegated women to the domestic realm at least in part based on the notion that women did not possess the appropriate mental or physical attributes that life in the public world demanded. In addition to being guided by emotion, impulse, and aesthetic considerations, women were portrayed in publicity materials as physically weak, further undercutting female claims to public space. Whereas men had the rational faculties and strong physical constitutions necessary to flourish in the public arena, women did not share these characteristics, according to popular ideology, and therefore belonged in the domestic realm.

Even when women were shown in the public sphere—a potentially liberating and empowering situation—such images served to assure that women's public forays were undertaken in guises consistent with their marital or maternal duties or that women were dependent on masculine guidance to participate in public life. Thus images of women driving in the public sphere almost always contained images of or references to children, family, or the need for a woman to get a man's help or opinion. Some scenes depicting women outdoors without a vehicle make use of similar techniques. Often picturing women with their children at a beach or other idyllic locale, these images placed women firmly in the realm of tradition rather than modernity.

The discursive process of modernizing the traditional elements of femininity proved quite diverse in its strategies and imagery. It turned out to be unshakable as well, persisting throughout the period between the world wars. It is a testament to the depth and breadth of such sentiments that they extended across socioeconomic, national-political, and even gender lines. Across the social and political spectrum, this cultural paradigm of gender met with relatively little resistance; in both France and Germany, these ideologies held hegemonic sway. Although each nation elaborated this gender discourse in its own way, both nations were responding to quite similar social concerns about gender and, in particular, women's place in society, and in the two countries the frame of reference for discussing and defining gender roles was remarkably equivalent. In an era of seemingly constant change and frequent upheaval and hardship, a firm attachment to traditional gender roles that incorporated elements of the modern provided an avenue through which French and German culture could envision slowing or reversing the pace of change in society, restoring a sense of stability and order, and ensuring national survival and well-being. The unanimity of this popular gender discourse reveals the deep and entrenched grasp in interwar society of an ideology of modernized yet traditional womanhood.

APPENDIX

The Popular Press in Interwar France and Germany

Between 1914 and 1939, the total circulation of newspapers in France increased just slightly, suffering several valleys in the intervening years due to the turbulent circumstances of the era. In 1914, the circulation of the whole of the French press stood at approximately 10 million or slightly less, while in 1939, the figure was as much as 12.5 million. The growth of the popular press in these years was often very uneven, as the number of daily newspapers diminished considerably and the vast majority of newspapers founded between the world wars failed fairly quickly in that difficult environment. Yet, seemingly paradoxically, the market share of the largest press publications declined during the interwar years, perhaps due to French readers' tendency to peruse disparate popular press publications rather than maintaining strict loyalty to one paper.[1] Thus no single newspaper dominated the interwar press landscape, which was characterized instead by many different papers of varying sizes.

There were a number of French daily newspapers of the political Right. One of the well-established, traditional "*quatre grands*" of the French press, *Le Matin* had an immediately recognizable name and reputation. As was the case with many other dailies, however, its circulation dipped in the interwar years, falling from approximately 1 million copies in 1918 to 312,000 by early 1939, a number that still qualified it as the fifth–most widely printed daily newspaper in France. Of these 312,000 daily editions, more than 200,000 were distributed and read in the provinces. The historically rightist political orientation and nationalistic tone of *Le Matin* intensified in the interwar years, especially in the 1930s, as became evident in its sympathetic treatment of Europe's fascist regimes. Located on the same wavelengths of the political spectrum was a much less widely read but still quite significant right-wing paper, *L'Action Française.* Its influence in rightist politics cannot be overstated, despite its meager circulation in 1939 of 45,000 copies. This newspaper was known for its virulent anti-Semitism and xenophobia. Even though this right-wing publication was sympathetic to Mussolini and Franco, it expressed powerful reservations about fascist Germany in the 1930s. It is important to note, as Pierre Albert points out, that this combative, confrontational publication was so notorious that many read it simply out of curiosity, not because they subscribed to its viewpoints.[2]

Among weeklies, a couple of other rightist-oriented publications should also be mentioned. One was *Gringoire,* a rare success story of the interwar press. Starting up in the late 1920s, it found an audience and managed to prosper in the interwar years, reaching a peak circulation of 650,000 by January 1937. Like *L'Action Française,* it was anti-Semitic, but *Gringoire* was not the violent, polemical publication that the former was. Although it was right-wing, it was not as predictable as many of its counterparts on the Right and the Left, choosing instead to be "[e]clectic in its affections."[3] A second rightist weekly publication was the internationally known *L'Illustration.* In an age of cheap, mass circulation papers, it continued to be expensive. Despite this fact, its circulation ran into the hundreds of thousands during the interwar years, reaching 400,000 before the onset of the Great Depression.[4] Partly thanks to its relatively high price, *L'Illustration* to an extent resisted the mass tendencies of other publications, remaining instead staunchly middle class.[5]

A number of nationally prominent dailies, by contrast, originated from a leftist political orientation. Perhaps most notable was *L'Oeuvre,* which, according to Pierre Albert, provided as close to a total image of the ideas and platforms of the radical political Left as any paper in interwar France. Its circulation figure of 236,000 to 274,000 in 1939 made it the seventh–most widely read daily newspaper in France. Anticlerical and, despite its leftist politics, somewhat ambivalent toward communism, *L'Oeuvre* was a leading supporter of the Popular Front government and vocal critic of the fascist regimes of Hitler and Mussolini. In turn, the Popular Front government of the 1930s, a coalition of leftist political parties united in their antifascist beliefs, had its main organ in the newspaper *Vendredi*. Founded in 1935 as the mouthpiece of the Popular Front, *Vendredi* was briefly a favorite of intellectuals, and almost immediately upon its creation enjoyed a circulation over the 100,000 mark. Yet the paper quickly fell out of favor with many readers along with the Popular Front itself, and survived (with a new name and focus on literary content after 1938) only until early 1939. For a brief moment, however, *Vendredi* had been a very important and prominent part of the French popular press. On a smaller scale, *La République* was a leftist publication with limited dissemination. Started in 1929 just before the Great Depression, its circulation was rather low through most of the 1930s, although with the ascension of the leftist Popular Front, its circulation momentarily ballooned, from around 20,000 in 1934 to 142,000 by October 1936. After this, its circulation figures dropped precipitously, and by the time *La République* closed down in 1939, its circulation approximated a paltry 6,000.[6]

One final daily newspaper must be discussed, although it belies easy classification on the political spectrum. *Paris-Soir* became in the 1930s the single-most widely read daily newspaper in France. By early 1939, its circulation of 1.7 million far exceeded that of its closest rival for that distinction, *Le Petit Parisien,* whose circulation barely topped 1 million.[7] The explosive growth of *Paris-Soir*—it had a circulation of only 130,000 in October 1931—is most likely attributable, as Pierre Albert argues, to its acquisition of readers who had previously read one of Paris's other *"quatre grands,"* whose audiences shrunk during the 1920s and 1930s. The success of *Paris-Soir* was in large part due to a change in format in the early 1930s in which the newspaper tried to reinvent itself as an illustrated daily magazine. It covered popular events like sports in greater depth and printed horoscopes, but without letting those features overtake the paper; the publication retained "serious" news and literary content as well.[8] Moreover, and of particular interest in the context of this study, *Paris-Soir* played a pioneering role in revolutionizing the placement and visibility of advertisements in its pages.[9] Pierre Albert writes: *"Paris-Soir* sought out the sensational, the colorful, the unusual, the fabulous, but presented it in a very different style than that of other popular sheets of the age." Moreover, unlike the other newspapers discussed above, it avoided taking a blatant political position (except for its disdain for the extremes of both the Left and Right). In most cases, it simply recounted events in as objective and neutral a manner as possible.[10]

GERMANY

While the French press was certainly not lacking in publications or circulations, Germany had more newspapers than any other industrialized nation (including the United States, and more, in fact, than Great Britain, France, and Italy combined), due in large part, as Oron Hale discusses, to strong regional loyalties that supported a more localized press, religious diversity, and the existence of numerous political parties, many of which published newspapers of their own. As a result, an unusually large number of newspapers with modest circulations existed in Germany.[11] As in France, the German press saw a number of small enterprises fail in the interwar era because of the difficult circumstances of the period, and while this created some concentration in the field, it did not always translate into larger circulation figures for bigger newspapers. In 1920, not a single daily publication approached a circulation of 1 million.[12] In that year, Germany had nearly 4,000 daily and weekly newspapers, of which two-thirds had print runs of 5,000 or fewer copies, while only 26 of them had a circulation of 100,000 or more.[13] Many of these did not openly espouse a political orientation, and those that did tended to identify themselves with a particular ideology broadly defined—for example, as liberal or republican. Although some of these papers expressed an affinity for a particular political party, they guarded their political independence and autonomy. As Modris Eksteins shows, as circulations grew, newspapers tended to tone down their political aggressiveness so as not to alienate potential readers who disagreed with a paper's political orientation.[14] By the beginning of 1933, the number of newspapers published on a daily or weekly basis in Germany had grown to just over 4,700, with a cumulative circulation of between 14 and 18.5 million copies.[15]

The situation of the popular press changed dramatically, of course, with Hitler's assumption of power and the Nazi *Gleichschaltung* of society and the press. The Nazi regime sought to control the content of newspapers, making editors culpable if the subject matter of their publications ran counter to government directives and policies. The Nazis quickly began the process of banning the newspapers of their political opponents, and the Nazi publishing house Eher Verlag (and its subsidiaries), run by Max Amann, gradually acquired ownership of more and more publications, owning more than two-thirds of the German popular press by 1939.[16]

Not all newspaper publishers objected vociferously to expanding Nazi censorship and control from 1933 onward. The Society of German Newspaper Publishers as well as the Reich Association of the German Press quickly moved to ingratiate themselves in many ways with the new Nazi leadership by, for example, removing Jews from positions of authority and replacing them with Nazis.[17] Indeed, the lack of indignation expressed by the left-liberal press regarding Nazi restrictions on newspapers has been noted by scholars such as Eksteins. Eksteins argues that events occurred at such a rapid pace in early 1933 that a gloomy resignation prevailed among liberal paper editors that—coupled with hopes that by not objecting to Hitler's regime, they might avoid the shuttered fate of their press counterparts further to the left—produced a liberal press that was for the most part reluctantly compliant with Nazi directives. As a result, the Nazis did not immediately outlaw many of these leftist papers, despite the obvious opposition between their political ideologies and that of the National Socialists. At any rate, the impact of the Nazi crackdown on press freedom was considerable and immediate. The number of newspapers published in Germany fell from 4,700 at the beginning of the Nazi era to just over 3,000 by 1934.[18]

The most prominent newspaper in Hitler's Germany, of course, was the Nazi mouthpiece, the *Völkischer Beobachter*. An obscure organ of a relatively obscure political party in the middle of the 1920s, it was not unlike numerous other politicized newspapers in terms of distribution. Its small circulation—just 4,000 or so copies in 1925—was not unusual for the German press. Its circulation had grown to about 18,000 by 1929, and with the onset of the Great Depression, it leapt to approximately 40,000 in 1930. With a circulation of over 100,000 by the time that Hitler became chancellor of Germany in January 1933, the *Völkischer Beobachter* grew from there as the official mouthpiece of the Nazi state, reaching a circulation figure of about 750,000 by 1939.[19] In addition, however, the Nazi press included dozens of other newspapers officially recognized by the party. By 1932, the Nazis could claim nearly 60 such daily outlets (not to mention weekly and biweekly ones, which brought the total near to 100). By 1935, the number of daily newspapers alone had risen to 100, and had a combined print run of nearly 4 million.[20]

In addition to the *Völkischer Beobachter*, a couple of rightist newspapers with national reputations and circulations during the interwar years deserve consideration. One was the central newspaper of the conservative German National People's Party, *Kreuz-Zeitung*, or *Neue Preussische Zeitung*, which had a circulation as high as 60,000 in the 1920s, a very high print figure for that decade.[21] Even more noteworthy, however, was the highly regarded *Deutsche Allgemeine Zeitung*. A rightist counterpart to the greatly respected leftist publication *Vossische Zeitung* (see below), the *Deutsche Allgemeine Zeitung* enjoyed relative success even into the Nazi years, having a circulation of approximately 90,000 shortly before the outbreak of World War II.[22] In part, its success—not to mention its ability to escape closure by the Nazis—was due to its international reputation. It was one of the best-known German newspapers both in its home country and abroad.[23]

Likewise, among the most respected newspapers within and outside Germany was Frankfurt's left-liberal newspaper of perhaps unsurpassed reputation, *Frankfurter Zeitung*. Published by the Jewish-owned Sonnemann firm, it was undoubtedly the most prominent German newspaper published outside Berlin. It was sympathetic to but not always perfectly in line with the liberal German Democratic Party. Like the *Deutsche Allgemeine Zeitung,* it was one of the most widely read German newspapers abroad, and its significance cannot be determined simply on the basis of its circulation figures, which fluctuated in the 1920s between 50,000 and 90,000. Indeed, *Frankfurter Zeitung,* despite its liberal orientation, was not conceived as a mass circulation newspaper, and did not seek a mass audience, but maintained an intellectually demanding and highbrow style and content. Indeed, many of its readers, largely drawn from the wealthier ranks of professional classes, did not at all share its leftist political views, but rather read it for its quality and reliability, particularly its news coverage and economic content.[24] Like *Deutsche Allgemeine Zeitung, Frankfurter Zeitung* was able to publish well into the Nazi era in part because of its reputation, yet like so many others, this paper also eventually was acquired by a subsidiary of the Nazis' Eher Verlag in 1938.[25]

My study also includes two publications each from Leipzig—*Leipziger Volkszeitung* and the popular *Illustrirte Zeitung*—and Munich. It is the publications from the latter city that I wish to describe briefly here; first, the weekly satirical publication *Simplicissimus.* Although its heyday preceded World War I, when it averaged as many as 100,000 readers, *Simplicissimus* was still an important part of the German press landscape in the 1920s, even though its circulation had fallen to 25,000—still a quite respectable number in the context of the era—by 1932.[26] The second publication from Munich was the very widely read *Münchner Illustrierte Presse.* Indeed, its circulation of 534,000 to 620,000 in the late 1920s and early 1930s made it—despite the fact that it was read mainly just in and around Munich—one of the most widely read publications of the German popular press in the late Weimar era.[27]

A number of important publications represented particular political parties. For example, the main organ of the Catholic Center Party, *Germania,* had a healthy, if not extraordinary, circulation of 35,000 by 1932.[28] In addition, the Social Democratic Party (SPD), on the eve of the Great Depression, published more than 200 newspapers whose total circulation was approximately 1.3 million, attesting to the popularity and influence of the SPD and its press, at the apex of which stood the best-known and most widely circulated SPD paper, *Vörwarts.*[29]

One final newspaper needs to be discussed. Alluded to previously as a liberal counterpart to the conservative *Deutsche Allgemeine Zeitung, Vossische Zeitung* was a highly respected newspaper read internationally. After 1914, it was a left-liberal publication of Ullstein, the most powerful publishing house in Weimar Germany (indeed, perhaps in all of Europe). *Vossische Zeitung* was Berlin's oldest newspaper, having been first published more than two hundred years earlier. Like *Frankfurter Zeitung,* it had a reputation as highbrow despite its liberal politics, and for the most part was aimed toward and read by more of an elite rather than a mass audience, although *Vossische Zeitung* did include in its content more popular culture items, such as sports, than the Frankfurt paper. *Vossische Zeitung* may best be remembered from the interwar years as the site where Erich Maria Remarque's famous novel *All Quiet on the Western Front* was first published, in serialized form.[30] The paper's circulation fluctuated considerably in the 1920s and early 1930s, from a nadir of 32,000 in 1923 to more than 70,000 in 1928 and an apogee of 81,000 in January 1931. When *Vossische Zeitung* ceased publication at the end of March 1934, its circulation had sunk to under 50,000.[31]

NOTES

ADP	Archives de Paris	LC	Library of Congress
AF	*L'Action Française*	*LV*	*Leipziger Volkszeitung*
BHVP	Bibliothèque Historique de la	*MAT*	*Le Matin*
	Ville de Paris	*MIP*	*Münchner Illustrierte Presse*
BMD	Bibliothèque Marguerite Durand	*NPZ*	*Neue Preussische Zeitung (Kreuz-*
BNF	Bibliothèque Nationale de France		*Zeitung)*
DAZ	*Deutsche Allgemeine Zeitung*	*OEU*	*L'Oeuvre*
FORN	Bibliothèque Forney	*PS*	*Paris-Soir*
FZ	*Frankfurter Zeitung*	SBB	Staatsbibliothek zu Berlin
GRIN	*Gringoire*	*SIMP*	*Simplicissimus*
GRM	*Germania*	*VB*	*Völkischer Beobachter*
ILL	*L'Illustration*	*VEN*	*Vendredi*
IZ	*Illustrirte Zeitung*	*VRW*	*Vörwarts*
KZ	*Kreuz-Zeitung*	*VZ*	*Vossische Zeitung*
LAB	Landesarchiv Berlin	*WM*	*Westermanns Monatshefte*

INTRODUCTION

1. Scholarly descriptions of this general postwar sense of crisis and displacement, as well as the importance of gender in responding to it, exist for all of the major belligerent nations. For just a few examples, see Roberts, *Civilization without Sexes;* von Ankum, ed., *Women in the Metropolis;* and Kent, *Making Peace.*

2. Showalter, *Sexual Anarchy,* 4.

3. Rosenhaft, "Women in Modern Germany," 148.

4. Edward Berenson, for instance, has explored the emasculation felt by defeated French

troops returning home after the Franco-Prussian War; see Berenson, *The Trial of Madame Caillaux.*

5. See Gilbert, "Soldier's Heart," 426–436; Roberts, *Civilization without Sexes,* 37–41; Petersen, *Women and Modernity in Weimar Germany,* 142–144; and Sherman, "Monuments, Mourning and Masculinity in France after World War I," 84.

6. Boxer and Quataert, "Overview, 1890 to the Present," 245; and Petersen, *Women and Modernity in Weimar Germany,* 142–143.

7. Maier, *Recasting Bourgeois Europe,* 7. See also Auffret, *La France de l'entre deux guerres,* 45–54.

8. Maier, *Recasting Bourgeois Europe,* 15.

9. For Germany, see Abrams and Harvey, "Gender and Gender Relations in German History," 25–26; Frevert, *Women in German History,* 179–180; and Petro, *Joyless Streets,* esp. 68–70. For France, see Frost, "Machine Liberation," 112; McMillan, *Housewife or Harlot,* 116–117; Roberts, *Civilization without Sexes,* 2–12; and Sherman, "Monuments, Mourning and Masculinity in France after World War I," 84–86.

10. Stephenson, *Women in Nazi Germany,* 8–9.

11. Boxer and Quataert, "Overview, 1890 to the Present," 246. See also van der Will, "Culture and the Organization of National Socialist Ideology," 105.

12. In the interest of clarity and economy of expression, I will employ the term *modern woman* (rather than *new woman*) when referring to this image.

13. The fashions of the "modern woman" have been the subject of much scholarly attention. For France, see McMillan, *Housewife or Harlot,* 163–167; Roberts, *Civilization without Sexes,* 19–21, 63–87; Roberts, "Samson and Delilah Revisited," 657–668; and Zdatny, "La mode à la garçonne," 23–56. For Germany, see Frevert, *Women in German History,* 176; Grossmann, "The New Woman and the Rationalization of Sexuality in Weimar Germany," 156; Harvey, "Culture and Society in Weimar Germany," 281–282; and Petro, *Joyless Streets,* 21–23, 103–105. For more on the *neue Frau,* see Frame, "Gretchen, Girl, Garçonne?" esp. 16–19. In a global framework, see Barlow et al., "The Modern Girl around the World," 245–294.

14. Roberts, *Civilization without Sexes,* 66. See also Petro, *Joyless Streets,* 105–107.

15. Roberts, "Samson and Delilah Revisited," 662–672. See also McMillan, *Housewife or Harlot,* 116–117, 163–167; and Roberts, *Civilization without Sexes,* 3–10, 63–87.

16. My overview of Margueritte's novel is drawn from Roberts, *Civilization without Sexes,* 52–57, which provides the best examination of the book.

17. Roberts, *Civilization without Sexes,* 52–53.

18. Ibid., 53.

19. Ibid., 52–57.

20. My overview of this novel is drawn from the excellent analysis in Petersen, *Women and Modernity in Weimar Germany,* 17–18, 35.

21. Petersen, *Women and Modernity in Weimar Germany,* 17–18, 35.

22. For just a couple of examples of scholarship that has taken part in or provided useful background and analysis of this line of thought, see Abrams and Harvey, "Gender and Gender Relations in German History," 18–19; and Goldstein, "From Service to Sales," 122–123. See also Lubar, "Men/Women/Production/Consumption," 31–32.

23. Rearick, *The French in Love and War,* 52–56.

24. This point has been made by Reynolds, *France between the Wars,* esp. 1–17. Commenting specifically on the French case, Reynolds notes that, while studies of women and gender at other times were proliferating, scholars were slow to turn to the question of women's place and roles between the world wars.

25. Among the most important works are Frost, "Machine Liberation"; Harp, *Marketing Michelin;* Martin, "Ménagère: Une profession?"; Offen, "Body Politics"; Reynolds, *France between the Wars;* Roberts, *Civilization without Sexes;* and Werner, "Du ménage à l'art ménager."

26. For studies of women and gender in interwar Germany, see Grossman, "*Girlkultur* or Thoroughly Rationalized Female"; Koonz, *Mothers in the Fatherland;* Lacey, *Feminine Frequencies;* Nolan, "Housework Made Easy," Reagin, "Comparing Apples and Oranges"; and von Ankum, ed., *Women in the Metropolis.*

27. Nolan, "Work, Gender and Everyday Life," 329–330.

28. Frost, "Machine Liberation," 109–130.

29. von Ankum, ed., *Women in the Metropolis,* esp. 1–40, 128–184.

30. Roberts, *Civilization without Sexes,* esp. 19–147.

31. Kent, *Making Peace;* Roberts, *Civilization without Sexes.* Indeed, both volumes' subtitles declare their subject to be the reconstructing of gender in their respective nations of study.

32. Grayzel, *Women's Identities at War.*

33. For more information on this subject, see the appendix.

34. In her work on gender ideologies in French and British industry during and after World War I, Downs has commented that examining two countries from a transnational, comparative point of view can illustrate "how national culture and differences in state structures defined distinctive routes to what were, in many important respects, rather similar outcomes." See Downs, *Manufacturing Inequality,* 12.

35. Several scholars have made the point regarding the relatively slow pace of scholarly efforts regarding German consumption specifically. See, for instance, Confino and Koshar, "Régimes of Consumer Culture," esp. 137, 143–144; Koshar, *German Travel Cultures,* 13; and Sherayko, "Selling the Modern," 4–6.

36. For example, based on their statistical analysis of the dissemination of household appliances in the interwar period, Bowden and Offer show that very few items of household technology actually were purchased by English consumers before World War II. See Bowden and Offer, "The Technological Revolution That Never Was," 244–274.

37. Frost, "Machine Liberation," 109–130; and Sherayko, "Selling the Modern," esp. 158–159.

38. Sherayko, "Selling the Modern," 252. See also Strasser, *Satisfaction Guaranteed,* 15–16; and Koshar, "Seeing, Traveling, and Consuming," 2.

39. Sherayko, "Selling the Modern," 2. See also Mort, "Paths to Mass Consumption," 10; and Sachs, *For Love of the Automobile,* 32–33, 40–42.

40. Confino and Koshar, "Régimes of Consumer Culture," 141.

41. Sherayko, "Selling the Modern," 247.

42. Stearns, *Consumerism in World History,* 50–52.

43. Confino and Koshar, "Régimes of Consumer Culture," 151–152, 159.

44. Breuilly, "The National Idea in Modern German History," 571–576.

45. Reagin, "*Marktordnung* and Autarkic Housekeeping," 163–166.

46. Multiple scholars have raised this point in a variety of national contexts. For a few examples, see Furlough, "Selling the American Way in Interwar France," esp. 509; Goldstein, "From Service to Sales," 151–152; Parkin, *Food Is Love,* esp. 12–29; and Stearns, *Consumerism in World History,* 44, 58. For the prewar era, see also Felski, *The Gender of Modernity;* and Tiersten, *Marianne in the Market.*

47. Mort, "Paths to Mass Consumption," 12. For conceptual connections between consumption, femininity, and modernity, see Felski, *The Gender of Modernity,* 61–90.

48. de Grazia, "The Arts of Purchase," 222–225; Sherayko, "Selling the Modern," 1; and Sneeringer, "The Shopper as Voter," 486. The advent of the *grands magasins* was also read as a sign of the modern, as Weber notes in his study on Ghent; see Weber, "Selling Dreams," esp. 161.

49. Sherayko, "Selling the Modern," 3. See also de Grazia, *Irresistible Empire;* and Harvey, "Culture and Society in Weimar Germany," 279, 283–288.

50. van der Will, "Culture and the Organization of National Socialist Ideology," 105.

51. Ibid., 106.

52. Herf, *Reactionary Modernism.*

53. Beale, *The Modernist Enterprise,* 5, 73; see also 6–7, 15–17, 72–77. See also Kuisel, *Seducing the French;* esp. 10–13. Beale's argument resonates with Alison Light's notion of "conservative modernity" in interwar England; see Light, *Forever England,* esp. 10–11.

54. See, for example, Bridenthal, Grossman, and Kaplan, "Women in Weimar and Nazi Germany," 13; Hales, "Woman as Sexual Criminal," esp. 116; and Petersen, *Women and Modernity in Weimar Germany,* esp. 3–4. See also Felski, *The Gender of Modernity,* esp. 61–63.

55. Petersen, *Women and Modernity in Weimar Germany,* 143. See also Bridenthal, Grossman, and Kaplan, "Women in Weimar and Nazi Germany," 13.

56. Peukert, *The Weimar Republic,* esp. 82.

57. See, for example, Crossick and Jaumain, "The World of the Department Store," esp. 8; and de Grazia, *Irresistible Empire,* 130–183.

58. For a fuller discussion of issues of readership levels and the political orientations of the press publications used in this study, see the appendix.

59. Gorman and McLean, *Media and Society in the Twentieth Century,* esp. 5–9, 21–23. See also de Grazia, "The Arts of Purchase," 249–251; and, for more on the increasing connection between the press's financial health and advertising revenue, Martin, *Trois siècles de publicité en France,* 191.

60. Schwartz, *Spectacular Realities,* 26–27, 39.

61. Ibid., 6.

62. See Albert, "La presse française de 1871 à 1940," esp. 458, 511.

63. Hale, *The Captive Press in the Third Reich,* 1–2.

64. See, for example, Eksteins, *The Limits of Reason,* 12–16. See also Hale, *The Captive Press in the Third Reich,* 1.

65. Cowan, "The Industrial Revolution in the Home," 294–295.

66. Beale, *The Modernist Enterprise,* 14; de Grazia, "The Arts of Purchase," 249–250; Gorman and McLean, *Media and Society in the Twentieth Century,* 66–67; Laird, *Advertising Progress,* 3–5; and Stearns, *Consumerism in World History,* 46.

67. de Grazia, "The Arts of Purchase," 249–251. See also de Certeau, *The Practice of Everyday Life,* 29–34, for a theoretical examination of consumers and mass media.

68. Marchand, *Advertising the American Dream,* 1, 7–9. Laird makes a similar claim; see Laird, *Advertising Progress,* 6.

69. Hultquist, "Americans in Paris," 471–472; and Merron, "Putting Foreign Consumers on the Map," 465–502, esp. 465–470. See also de Grazia, *Irresistible Empire,* 230–242; Reinhardt, *Von der Reklame zum Marketing,* 126–128; and Schug, "Wegbereiter der modernen Absatzwerbung in Deutschland," 39–42. It should be noted in the German case that the Nazi regime ultimately excluded foreign ad agencies from operating in Germany; see Berghoff, "Times Change and We Change with Them," 133.

70. See, in particular, Beale, *The Modernist Enterprise,* esp. 6–7, 15–16, 72–77, which deals with the French case. See also Chessel, "Une methode publicitaire americaine?" 61–76; and Martin, *Trois siècles de publicité en France,* 207–211. In the German context, Berghoff has noted the widening gap separating American and German advertising styles; see Berghoff, "Times Change and We Change with Them," 140, 145. Perhaps the best example of this is provided by French auto manufacturer André Citroën, who famously had his name placed in lights on the Eiffel Tower starting in 1925; for a discussion of this, see de Grazia, *Irresistible Empire,* 249–250.

71. Sherayko, "Selling the Modern," 14–60. See also Berghoff, "Times Change and We Change with Them," 128–129; and Reinhardt, *Von der Reklame zum Marketing,* 44–48, 130–137.

72. Schug, "Wegbereiter der modernen Absatzwerbung in Deutschland," 35–38.

73. Berghoff, "Times Change and We Change with Them," 130–131; see also 135.

74. Ibid., 136–137. See also Reinhardt, *Von der Reklame zum Marketing,* 137–145.

75. Berghoff, "Times Change and We Change with Them," 136–138. Nonetheless, Reinhardt shows that advertising in the German press continued to increase over the course of the middle and late 1930s; see Reinhardt, *Von der Reklame zum Marketing,* 201.

76. Chessel, *La publicité,* esp. 23–49 ; see also 211. See also Beale, *The Modernist Enterprise,* 56–57; Chessel, "Die Werbefachleute in Frankreich," 79–92; Hultquist, "Americans in Paris," 473; and Martin, *Trois siècles de publicité en France,* 247–274, esp. 254–265.

77. Chessel, "Die Werbefachleute in Frankreich," 79–92.

78. Hultquist, "Americans in Paris," 474. As Hultquist notes, Havas was more than just an ad agency—for example, it ran a wire service as well. See also Beale, *The Modernist Enterprise,* 53–58; and Martin, *Trois siècles de publicité en France,* 99–103, 259–260.

79. Hultquist, "Americans in Paris," 472–480, esp. 479–480.

80. Sneeringer, "The Shopper as Voter," 478.

81. de Grazia, *Irresistible Empire,* 235–237; Hultquist, "Americans in Paris," 474–478; and Merron, "Putting Foreign Consumers on the Map," 465–484.

82. Merron, "Putting Foreign Consumers on the Map," 486.

83. See, for example, de Grazia, *Irresistible Empire,* 244–245.

84. Gorman and McLean, *Media and Society in the Twentieth Century,* 65–68; Marchand, *Advertising the American Dream,* xxi–xxii, 11–12; Sherayko, "Selling the Modern," 207–210; and Weber, "Selling Dreams," 175–176. See also de Grazia, *Irresistible Empire,* 273–275; Pollay, "The Subsiding Sizzle," 30–32; and Reinhardt, *Von der Reklame zum Marketing,* 222–230.

85. Sherayko, "Selling the Modern," 208.

86. Ibid., 219–220.

87. The association of femininity with emotionality extended well beyond Europe. See Reekie, "Impulsive Women, Predictable Men," esp. 366–371.

88. Marchand, *Advertising the American Dream,* xxi–xxii, 9–10.

89. Laird, *Advertising Progress,* 2. See also Lears, *Fables of Abundance,* 1; Leiss, Kline, and Jhally, *Social Communication in Advertising,* 5; and Sherayko, "Selling the Modern," 9.

90. Williamson, *Decoding Advertisements,* 40; emphasis in original.

91. Stearns, "Stages of Consumerism," 114. See also Goffman, *Gender Advertisements,* 84; and McCracken, *Culture and Consumption,* 131.

92. Williamson, *Decoding Advertisements,* 47–48.

93. Marchand, *Advertising the American Dream,* xvi–xvii; Sherayko, "Selling the Modern," 238; and Weber, "Selling Dreams," 174.

94. Marchand, *Advertising the American Dream,* xviii. Quite often, as Gorman and McLean argue, this could mean perpetuating dominant discourses, such as codifying masculine authority over women in a culture's gender discourse; see Gorman and McLean, *Media and Society in the Twentieth Century,* 70–74.

95. Gorman and McLean, *Media and Society in the Twentieth Century,* 90–92; and Welch, *The Third Reich,* 5, 50.

96. Welch, *The Third Reich,* 5, 50.

97. Marchand, *Advertising the American Dream,* xviii–xix.

98. Ibid., xix; emphasis in original.

99. Ibid., xviii–xix.

100. Leiss, Kline, and Jhally, *Social Communication in Advertising,* 1; emphasis in original. See also de Certeau, *The Practice of Everyday Life,* 29–34; and Sachs, *For Love of the Automobile,* 58.

101. Goubert makes an analogous assertion with respect to publications of differing political perspectives and readerships in France, finding that advertising messages were often quite similar in the pages of newspapers as diverse as *Le Petit Journal,* a cheap daily paper that was geared in many ways toward a more working-class audience, and the expensive, conservative *L'Illustration,* whose readership was largely middle class. See Goubert, *The Conquest of Water,* 124–125. Sherayko provides a similar example from Germany by comparing the bourgeois *Berliner Illustrirte Zeitung* with the Communist *Arbeiter Illustrierte Zeitung.* Sherayko notes that, alongside advertisements for trips to Moscow and books with transcripts of Communist speeches, the pages of the *Arbeiter Illustrierte Zeitung* carried advertisements of the same ilk as the *Berliner Illustrirte Zeitung,* for products such as shampoo, coffee, and cigarettes, among others. Sherayko argues that there was a relative homogenization in the advertisements in both papers that actually reflected capitalist, middle-class values (although the content of articles in *Arbeiter Illustrierte Zeitung* remained true to Communist ideology). See Sherayko, "Selling the Modern," 241–246. De Grazia suggests a consistency of advertising images across sociopolitical lines as well, commenting that advertising in interwar France and Germany, facilitated by advances in technology and the growth and development of the advertising industry, contributed to a more uniform control over consumer tastes on a national scale. See de Grazia, "The Arts of Purchase," 250–251.

102. Marchand, *Advertising the American Dream*, xv–xvi. See also Sachs, *For Love of the Automobile*, 58.

ONE. DUTY AND EMPOWERMENT

1. Nolan, *Visions of Modernity*, 6–7. The prominence of ideologies of rationalization or Taylorism in interwar industry has been analyzed at length in the scholarly literature. See, for instance, Cross, *A Quest for Time*, 194–214; and Nolan, *Visions of Modernity*, esp. 30–57. See also Gagnon, "La Vie Future," 172–176.

2. Grossmann, "*Girlkultur* or Thoroughly Rationalized Female," 66–67; Nolan, "Housework Made Easy," esp. 549–552; and Nolan, *Visions of Modernity*, 206–226.

3. Nolan, *Visions of Modernity*, 206–226.

4. Frevert, *Women in German History*, 195. See also Simonton, *A History of European Women's Work*, 200. Reagin finds that the Hanover Housewives' Association made efforts to bring rationalization into the household as a means of modernizing and professionalizing housework. See Reagin, *A German Women's Movement*, 228–230. Nolan makes a similar case regarding German bourgeois feminists, who, she claims, appropriated the language of industrial rationalization as a means of legitimizing household labor. See Nolan, *Visions of Modernity*, 206–226, esp. 207.

5. Giles makes this point with respect to interwar England; see Giles, "A Home of One's Own," 244.

6. For France, see Frost, "Machine Liberation," 109–130; Martin, "Ménagère: Une profession?" 96–106; and Werner, "Du ménage à l'art ménager," 70–71, 74–76, 84–87. For Germany, see Nolan, *Visions of Modernity*, 206–226; and Reagin, *A German Women's Movement*, 228–233.

7. Peukert, *The Weimar Republic*, 100.

8. Goldstein, "From Service to Sales," 151–152.

9. Nolan, *Visions of Modernity*, 225; and Reagin, "Comparing Apples and Oranges," 245.

10. Nolan, *Visions of Modernity*, esp. 212–217; and Reagin, "*Marktordnung* and Autarkic Housekeeping," 162–184.

11. Frost, "Machine Liberation," 111–112; and Weber, *The Hollow Years*, 60–62.

12. For Germany, see Reagin, "Comparing Apples and Oranges," 245–247. For France, see Furlough, "Selling the American Way in Interwar France," esp. 491–493, 503–511; and Werner, "Du ménage à l'art ménager," 72–74.

13. Nolan, *Visions of Modernity*, 206–226; and Nolan, "Housework Made Easy," 549–577. See also Frevert, *Women in German History*, 195–196.

14. Nolan, *Visions of Modernity*, 224. See also Grossmann, *Reforming Sex*, 5; and Petro, *Joyless Streets*, 75–76.

15. For some statistics on the employment of domestic servants, see, for Germany, Frevert, *Women in German History*, 218; Peukert, *The Weimar Republic*, 96; and Stephenson, *Women in Nazi Germany*, 65–66. For France, see McBride, *The Domestic Revolution*, 111–112; Singer, "Technology and Social Change," 325; Tilly and Scott, *Women, Work, and Family*, 153–154; and Weber, *The Hollow Years*, 55.

16. Bridenthal, "Class Struggle around the Hearth," 254; Frevert, *Women in German History*, 195; Reagin, *A German Women's Movement*, 231–233; Simonton, *A History of European Women's Work*, 183, 201–205; and Tilly and Scott, *Women, Work, and Family*, 153–154, 181–182. The low es-

teem in which domestic service was held was common to the United States as well; see Cowan, *More Work for Mother,* esp. 120–125.

17. Bridenthal, "Class Struggle around the Hearth," 248; Frevert, *Women in German History,* 195; Reagin, *A German Women's Movement,* 231–233; Simonton, *A History of European Women's Work,* 200; and Tilly and Scott, *Women, Work, and Family,* 153–154.

18. Weber, *The Hollow Years,* 26–27. See also Auffret, *La France de l'entre deux guerres,* 67–82.

19. Frost, "Machine Liberation," 113–115; McBride, *The Domestic Revolution,* 113–116; Reagin, *A German Women's Movement,* 224; and Simonton, *A History of European Women's Work,* 200.

20. Bridenthal, "Class Struggle around the Hearth," 251; and Furlough, "Selling the American Way in Interwar France," 506. See also Cowan, *More Work for Mother,* 174–181.

21. Meyer, "The Tiresome Work of Conspicuous Leisure," 185–193.

22. *DAZ,* LAB (2 October 1922): n.p.

23. *LV,* LAB (28 May 1921): n.p.

24. For one such example, see *IZ* (26 July 1923): 45.

25. See, for example, *IZ* (13 May 1926): 611 and (27 May 1926): 718.

26. *VRW,* LAB (15 January 1927): n.p. For another example in which a housewife and servant appear together, see the Schwerter soap ad in *LV,* LAB (7 May 1921): n.p.

27. For just one example, see the Henko ad in *VB* (8 February 1938): 15.

28. Stephenson, *Women in Nazi Germany,* 66.

29. For a few examples, see *OEU* (13 August 1921): n.p. and (5 July 1923): n.p.; and *MAT,* LC (28 June 1924): n.p.

30. BHVP, Bon Marché agenda, 1923, 98.

31. Ibid., 162.

32. See, for example, *AF* (13 July 1922): 4, (3 February 1926): 4, and (5 October 1927): 4.

33. For an example of one such exception—namely, an ad featuring a servant after the middle of the 1920s, see the Byrrh advertisement from *ILL* (14 February 1931): xix.

34. BHVP, Bon Marché agenda, 1925, 147–148.

35. FORN, Bon Marché agenda, 1933, 18.

36. Ibid., 19.

37. This ad appeared in FORN, Magasins Réunis agenda, 1927, 53; and *MAT,* LC (13 November 1925): 8.

38. ADP, Publicité (D 18 Z cart. 9), Folder Installation—Subfolder Electricité, Gaz, Téléphone, 16. While the brochure is undated, it is unmistakably from the interwar years. See also the 1927 advertising flyer for Probus vacuums in ADP, Publicité (D 18 Z cart. 9), Folder Installation—Subfolder Entretien, Désinfection; the ad for Lux vacuums in *OEU* (17 December 1930): 8; and another Lux vacuum ad in *GRIN* (12 December 1930): 12.

39. For examples, see *LV,* LAB (30 June 1921): n.p.; *VRW,* LAB (27 November 1921): n.p.; *IZ* (18 February 1926): 206; *VB* (20 January 1934): n.p.; *IZ* (31 January 1935): 149; and *KZ,* LAB (26 January 1936): n.p.

40. A few examples can be found in *LV,* LAB (22 June 1921): n.p.; *IZ* (2 August 1923): 81; *VRW,* LAB (21 November 1926): n.p.; *GRM,* LAB (11 December 1927): n.p.; *SIMP* (21 May 1928): 102; *NPZ,* LAB (20 April 1930): n.p.; *WM* (December 1934, advertising section): 22; *IZ* (11 April 1935): 502; *MIP,* SBB (12 November 1936): 1605; *KZ,* LAB (26 October 1938): n.p.; and *VB* (26 March 1939): 24.

41. While these designations were to some degree interchangeable, *maîtresse de maison,* the "mistress of the house," was a bit broader in scope; it connoted all of women's responsibilities in the home, from ornamenting the home interior to mothering to entertaining guests. Meaning "housewife" more literally, *ménagère* tended to refer more strictly to issues involving the chores of housekeeping.

42. For a few examples of such ads, see *MAT,* LC (1 February 1924): 6; *OEU* (15 April 1924): n.p.; and *ILL* (14 May 1938): xviii. In addition, see the advertisements for O-Cedar in FORN, Printemps agenda, 1920, 422; 1921, 492; and 1922, 458.

43. For just a small sample of such ads, see *MAT,* LC (6 October 1922): 5; *OEU* (5 July 1923): n.p.; *AF* (15 January 1926): 4; *ILL* (14 March 1931): xxxi; *GRIN* (17 August 1934): 14; *PS* (24 November 1935): 11; and *ILL* (4 March 1939): x. See also the advertising flyer for Félix Potin from 1929 that features a woman pouring drinks for her husband and guests; ADP, Publicité (D 18 Z cart. 8), Folder Félix Potin, 1868–1933.

44. This point has been discussed by Werner, "Du ménage à l'art ménager," 66–70.

45. At times, such ads offered to provide a copy of a company cookbook upon request of the consumer, usually at no charge. *VRW,* LAB (17 December 1926): n.p.; *VZ* (7 July 1933): n.p.; *VB* (24 January 1934, supplement): n.p.; *KZ,* LAB (24 November 1935): 5; *IZ* (21 May 1936): 656; and *KZ,* LAB (21 October 1938): n.p.

46. See, for instance, *GRM,* LAB (22 May 1932): n.p.; and *KZ,* LAB (7 December 1938): n.p. and (30 December 1938): n.p.

47. For a couple of instances in which recipes did appear, see the ads for Sauter electric stoves in *GRIN* (25 May 1934): 10 and (22 June 1934): 12.

48. Frequently an entire meal, including main courses and side dishes, would be proposed; sometimes an entire set of meals for a whole day would be listed. In many *agendas,* such recipe and meal suggestions were offered on every calendar day, or sometimes on a page separating each of the months of a particular year. BNF, Galeries Lafayette agenda, 1934, provides an example of an *agenda* wherein a suggested meal appears on each day of the calendar. See also BHVP, Bon Marché agenda, 1920; FORN, Grands Magasins du Louvre agenda, 1921, 32, 60, 120; FORN, Nouvelles Galeries "A La Ménagère" agenda, 1923; FORN, Galeries Lafayette agenda, 1928, 8–15 and 1933; FORN, Bon Marché agenda, 1938; and BHVP, Galeries Lafayette agenda, 1938. In addition, see the *agendas* of Printemps at FORN for each year from 1920 to 1926, as well as 1929, 1932, 1934, 1936, 1937, and 1938.

49. FORN, Galeries Lafayette agenda, 1924.

50. BHVP, Galeries Lafayette agenda, 1923, 163. See also the advice offered in FORN, Grands Magasins du Louvre agenda, 1926; and FORN, Printemps agenda, 1929.

51. See, for instance, FORN, Grands Magasins du Louvre agenda, 1922, 47–52; and BHVP, Bon Marché agenda, 1934. See also FORN, Grands Magasins du Louvre agenda, 1924, 85–90.

52. *LV,* LAB (4 June 1921): n.p.

53. BHVP, Bon Marché agenda, 1925, 147–148.

54. *WM* (December 1927): 455–457. In the French case, see the article in *ILL* (20 May 1939): 104–107.

55. *WM* (September 1934, advertising section): 7. In addition, various other sources from France elaborated upon such professionalization of housewifery. See, for example, a 1938 article from the weekly feminist newspaper *La Française* documenting the creation of the "professional

syndicate of maîtresses de maison" in BMD, Dossier Maîtresse de Maison. In addition, see the article detailing a contest held in 1938 to determine "the best ménagère in France," ibid. Unfortunately, it is not clear where this article, included in the dossier among a number of other press clippings collected by the BMD, was published.

56. Furlough, "Selling the American Way in Interwar France," 508.

57. Indeed, in his analysis of the marketing of electricity in early twentieth-century America, Williams shows how electricity was a vital symbol of modernity and technological advancement; Williams, "Getting Housewives the Electric Message," esp. 100–101. For just a few examples from the primary sources, see, for France, *MAT,* LC (29 November 1923): 8; *OEU* (7 November 1925): 6; *AF* (2 March 1926): 4; *MAT,* LC (22 May 1931): 2; *GRIN* (1 July 1932): 12; and *ILL* (21 April 1934): xx. See also the illustration and accompanying text in BHVP, Bon Marché agenda, 1928, 78.; and the advertising brochure for Calor electric washing machines in ADP, Publicité (D 18 Z cart. 9), Folder Installation—Subfolder Electricité, Gaz, Téléphone, 16. Additionally, FORN, Grands Magasins du Louvre agenda, 1924, 123–128, contains an article entitled "Modern Decoration" that details how to modernize the décor of the home interior. For Germany, see *VB* (6–7 January 1934): n.p.; *WM* (October 1934, advertising section): 5; and *VB* (14 June 1939): 7.

58. *VB* (14 June 1937): 16.

59. *ILL* (6 June 1936): xxiii.

60. *MAT* (23 September 1927): 3.

61. This fits with Simonton's contention that a drive for organizational planning took especially strong hold in interwar Germany. See Simonton, *A History of European Women's Work,* 195–196. See also Frevert, *Women in German History,* 194; Reagin, "Comparing Apples and Oranges," esp. 245–246; and Reagin, "*Marktordnung* and Autarkic Housekeeping," 178–179.

62. *WM* (December 1927): 455–457. See also advertisements for modern kitchens in *DAZ,* LAB (20 June 1926): n.p.; and *VZ* (9 July 1933): n.p. and (13 August 1933): n.p.

63. *GRIN* (19 January 1939): 12. See also the Banania ad regarding the streamlining of breakfast meals for the family in *GRIN* (26 January 1939): 9.

64. ADP, Publicité (D 18 Z cart. 9), Folder Installation—Subfolder Electricité, Gaz, Téléphone, 1. A less dramatic example from Germany is an ad for Johns washing machines that promises the Hausfrau that she will be "freed" of difficult laundry if she utilizes this brand of washer. See *WM* (September 1934, advertising section): 7.

65. For some German advertisements of this sort, see *LV,* LAB (18 June 1921): n.p.; *VRW,* LAB (27 July 1930): n.p.; *WM* (September 1934, advertising section): 7; and *VB* (8 December 1936): 16 and (14 June 1939): 7. For French ads of the same ilk, see *MAT,* LC (22 February 1924): 6; *GRIN* (9 May 1930): 12; *ILL* (14 March 1931): xxx; *PS* (19 November 1935): 11; and *GRIN* (19 November 1937): 16. See also two articles from *ILL* that touch on these same topics—the first, an article entitled "Domestic Electricity" (28 May 1932): xxxi; and the second, an article on domestic technologies (20 May 1939): 104–107. See also the article "The Domain of the Kitchen" in BHVP, Bon Marché agenda, 1925, 147–148.

66. For France, see *MAT,* LC (13 November 1925): 5 and (22 May 1931): 8; and *GRIN* (28 September 1934): 12. A number of materials in Parisian archival collections emphasized in particular the issue of being able to perform housework without fatigue; see the 1931 advertising flyer for

the Compagnie Parisienne de Distribution d'Electricité in Publicité, the advertising flyer from 1927 for Probus vacuum cleaners, and the ad booklet for Lux vacuums from 1927, all of which are to be found in ADP, Publicité (D 18 Z cart. 9), Folder Installation—Subfolder Electricité, Gaz, Téléphone. Additionally, the point about the ability to use technological items in the home without watching them closely is made in an article on using gas in the home in *ILL* (28 May 1932): xxx. For Germany, see *SIMP* (23 November 1921): 475; *VRW,* LAB (14 November 1926): n.p.; and *VB* (10 June 1937): 20 and (24 July 1938): 5.

67. This ad appears in two issues of *GRIN:* (16 April 1937): 18 and (28 January 1938): 14.

68. *OEU* (8 December 1931): 8. See also *ILL* (7 April 1934): xxix; and *OEU* (22 April 1924): n.p.

69. *VB* (10 March 1939): 13. See also ibid. (14 March 1935): n.p.

70. Ibid. (30 March 1937): 18.

71. Interestingly, in his essay on the marketing of electricity to American housewives in the United States in the early twentieth century, Williams finds a similar vocabulary; he comments on the perception that electricity "seemed to possess magical qualities that made it an indisputable force for better living." See Williams, "Getting Housewives the Electric Message," 100.

72. *ILL* (11 December 1937): xxv.

73. *GRIN* (25 May 1934): 10 and (22 June 1934): 12. See a similar ad for Arthur Martin stoves in *ILL* (28 April 1934): xxv.

74. *IZ* (18 February 1926): 206.

75. *MAT,* LC (11 December 1925): 8. See similar ads for Electro-Lux in *MAT,* LC (29 November 1923): 8; and for Calor electric washing machines in *ILL* (7 April 1934): xxix.

76. *ILL* (31 August 1929): x; *GRIN* (10 June 1932): 10; and *ILL* (23 May 1936): xxxix.

77. *VB* (22 November 1935): n.p. See also the ad for Ozonil detergent in *VRW,* LAB (7 November 1926): n.p. An article on housekeeping from *WM* also mentions the short time involved in cleaning the household thoroughly; see *WM* (December 1927): 455–457.

78. *VB* (26 February 1939): 5. See also the iMi ads in *VB* (19 March 1939): 5 and (26 March 1939): 9.

79. *GRIN* (12 February 1937): 10. See also *ILL* (11 June 1938): xxiv.

80. *MAT,* LC (25 March 1924): 5.

81. This argument has been made most often with respect to the United States and England. See, for example, Cowan, "The Industrial Revolution in the Home," esp. 289–291; Cowan, *More Work for Mother,* esp. 97–101; Hardyment, *From Mangle to Microwave;* and Thomas and Zmroczek, "Household Technology," esp. 101–102. For Germany, see Petro, *Joyless Streets,* 75–76.

82. Furlough, "Selling the American Way in Interwar France," 506.

83. *ILL* (16 May 1936): xxii. See also the article entitled "The Art of Staying Home" in FORN, Grands Magasins du Louvre agenda 1922, 85–90; and ads in *GRIN* (30 November 1928): 12; and *ILL* (1 October 1932): xlviii.

84. *IZ* (21 January 1926): 98.

85. See the Persil ad in *LV,* LAB (25 June 1921): n.p.; and the ad for iMi in *VRW,* LAB (3 September 1930): n.p. See also *VB* (3 June 1934): n.p. and (11 June 1939): 23.

86. *VRW,* LAB (14 September 1930): n.p. See also the ad for Gefest in *VB* (14 June 1934): n.p., which is quite similar in tone and spirit.

87. *GRIN* (24 June 1932): 12.

88. *ILL* (21 January 1933): ix. See also materials discussing "the joy of the *foyer*" in FORN, Galeries Lafayette agenda, 1932, 6–7; and *GRIN* (21 September 1934): 20.

89. *VB* (10 June 1937): 20. See also the ad for Degea irons in *GRM*, LAB (14 December 1920): n.p.; and the ad for Ralatum floor polish in *VB* (6 December 1936): 19.

90. *ILL* (28 April 1934): xxv.

91. Ibid. (6 June 1936): xxiii.

92. Furlough's examination of Americanized merchandising in interwar France notes this strategy, arguing that exhibitions of domestic technologies deliberately changed their designation from a display of "housework devices" to the "household arts" as a means of attempting to portray household labor as "elegant and refined." Furlough, "Selling the American Way in Interwar France," 504.

93. *FZ*, LAB (11 September 1920): 3.

94. *VB* (14 March 1937): 14.

95. See, for instance, FORN, Grands Magasins du Louvre agenda, 1922, 85–90; *GRIN* (3 October 1930): 10; and *OEU* (17 November 1930): 6. Indeed, Furlough highlights the "assertions of French superiority in matters of taste and elegance" in interwar domestic technology exhibitions; see Furlough, "Selling the American Way in Interwar France," 511.

96. *ILL* (21 January 1933): ix.

97. Ibid. (7 May 1932): xx. For discussion of the gendering of sewing as a female engagement, see Coffin, *The Politics of Women's Work*. For similar ads, see also the ad for Birum vacuum cleaners in FORN, Printemps agenda, 1921, 424; the ad for Thomson appliances in *ILL* (14 March 1931): xxx; the ad for Sauter electric stoves in *GRIN* (24 June 1932): 12; and the Frigidaire ads in *ILL* (28 June 1930): xxxiii; and *MAT*, LC (10 July 1930): 8.

98. *ILL* (11 December 1937): xxv. See also the *ILL* article on electrification in the kitchen (7 March 1936): xxiii.

99. Williams, "Getting Housewives the Electric Message," 102–103.

100. *VB* (14 March 1937): 14. See also *WM* (October 1934, advertising section): 17.

101. *GRIN* (9 May 1930): 12. See also *ILL* (25 August 1928): xii and (7 May 1932): xx; *GRIN* (24 June 1932): 12 and (9 March 1934): 12; *VEN* (18 June 1937): 8; and FORN, Bon Marché agenda, 1938, 352. Additionally, see the advertising booklet for Lux vacuum cleaners from 1927 in ADP, Publicité (D 18 Z cart. 9), Folder Installation—Subfolder Entretien, Désinfection.

102. *ILL* (28 May 1932): xxxi. See also the article entitled "The Home and the Technique of Comfort" in *ILL* (20 May 1939): 104–107.

103. *VB* (6 July 1938): 12.

104. A Frigidaire ad of this variety can be found in *MAT*, LC (10 July 1930): 8; a Kelvinator ad appears in *ILL* (21 April 1934): xx; an ad for Crosley is in *GRIN* (28 September 1934): 12; and Electro-Lux ads appear in *VEN* (5 June 1936): 9 and (18 June 1937): 8.

105. See, for example, *MAT*, LC (4 May 1930): 8; *OEU* (10 October 1930): 8; *GRIN* (28 November 1930): 10; *OEU* (1 May 1931): 8; and *MAT*, LC (22 May 1931): 8.

106. *MAT*, LC (17 October 1923): 6.

107. *GRIN* (13 May 1932): 10.

108. In other cases, advertisements made similar points about their products' superiority, but without directly invoking the notion of perfection. For Germany, see *IZ* (26 July 1923): 45

and (1 April 1926): 438; *VRW,* LAB (13 August 1930): n.p.; and *VB* (9 September 1937): 19. For France, see *MAT,* LC (18 February 1927): 6; *ILL* (31 August 1929): xii; *GRIN* (20 May 1932): 10; *PS* (6 November 1935): 13 and (13 November 1935): 13; and *GRIN* (9 February 1939): 9.

109. *ILL* (15 December 1928): xxxix. See also ibid. (21 April 1934): xxi.

110. *GRIN* (30 November 1928): 12. There are plenty of other examples of French ads that explicitly claimed perfection for their products. For a few more instances of this, see *MAT,* LC (11 December 1925): 8; *OEU* (17 November 1930): 6; *ILL* (24 January 1931): xxii; *GRIN* (1 July 1932): 12; *PS* (19 November 1935): 11; and *GRIN* (15 April 1938): 12. Along similar lines, "magnificent results" are promised by an advertising booklet for the cleaning product Furmoto; see ADP, Publicité (D 18 Z cart. 9), Folder Installation—Subfolder Entretien, Désinfection.

111. *VRW,* LAB (6 November 1921): n.p. and (13 November 1921): n.p. Other ads similarly vow to provide "the highest performance" or "wonderful" results. See, for instance, *VRW,* LAB (3 August 1930): n.p.; *VB* (6–7 January 1934): n.p.; *IZ* (31 January 1935): 149; *KZ,* LAB (26 January 1936): n.p.

112. For some examples, see *VRW,* LAB (17 September 1930): n.p.; and *VB* (24 January 1936): n.p. and (2 June 1939): 9.

113. For some examples, see *PS* (6 November 1935): 6; and *GRIN* (16 April 1937): 18 and (14 January 1938): 16.

114. For a couple of examples of this type of ad, see *GRIN* (5 August 1938): 16 and (2 February 1939): 10. Lux occasionally used ads like this as well; for a couple of good examples, see *PS* (8 November 1935): 8 and (3 December 1935): 9.

115. *GRIN* (9 March 1939): 14 and (23 March 1939): 16. Similar ads for Lux appear in *PS* (8 November 1935): 13 and (3 December 1935): 9.

116. The very application of the language and practice of industrial rationalization into the realm of the household, according to Mary Nolan, ultimately proved revelatory of the limits of female empowerment with respect to the household. Despite the fact that one of the central tenets of industrial rationalization was the specialization of labor in the workplace, Nolan shows, housewives themselves were to perform all of the diverse domestic tasks that had to be completed. Rationalization advocates feared that the wholesale application of the notion of specialization to the home would threaten the traditional meaning and stability of the family household. Such limits to female empowerment, as Nolan claims, demonstrate the underlying traditionalism of the ideology of modern housewifery. See Nolan, *Visions of Modernity,* 216.

117. Ibid., esp. 206, 221.

118. Frevert, *Women in German History,* 195–196; Nolan, *Visions of Modernity,* esp. 218–219; and Reagin, *A German Women's Movement,* 230–231.

119. ADP, Publicité (D 18 Z cart. 9), Folder Installation—Subfolder Electricité, Gaz, Téléphone.

120. Reagin, "*Marktordnung* and Autarkic Housekeeping," 168–178. See also Kessler, *"Die deutsche Frau,"* 16–17.

121. FORN, Bon Marché agenda, 1933, 3; ellipses in original.

122. Ibid, 17; emphasis added.

123. Furlough, "Selling the American Way in Interwar France," 507.

124. Stewart, *For Health and Beauty,* 56–57. See also Simonton, *A History of European Women's Work,* 195–199.

125. Frevert, *Women in German History*, 195.

126. In the French case, examples can be found in *ILL* (23 November 1929): xxxviii; *GRIN* (9 March 1934): 12; and *VEN* (18 June 1937): 8. See also the article on electricity in the home in *ILL* (28 May 1932): xxxi; and the *ILL* article entitled "The Home and the Technique of Comfort" (20 May 1939): 104–107. See also the 1927 advertising flyer for Probus vacuums as well as the 1927 advertising booklet for Lux vacuums, both of which are to be found in ADP, Publicité (D 18 Z cart. 9), Folder Installation—Subfolder Entretien, Désinfection. See also BHVP, Bon Marché agenda, 1928, 78. For Germany, see, for instance, *VB* (22 June 1937): 20 and (24 July 1938): 5. See also the article entitled "Economy in Housekeeping" in *WM* (December 1927): 455–457.

127. *VB* (19 March 1939): 5. For other ads with a powerful emphasis on sparkling cleanliness, see *VRW*, LAB (4 November 1926): n.p. and (14 September 1930): n.p.; and *VB* (26 March 1939): 9. Such notions are not altogether surprising given Frevert's observation that, in the interwar period, housewives took advantage of new domestic cleaning-related technologies in order "to declare war on infectious germs"; Frevert, *Women in German History*, 195. See also Cowan, "The Industrial Revolution in the Home," 290.

128. *MAT*, LC (29 November 1923): 8. For similar (albeit less dramatic) ads, see ibid. (13 November 1925): 5; and *GRIN* (28 November 1930): 10.

129. For some German examples, see *VB* (5 August 1936): n.p., (27/28/29 March 1937): 25, and (1 June 1937): 20. For French examples, see *MAT*, LC (19 March 1928): 3; *GRIN* (20 May 1932): 10; and *ILL* (6 June 1936): xxiii. See also the advertising booklet for Viandox from May 1927 in ADP, Publicité (D 18 Z cart. 8), Folder Alimentation (Produits d').

130. See, for example, *GRIN* (26 February 1932): 6; and *VEN* (5 June 1936): 9 and (14 May 1937): 7.

131. In the German context, Frevert makes note of this concern for high nutritional value among interwar middle-class German housewives, claiming that this was yet another responsibility that they were to accept in light of the time and effort they were saving in their domestic labor through household rationalization; Frevert, *Women in German History*, 195. Reagin points out the focus on healthier foods as well, although she argues that much of the political impetus for it originated not simply in a desire to improve nutrition, but rather in an effort to meet the needs of the Nazis' plans for autarky; Reagin, "*Marktordnung* and Autarkic Housekeeping," 172–173, 179. Similarly, Parkin has noted, in American food advertising directed at women, an emphasis on familial health; see Parkin, *Food Is Love*, 159–164.

132. *VB* (2 June 1934): n.p. See also ibid. (17 September 1937): 4.

133. *VRW*, LAB (8 November 1926): n.p.

134. *GRIN* (19 August 1932): 10. In addition, French sources occasionally reminded housewives of the importance of variety as the capstone of a healthy diet. For examples of this sort, see the Frigidaire ad in *GRIN* (23 February 1939): 5; and the note preceding the introduction of new recipes in FORN, Printemps agenda, 1923, 2.

135. See Gilbert, "Soldier's Heart," 426–436; and Roberts, *Civilization without Sexes*, 37–41.

136. McMillan, *Housewife or Harlot*, 128. In the German case, see Kessler, "*Die deutsche Frau*," 51–52, 87–89.

137. *PS* (24 November 1935): 11. See also ibid. (10 November 1935): 11. Parkin has discussed a similar phenomenon in American food advertising; see Parkin, *Food Is Love*, 125–158.

138. *GRIN* (23 February 1939): 5. See also ibid. (23 March 1939): 9.

139. *VB* (26 March 1939): 9.

140. Ibid. (5 September 1937): 23; ellipsis in original.

141. Ibid. See also *VRW,* LAB (7 November 1926): n.p. and (14 September 1930): n.p.; and *VB* (17 January 1934, supplement): n.p. and (9 March 1937): 19.

142. *GRIN* (9 March 1934): 12. See also *MAT,* LC (9 January 1921): 6; *VEN* (17 April 1936): 8; and the May 1927 advertising booklet for Viandox in ADP, Publicité (D 18 Z cart. 8), Folder Alimentation (Produits d').

143. FORN, Galeries Lafayette agenda, 1928, 6; ellipsis in original. See also ibid., 1929, 6–16, which performs a similar function with respect to cooking rather than cleaning.

144. Lubar, "Men/Women/Production/Consumption," 30; and Williams, "Getting House-wives the Electric Message," 103–104.

145. FORN, Printemps agenda, 1938, 76.

146. FORN, Grands Magasins du Louvre agenda, 1922, 123–128. For a similar example, see the ad for Arthur Martin stoves in *ILL* (28 April 1934): xxv. Interestingly, ledgers for tracking household incomes and expenditures were incorporated into several *agendas* of the Grands Magasins du Louvre in the 1920s. See FORN, Grands Magasins du Louvre agenda 1921, 1922, 1924, and 1926.

147. FORN, Nouvelles Galeries "A La Ménagère" agenda, 1923, n.p.

148. Nolan, *Visions of Modernity,* 208–222. See also Lacey, "Driving the Message Home," 190–191. Sneeringer points out the contradictions embedded in advertising that portrayed female consumers as, on the one hand, capable managers of the domestic sphere, and on the other, wasteful and irrational spenders; see Sneeringer, "The Shopper as Voter," 493–494.

149. Stephenson, "Propaganda, Autarky, and the German Housewife," 121–131. See also Lacey, "Driving the Message Home," 190–191. Moreover, Reagin contends that this connection between domestic and national economy was highlighted by Nazi women's leader Gertrude Scholz-Klink to demonstrate a further aspect of housewives' empowerment, since they thus played such a vital role in the fate of the nation. See Reagin, "*Marktordnung* and Autarkic House-keeping," 163–167, 183.

150. As Reagin demonstrates, the hope was that the intensified thrift of already selective Hausfrauen would negate the impact of Nazi-imposed wage freezes. Reagin, "*Marktordnung* and Autarkic Housekeeping," 176–177.

151. For some examples from France, see *MAT,* LC (16 October 1922): 5 and (18 February 1927): 6; *ILL* (31 August 1929): x; *GRIN* (1 July 1932): 12; *PS* (13 November 1935): 13; *ILL* (23 May 1936): xxxix; and *VEN* (14 May 1937): 7. See also the article entitled "The Domain of the Kitchen" in BHVP, Bon Marché agenda, 1925, 147–148. For German examples, see *FZ,* LAB (11 September 1920): 3; *LV,* LAB (4 June 1921): n.p.; *IZ* (1 April 1926): 438; *VRW,* LAB (23 September 1930): n.p.; *VZ* (3 August 1933): n.p.; *IZ* (28 March 1935): 425; *KZ,* LAB (26 January 1936): n.p.; *VB* (9 March 1937): 19; *IZ* (9 September 1937): 440; and *VB* (17–18 May 1939): 12.

152. For examples from Germany, see *IZ* (14 March 1935): 320 and (22 April 1937): 540. For French examples, see *ILL* (31 August 1929): xii; *GRIN* (12 December 1930): 12 and (21 September 1934): 20; and *ILL* (16 May 1936): xxii; and (11 June 1938): xxiv. A number of French articles related to housework and electrical or gas power addressed this issue; see *ILL* (21 January 1933): ix, (7 March 1936): xxiii, and (11 December 1937): xxv.

153. For Germany, see *VRW,* LAB (24 November 1926): n.p.; and *VB* (6 December 1936): 19 and (27 June 1937): 14. See also the article entitled "The Economy of Housekeeping" in *WM* (December 1927): 455-457. For France, see *ILL* (28 June 1930): xxxiii; *MAT,* LC (22 May 1931): 8; *GRIN* (26 February 1932): 6; and *ILL* (9 December 1933): xxxvii. Historians have likewise noted an emphasis on consumer conservation, especially in Nazi Germany. See Reagin, "Comparing Apples and Oranges," esp. 258-259; Reagin, "*Marktordnung* and Autarkic Housekeeping," 172-173; and Stephenson, "Propaganda, Autarky and the German Housewife," 137.

154. Furlough, "Selling the American Way in Interwar France," 510.

155. For analyses of this ambiguity toward American methods, see, for Germany, Nolan, *Visions of Modernity,*" 206-226; and Reagin, "Comparing Apples and Oranges," esp. 246-247. For France, see Furlough, "Selling the American Way in Interwar France," esp. 491-493, 509-511; and Martin, "Ménagère: Une profession?" 97-99. See also de Grazia, *Irresistible Empire.*

156. Frevert, *Women in German History,* 194.

157. FORN, Printemps agenda, 1920, 422; 1921, 492; and 1922, 458.

158. de Grazia, *Irresistible Empire,* esp. 3.

159. Nolan, *Visions of Modernity,* 207-221. See also Reagin, *A German Women's Movement,* 230-231.

160. Nolan, *Visions of Modernity,* 213.

161. Ibid., 221.

162. For a few examples, see *MAT,* LC (16 September 1927): 6; *PS* (19 November 1935): 11; *GRIN* (19 November 1937): 16; *ILL* (14 May 1938): xviii; and *GRIN* (9 March 1939): 14. See also a 1936 article on electricity in the kitchen in *ILL* (7 March 1936): xxiii. See also the May 1927 advertising booklet for Viandox in ADP, Publicité (D 18 Z cart. 8), Folder Alimentation (Produits d'); and the 1927 advertising flyer for Probus vacuum cleaners in ADP, Publicité (D 18 Z cart. 9), Folder Installation—Subfolder Entretien, Désinfection.

163. Reagin, "*Marktordnung* and Autarkic Housekeeping," 168-171. See also de Grazia, *Irresistible Empire,* 124-126, 215-216, which notes the mixed results of such "buy national" campaigns; Lacey, "Driving the Message Home," 190-191, which makes a similar point about calls for "patriotic consumption"; and Reagin, "Comparing Apples and Oranges," 248-253.

164. For a few examples, see *VB* (17 January 1934, supplement): n.p.; *IZ* (31 January 1935): 149; *VB* (17 November 1935): n.p.; and *KZ,* LAB (26 January 1936): n.p.

165. *DAZ,* LAB (9 May 1926): n.p.

166. *VRW,* LAB (10 August 1930): n.p. See also *IZ* (12 July 1923): 6; and *WM* (October 1934, advertising section): 17.

167. The vacuum ad is in *GRIN* (9 March 1934): 12. The refrigerator ad can be found in *VEN* (18 June 1937): 8.

TWO. WOMEN'S "DELIGHTFUL DUTY"

1. BHVP, Bon Marché agenda, 1920, 3; and 1922, 2.

2. As just one example of the primacy of motherhood in cultural definitions of femininity, see Grayzel, *Women's Identities at War.*

3. For some examples of this in German scholarship, see Abrams and Harvey, "Gender and

Gender Relations in German History," 24–25; Klinksiek, *Die Frau im NS-Staat,* 23–24; Lacey, "Driving the Message Home, 191; Vinken, *Die deutsche Mutter,* 280; and Wiggershaus, *Frauen unterm Nationalsozialismus,* 21. For a couple of examples from France, see Offen, "Body Politics," esp. 138; and Roberts, *Civilization without Sexes,* esp. 91–131.

4. Seccombe, "Men's 'Marital Rights' and Women's 'Wifely Duties,'" esp. 66–74.

5. See, for example, Mason, "Women in Germany, 1925–1940," 76; and Vinken, *Die deutsche Mutter,* 266–267.

6. For instance, see Frevert, *Women in German History,* 230–231; Hausen, "Mothers, Sons, and the Sale of Symbols and Goods," 391; Peukert, *The Weimar Republic,* 7–9, 102; and Pine, "Women and the Family," 200.

7. See, for example, Jenson, "Gender and Reproduction," 40; and Teitelbaum and Winter, *The Fear of Population Decline,* 36–39.

8. For instance, see Jenson, "Gender and Reproduction," 16; Klaus, "Depopulation and Race Suicide," 194; Odgen and Huss, "Demography and Pronatalism in France," 283–284; and Pedersen, *Family, Dependence, and the Origins of the Welfare State,* 359–360.

9. A number of scholars have pointed out the increased interference of the government in the affairs and machinations of reproduction and motherhood. For a few examples, see Allen, *Feminism and Motherhood in Western Europe,* esp. 139; Pedersen, *Family, Dependence, and the Origins of the Welfare State,* 359–360; Pine, *Nazi Family Policy,* 8; Pine, "Women and the Family," 205; Reynolds, *France between the Wars,* 31–32; and Stephenson, "Women, Motherhood and the Family in the Third Reich," 168.

10. Frevert, *Women in German History,* 186. See also Usborne, *The Politics of the Body in Weimar Germany,* xi; and Vinken, *Die deutsche Mutter,* 269. In the French context, see Thebaud, *Quand nos grand-mères donnaient la vie,* 14–15.

11. For example, see Huss, "Pronatalism in the Inter-war Period in France," 39, 42; Klaus, "Depopulation and Race Suicide," 199–200, who illustrates that most women accepted such ideas strengthening their connection to motherhood; Ogden and Huss, "Demography and Pronatalism in France," 293; Reynolds, *France between the Wars,* 18; and Usborne, *The Politics of the Body in Weimar Germany,* 210.

12. For France, see Auffret, *La France de l'entre deux guerres,* 43; Klaus, "Depopulation and Race Suicide," 189–194; Ogden and Huss, "Demography and Pronatalism in France," 283; Thebaud, *Quand nos grand-mères donnaient la vie,* esp. 13–14; and Winter, "War, Family, and Fertility in Twentieth-Century Europe," 294.

For Germany, see Bessel, *Germany after the First World War,* 224–225; Marschalck, *Bevölkerungsgeschichte Deutschlands,* 53–67; Spree, "The German Petite Bourgeoisie and the Decline of Fertility," 15–17; and Usborne, *The Politics of the Body in Weimar Germany,* xii, 31.

13. Huss, "Pronatalism in the Inter-war Period in France," 39–42. See also Accampo, "Private Life, Public Image," 250.

14. Accampo, "Private Life, Public Image," 247–248; Cova, *Maternité et droits des femmes en France,* 254–265; Huss, "Pronatalism in the Inter-war Period in France," 55; Lees, "Safety in Numbers," 318; Reynolds, *France between the Wars,* 18; and Thebaud, *Quand nos grand-mères donnaient la vie,* 26.

15. Accampo, "Private Life, Public Image," 247–248.

16. Cova, *Maternité et droits des femmes en France,* 362–373; Huss, "Pronatalism in the Inter-war Period in France," 56–63; Ogden and Huss, "Demography and Pronatalism in France in the Nineteenth and Twentieth Centuries," 293; and Reynolds, *France between the Wars,* 29–30.

17. Dyer, *Population and Society in Twentieth-Century France,* 82–83. See also Accampo, "Private Life, Public Image," 250; Cova, *Maternité et droits des femmes en France,* 234; Ogden and Huss, "Demography and Pronatalism in France," 286; Thebaud, *Quand nos grand-mères donnaient la vie,* 13, 295; Tilly and Scott, *Women, Work, and Family,* 167; and Weber, *The Hollow Years,* 13.

18. Dyer, *Population and Society in Twentieth-Century France,* 63–64; Huss, "Pronatalism in the Inter-war Period in France," 56–62; and Ogden and Huss, "Demography and Pronatalism in France," 286.

19. Huss, "Pronatalism in the Inter-war Period in France," 63. See also Weber, *The Hollow Years,* 13.

20. Unlike in France, though, pronatalism was not a major element in interwar German population discourse, at least not directly. As Usborne shows, the Wilhelmine government had begun to advocate a pronatalist policy in response to the declining birth rate in the prewar era, and as such, with the overthrow of that regime and the creation of the Weimar Republic, pronatalism was viewed as a discredited imperial ideology (with some exceptions among a small number of rightist groups). See Usborne, *The Politics of the Body in Weimar Germany,* xii, 36–38, 69–71.

21. David, Fleischhacker, and Höhn, "Abortion and Eugenics in Nazi Germany," 83–87; Petersen, *Women and Modernity in Weimar Germany,* 31–32; Usborne, *The Politics of the Body in Weimar Germany,* 157–181, 202; and Weindling, *Health, Race, and German Politics,* 421.

22. Lefko, "'Truly Womanly' and 'Truly German,'" 133. See also Grossmann, "The New Woman and the Rationalization of Sexuality in Weimar Germany," 154–155; and Usborne, *The Politics of the Body in Weimar Germany,* 99–101.

23. Bessel, *Germany after the First World War,* 229; David, Fleischhacker, and Höhn, "Abortion and Eugenics in Nazi Germany," 87–88; Kessler, *"Die deutsche Frau,"* 22; Klinksiek, *Die Frau im NS-Staat,* 158; Knodel, *The Decline of Fertility in Germany,* 4–5; Mouton, *Nurturing the Nation,* 108–109; and Stephenson, *Women in Nazi Society,* 37–41.

24. Qtd. in Boxer and Quataert, "Overview, 1890 to the Present," 244; Frevert, *Women in German History,* 207; and Vinken, *Die deutsche Mutter,* 260. See also Frevert, "Gender in German History," 516; and Klinksiek, *Die Frau im NS-Staat,* 84.

25. David, Fleischhacker, and Höhn, "Abortion and Eugenics in Nazi Germany," 89–90; Frevert, *Women in German History,* 231–232; Kudlien, "The German Response to the Birth-Rate Problem during the Third Reich," 229; and Stephenson, *Women in Nazi Germany,* 38. As with so many other facets of Nazi belief and policy, National Socialist motherhood ideology was not without considerable contradictions; for more on this subject, see Bock, "Racism and Sexism in Nazi Germany," 273; Klinksiek, *Die Frau im NS-Staat,* 73–75; Stephenson, "Reichsbund der Kinderreichen," 350–352; and Vinken, *Die deutsche Mutter,* 295–296.

26. Frevert, *Women in German History,* 231–232; Kessler, *"Die deutsche Frau,"* 22; Klinksiek, *Die Frau im NS-Staat,* 158; and Stephenson, *Women in Nazi Germany,* 24. See also Knodel, *The*

Decline of Fertility in Germany, 5; Stephenson, "Reichsbund der Kinderreichen," 367–368; and Stephenson, "Women, Motherhood and the Family in the Third Reich," 175.

27. Bock, "Racism and Sexism in Nazi Germany," 277–278; Frevert, *Women in German History,* 231–232; and Mason, "Women in Germany, 1925–1940," 102–103.

28. Usborne, *The Politics of the Body in Weimar Germany,* 46–48. Usborne notes that rapid inflation soon made these benefits all but worthless in economic terms, but that should not alter the perception of their purpose and intent.

29. Ibid., 36, 48–49. In the French context, see Cova, *Maternité et droits des femmes en France,* 271–272.

30. Mason, "Women in Germany, 1925–1940," 97.

31. Czarnowski, "The Value of Marriage for the *Volksgemeinschaft,*" 98; Frevert, *Women in German History,* 233–234; Mouton, *Nurturing the Nation,* 49, 169–171; Pine, *Nazi Family Policy,* 23–28, 34; and Pine, "Women and the Family," 209–212.

32. For descriptions of this system, see, for example, Pedersen, "Catholicism, Feminism, and the Politics of the Family during the Late Third Republic," 254–255; and Pedersen, *Family, Dependence, and the Origins of the Welfare State,* 229–232, 357–379. Further, the 1920 and 1922 *agendas* of the Bon Marché laid out the store's program of maternity benefits for its workers; see BHVP, Bon Marché agenda, 1920, 3; and 1922, 2.

33. Pedersen, "Catholicism, Feminism, and the Politics of the Family during the Late Third Republic," 254; and Pedersen, *Family, Dependence, and the Origins of the Welfare State,* 232. See also Cova, *Maternité et droits des femmes en France,* 378.

34. Pedersen, *Family, Dependence, and the Origins of the Welfare State,* 379. See also Cova, *Maternité et droits des femmes en France,* 338–345.

35. Huss, "Pronatalism in the Inter-war Period in France," 42–43; and Offen, "Body Politics," 138.

36. Boxer and Quataert, "Overview, 1890 to the Present," 244; Offen, "Body Politics," 138; Simonton, *A History of European Women's Work,* 189; and Thebaud, *Quand nos grand-mères donnaient la vie,* 21.

37. Klinksiek, *Die Frau im NS-Staat,* 84; Kudlien, "The German Response to the Birth-Rate Problem during the Third Reich," 235; Marschalck, *Bevölkerungsgeschichte Deutschlands,* 77; Mouton, *Nurturing the Nation,* 124–127; Stephenson, "Women, Motherhood and the Family in the Third Reich," 173; and Weyrather, *Muttertag und Mutterkreuz,* esp. 55–84.

38. Rupp, "Mother of the *Volk,*" 370–371; Stephenson, *Women in Nazi Germany,* 31. For honors bestowed on mothers in the Weimar era, see Usborne, *The Politics of the Body in Weimar Germany,* 44; and Weindling, *Health, Race, and German Politics,* 448–449.

39. Kudlien, "The German Response to the Birth-Rate Problem during the Third Reich," 235; Stephenson, "Reichsbund der Kinderreichen," esp. 352–357; Stephenson, *Women in Nazi Germany,* 31; and Stephenson, "Women, Motherhood and the Family in the Third Reich," 173.

40. Hausen, "Mother's Day in the Weimar Republic," 132–133; Hausen, "Mothers, Sons, and the Sale of Symbols and Goods," 374–378; Weindling, *Health, Race, and German Politics,* 423–424; and Weyrather, *Muttertag und Mutterkreuz,* 18–39.

41. Hausen, "Mothers, Sons, and the Sale of Symbols and Goods," 380–383; and Hausen, "Mother's Day in the Weimar Republic," 140–141. See also Mouton, *Nurturing the Nation,* 110–113.

42. Badinter, *Mother Love*, 275–276.

43. For some examples, see *MAT*, LC (15 April 1920): 4 and (19 March 1928): 3; *GRIN* (19 January 1934): 10; *PS* (20 November 1935): 6; and *GRIN* (23 February 1939): 9.

44. See, for example, FORN, Grands Magasins du Louvre agenda, 1922, 11; FORN, Nouvelles Galeries "A La Ménagère" agenda, 1923, n.p; ADP, Publicité Commerciale (D 18 Z cart. 7), Folder Palais de la Nouveauté, 1925–1927; and ADP, Publicité (D 18 Z cart. 9), Folder Bonneteries.

45. BHVP, Bon Marché agenda, 1920, 3; and 1922, 2.

46. See, for instance, *MAT*, LC (4 December 1923): 5; *OEU* (26 March 1925): 3; *GRIN* (9 November 1928): 8; *AF* (10 April 1930): 7; *MAT*, LC (23 September 1932): 7; *PS* (10 November 1935): 7; and *GRIN* (19 March 1937): 18. See also ADP, Publicité Commerciale (8 AZ 891); and ADP, Publicité Commerciale (D 18 Z cart. 7), Folder Palais de la Nouveauté, 1925–1927.

47. FORN, Grands Magasins du Louvre agenda, 1921, 123–128.

48. For a few examples, see *MAT*, LC (28 December 1923): 6; *OEU* (10 June 1928): 8; *AF* (1 August 1928): 3; *MAT*, LC (25 July 1931): 3; and *GRIN* (23 February 1939): 16. See also the illustration in FORN, Grands Magasins du Louvre agenda, 1922, 89.

49. ADP, Publicité Commerciale (D 18 Z cart. 7), Folder Palais de la Nouveauté, 1925–1927.

50. For a few instances of this, see *AF* (26 June 1921): 4; *OEU* (8 August 1921): n.p.; *MAT*, LC (7 July 1925): 3; *GRIN* (28 May 1937): 14; and *ILL* (28 May 1938): lxxii.

51. Rearick, *The French in Love and War*, 154–178, esp. 154–157.

52. For some examples, see *GRM*, LAB (18 March 1921): n.p.; *DAZ*, LAB (16 May 1926): n.p.; *VRW*, LAB (21 November 1926): n.p.; *VB* (13 June 1934, supplement): n.p. and (5 August 1936): n.p.; and *IZ* (22 April 1937): 540.

53. See, for instance, *VRW*, LAB (29 November 1926): n.p. and (17 December 1926): n.p.; and *VB* (9 January 1934): n.p. and (26 January 1936): n.p.

54. For one example, see *WM* (September 1934, advertising section): 19. See also the Alva cigarette ad in *MIP*, SBB (31 January 1935): 135.

55. For some examples, see *LV*, LAB (26 August 1921): n.p.; *IZ* (4 February 1926): 163; *VB* (17 October 1934): n.p.; *MIP*, SBB (10 December 1936): 1797; and *VB* (19 September 1937): 19.

56. See Frevert, *Women in German History*, 233; Vinken, *Die deutsche Mutter*, 264–265; and Weyrather, *Muttertag und Mutterkreuz*.

57. *SIMP* (15 July 1934): 187.

58. For a few examples, see *MIP*, SBB (31 January 1935): 140; *SIMP* (10 February 1935): 547; and *IZ* (23 February 1939): 278.

59. For instance, see *SIMP* (21 September 1925): 353; *VZ* (12 July 1933): n.p.; *SIMP* (9 September 1934): 283; *VB* (26 July 1935): n.p.; *IZ* (14 May 1936): 626; and *IZ* (11 May 1939): 700.

60. Frevert, *Women in German History*, 193.

61. Domansky, "Militarization and Reproduction in World War I Germany," 427–463.

62. BHVP, Bon Marché agenda, 1932, 1.

63. Simonton, *A History of European Women's Work*, 189.

64. Badinter, *Mother Love*, 272–278.

65. *GRIN* (15 February 1929): 1. At the same time, it should be noted that an alternate reading of this cartoon suggests that the man and woman are a wealthy Jewish couple, and thus the

cartoon's intended message is as likely to have been anti-Semitic (which was certainly not unusual for *Gringoire;* see the appendix) as about maternity.

66. Several scholars have noted this emphasis on infant health. For one example from German scholarship, see Abrams and Harvey, "Gender and Gender Relations in German History," 24. For the French case, see, for instance, Stewart, *For Health and Beauty,* esp. 2–3, 59.

67. *VB* (12 January 1936): n.p.

68. See, for example, *KZ,* LAB (30 October 1935): 5; and *VB* (5 November 1935): n.p.

69. Indeed, Cowan claims that, in the American context, maintaining a clean household was seen as one of mothers' foremost duties and as a demonstration of maternal instinct. Moreover, she contends, women who did not accomplish sufficiently such cleaning tasks were expected to feel guilt and even humiliation at this sign of their failure as mothers. Cowan, "The Industrial Revolution in the Home," 291–292.

70. Such ads were particularly plentiful in the Nazi era. For a few examples, see *VB* (13 June 1934, supplement): n.p., (12 March 1935): n.p., and (10 July 1935): n.p.

71. Ibid. (17 October 1934): n.p.

72. See, for instance, *IZ* (6 May 1926): 607; and *VB* (9 June 1934): n.p.

73. For a few examples, see *VRW,* LAB (29 November 1926): n.p.; and *VB* (10 January 1934): n.p. and (27/28/29 March 1937): 25.

74. Coward, *Female Desires,* 119–121. See also Parkin, *Food Is Love,* esp. 193–221.

75. Cowan, "The Industrial Revolution in the Home," 291–292, 295. See also Parkin, *Food Is Love,* esp. 30–78.

76. *IZ* (11 May 1939): 700.

77. *SIMP* (2 December 1934): 427.

78. For just a few examples, see *PS* (14 November 1935): 6; and *GRIN* (4 February 1938): 14 and (12 January 1939): 16.

79. *ILL* (14 March 1931): xxx.

80. *MAT,* LC (4 March 1927): 6. Some ads did mention health-related issues, but usually in a limited context. See, for instance, *GRIN* (16 March 1934): 10.

81. For a selection of such ads, see *MAT,* LC (15 April 1920): 4; *OEU* (26 March 1925): 3; *AF* (10 July 1928): 5; *GRIN* (1 August 1930): 10; *MAT,* LC (30 June 1931): 6; *PS* (3 November 1935): 3; and *GRIN* (30 March 1939): 9.

82. *MAT,* LC (16 April 1928): 6. See also *GRIN* (19 March 1937): 18.

83. *PS* (20 November 1935): 6.

84. Cowan, "The Industrial Revolution in the Home," 295.

85. BHVP, Bon Marché agenda, 1928, 28. See also a Nestlé ad showing a mother weighing her child that appeared in both *OEU* (21 September 1927): 3; and *AF* (20 July 1928): 3.

86. Cova, *Maternité et droits des femmes en France,* 315–316.

87. For a few examples of such ads, see *MAT,* LC (12 July 1923): 4; *OEU* (12 July 1923): n.p.; *MAT,* LC (12 June 1929): 6; and *AF* (30 April 1930): 5. The 1920 and 1922 agendas of the Bon Marché also encouraged women to breastfeed their children. See BHVP, Bon Marché agenda, 1920, 3; and 1922, 2.

88. *MAT,* LC (20 October 1923): 7. See also *AF* (8 March 1924): 4; and *MAT,* LC (8 March 1924): 6.

89. *MAT,* LC (21 January 1927): 6; emphasis shown in bold type in original. See also *AF* (22 November 1921): 4 and (30 May 1927): 4; and *GRIN* (9 November 1928): 8.

90. Stewart, *For Health and Beauty,* 59. See also Thebaud, *Quand nos grand-mères donnaient la vie,* 181–184.

91. *GRIN* (17 October 1930): 14.

92. Hermand, *"All Power to the Women,"* 652.

93. Rupp, "Mother of the *Volk,*" 372. German celebrations of Mother's Day also possessed overtones of national responsibility. See, for instance, Hausen, "Mothers, Sons, and the Sale of Symbols and Goods," 374–378; and Weyrather, *Muttertag und Mutterkreuz,* 40–48.

94. *VB* (17 October 1934): n.p. The fact that such an advertisement appeared early in the Nazi regime should not be surprising given Lisa Pine's observation that the National Socialists felt that the promotion of traditional and distinctly German familial relations was necessary in order to offset what they viewed as the rampant "internationalism" of the Weimar years. See Pine, *Nazi Family Policy,* 9; and Pine, "Women and the Family," 201.

95. *IZ* (14 May 1936): 626.

96. *MAT,* LC (7 October 1922): 4.

97. Teitelbaum and Winter, *The Fear of Population Decline,* 47, point out that the term "race" was frequently used in such contexts as a synonym for nation.

98. BHVP, Bon Marché agenda, 1920, 3; and 1922, 2.

99. For France on this subject, see McMillan, *Housewife or Harlot,* 128. For Germany, see Petersen, *Women and Modernity in Weimar Germany,* 19; Pine, *Nazi Family Policy,* 5; Pine, "Women and the Family," 199; and Rosenhaft, "Women in Modern Germany," 148–150.

100. Hausen, "Mothers, Sons, and the Sale of Symbols and Goods," 402–403.

101. Stephenson, "Women, Motherhood and the Family in the Third Reich," 168. See also Rupp, "Mother of the *Volk,*" 369.

102. Gunn, "The Public Sphere, Modernity and Consumption," 20–22.

103. Peukert, *The Weimar Republic,* 105.

104. Badinter, *Mother Love,* 284–285.

105. *IZ* (2 March 1939): 282.

106. *VB* (28 March 1935): n.p. See also *GRM,* LAB (10 April 1921): n.p.; and *VB* (14 January 1934): n.p.

107. *VRW,* LAB (21 September 1930): n.p.

108. *OEU* (10 June 1928): 8. See also *GRIN* (3 August 1934): 14 and (14 January 1938): 12.

109. This ad appeared in both *OEU* (21 September 1927): 3; and *AF* (20 July 1928): 3.

THREE. GENDERING THE BOUNDARIES OF PUBLIC AND PRIVATE

1. Lerman, Mohun, and Oldenziel, "The Shoulders We Stand On and the View from Here," 24.

2. BHVP, Bon Marché agenda, 1925, 129.

3. For literature on interwar fashions, see, for France, Fourny, "Discours de la mode," 214–230; Gronberg, "Beware Beautiful Women," 375–382; Roberts, *Civilization without Sexes,* 19–21, 63–87; Roberts, "Prêt-à-déchiffrer," 57–73; Roberts, "Samson and Delilah Revisited," 657–668;

Zdatny, "Hair and Fashion," 335–345; and Zdatny, "La mode à la garçonne," 23–56. For Germany, see Guenther, "Nazi 'Chic'?" esp. 29–45; Gustavus, "WKS," 72–75; Heinze, "Schick, selbst mit beschränkten Mitteln!" 9–17; Loreck, "Das Kunstprodukt 'Neue Frau,'" 12–19; McDonald, "Creating a 'Nazi Style,'" 51–62; Petro, *Joyless Streets,* 110–114; and Waidenschlager, "Berliner Mode," 20–31.

4. For just a few examples of ads featuring men in public or social contexts from France, see *AF* (27 July 1920): 4; *MAT,* LC (18 April 1921): 4; *OEU* (19 September 1923): n.p.; and *ILL* (2 July 1932): xvii and (8 April 1939): xii. For Germany, see *VRW,* LAB (12 November 1926): n.p.; and *VB* (2 December 1936): 23 and (19 May 1939): 7.

5. Examples of such ads showing women devoid of any background context or inside a household setting are seemingly endless. For just a few examples, see, in the German case, *NPZ,* LAB (1 February 1920): n.p.; *GRM,* LAB (27 March 1921): n.p.; *DAZ,* LAB (18 May 1926): n.p.; *VRW,* LAB (14 September 1930): n.p.; *GRM,* LAB (1 May 1932): n.p.; *VZ* (13 August 1933): n.p.; *KZ,* LAB (17 November 1935): 12; and *VB* (1 December 1936): 19; and (13 March 1937): 20. For France, see *AF* (5 July 1922): 4; *MAT,* LC (19 October 1922): 3; *OEU* (28 September 1923): n.p.; *AF* (1 October 1924): 4; *OEU* (4 October 1926): 6; and *GRIN* (2 May 1930): 8 and (27 April 1934): 12.

6. For a couple of examples, see *AF* (12 September 1922): 4; and *GRIN* (7 October 1932): 8. See also the winter 1931 catalog of the Bon Marché in ADP, Publicité Commerciale (D 18 Z cart. 7), Folder Bon Marché, 1847–1933.

7. *VRW,* LAB (20 January 1924): n.p.

8. *DAZ,* LAB (15 April 1926): n.p. For a French clothing ad in which business clothes are cited, see *AF* (27 July 1920): 4. See also the winter 1931 catalog of the Bon Marché in ADP, Publicité Commerciale (D 18 Z cart. 7), Folder Bon Marché, 1847–1933.

9. BNF, Bazar de l'Hôtel de Ville, catalogues, 1910–. In the German case, an advertisement for Koltermann clothing that features a male figure does mention "work clothes" as one of its specialties; see *VRW,* LAB (27 January 1924): n.p.

10. For an example in the German case, see *VRW,* LAB (23 October 1921): n.p. For France, see the advertising booklet for Grands Magasins Sigrand & Cie from autumn-winter 1925–1926 in ADP, Publicité (D 18 Z cart. 9), Folder Habillement—Subfolder Tailleurs. For advertisements in the French press, see *MAT,* LC (18 October 1923): 7; *AF* (10 June 1925): 3; *OEU* (17 October 1926): 6; *La République* (24 April 1931): 4; and *GRIN* (7 October 1932): 8.

11. For France, see the 1933 advertising sheet for Samaritaine in ADP, Publicité Commerciale (D 18 Z cart. 7), Folder Samaritaine, 1910–1933. For advertisements in the French press, see *AF* (21 August 1920): 4; *MAT* (24 August 1922): 6; *AF* (18 August 1926): 4; *OEU* (3 September 1927): 6; *GRIN* (15 August 1930): 12; and *OEU* (25 August 1932): 8. For a German example, see *DAZ,* LAB (15 April 1926): n.p.

12. *AF* (1 August 1920): 3.

13. *VRW,* LAB (19 September 1930): n.p.

14. For one German example, see *GRM,* LAB (3 April 1932): n.p. For France, see *AF* (20 April 1921): 4 and (6 October 1921): 4.

15. BNF, *La Mode et L'Ameublement Au Bon Marché,* 1920, n.p.

16. Ibid.

17. Rearick, *The French in Love and War,* 154–178, esp. 154–157.

18. *VRW,* LAB (11 December 1921): n.p.

19. ADP, Publicité Commerciale (D 18 Z cart. 7), Folder Galeries Lafayette, 1912–1933.

20. *MAT,* LC (18 April 1921): 4.

21. *AF* (27 July 1920): 4. See also ADP, Publicité Commerciale (D 18 Z cart. 7), Folder Bon Marché, 1847–1933; and *GRIN* (27 May 1938): 13. Moreover, several ads for coats cite their waterproof qualities; see, for example, *AF* (12 September 1922): 4; and *GRIN* (15 August 1930): 12 and (7 October 1932): 8.

22. *VRW,* LAB (12 November 1926): n.p. See also *NPZ,* LAB (5 April 1925): n.p.

23. See, for example, *VRW,* LAB (23 October 1921): n.p. and (19 September 1930): n.p.; and *VB* (30 October 1934): n.p.

24. *ILL* (9 May 1936): xxv. See also *OEU* (17 October 1926): 6; and *GRIN* (4 June 1937): 12.

25. *MAT,* LC (18 October 1923): 7; emphasis in original. See also *GRIN* (9 March 1939): 9.

26. The prominence of ads from such English firms as Burberrys and Nicoll should not be entirely surprising, as British fashions had historically played an important role influencing French ones as far back as the eighteenth century. See, for example, Ribeiro, *The Art of Dress;* Ribeiro, *Fashion in the French Revolution;* and Steele, *Paris Fashion.*

27. *OEU* (13 October 1926): 6. See also *AF* (10 June 1925): 3.

28. *AF* (6 October 1921): 4; emphasis in original. See also ADP, Publicité Commerciale (D 18 Z cart. 7), Folder Le Printemps, 1916–1927; and *ILL* (27 November 1937): xxi.

29. *ILL* (2 July 1938): xi; emphasis in original.

30. FORN, Galeries Lafayette agenda, 1924, 44. See also FORN, Nouvelles Galeries "A La Ménagère" agenda, 1923.

31. See, for instance, ADP, Publicité Commerciale (D 18 Z cart. 7), Folder Le Printemps, 1916–1927; BHVP, Printemps catalogue, 1930. See also BHVP, Printemps catalogue publicitaire, 1929.

32. See, for example, *VRW,* LAB (4 December 1921): n.p.; *DAZ,* LAB (1 October 1922): n.p.; *VRW,* LAB (24 February 1924): n.p. and (24 August 1930): n.p.; and *GRM,* LAB (29 May 1932): n.p.

33. For instance, see *VRW,* LAB (11 December 1921): n.p.; *GRM,* LAB (15 May 1932): n.p.; *VZ* (27 August 1933): n.p.; and *KZ,* LAB (17 November 1935): 12.

34. *VRW,* LAB (11 November 1926): n.p.

35. *AF* (21 June 1927): 4. See also advertising materials of the department store Samaritaine in ADP, Publicité Commerciale (D 18 Z cart. 7), Folder Bon Marché, 1847–1933; ADP, Publicité Commerciale (D 18 Z cart. 7), Folder Le Printemps, 1916–1927, Folder Le Louvre, 1877–1933, Folder Belle Jardinière, 1862–1931, Folder Bazar de l'Hôtel de Ville, 1913–1931; BNF, Grands Magasins du Louvre, documents publicitaires, 1925–; BNF, Magasins Réunis Rive Gauche, catalogues, 1926–; BNF, Grands Magasins Royal Haussman, catalogues, 1930–; and BNF, Trois Quartiers, documents publicitaires, 1925–.

36. *GRM,* LAB (19 February 1921): n.p. It should be noted that ads directed at women did sometimes mention issues such as quality and durability, just as some ads for men's fashions made mention of the aesthetic features of items of clothing. In those cases, however, quality in women's fashion ads and elegance in men's fashion ads gained only a passing mention, when

they were discussed at all, and played a subordinate role to issues more closely linked to purportedly typical masculine and feminine characteristics, respectively.

37. Hau has noted this phenomenon in *The Cult of Health and Beauty in Germany*, 69. In addition, scholars dealing with other national contexts have found similar ideologies at work; see, for example, Greenfield, O'Connell, and Reid, "Gender, Consumer Culture and the Middle-Class Male," 190; Parkin, *Food Is Love*, 16–17; Reekie, "Impulsive Women, Predictable Men," 368–371; and Hosgood, "Mrs Pooter's Purchase," 152–157.

38. *AF* (21 March 1929): 8; ellipsis and capitalization in original.

39. *VRW*, LAB (9 October 1921): n.p.

40. Peiss, "Making Faces," 143. See also Stewart, *For Health and Beauty*, 13–14.

41. Stewart, *For Health and Beauty*, 60. See also Hau, *The Cult of Health and Beauty in Germany*, 8.

42. Peiss, "Making Faces," 147. See also Hau, *The Cult of Health and Beauty in Germany*, 34.

43. Stewart, *For Health and Beauty*, 13.

44. Hau, *The Cult of Health and Beauty in Germany*, 70.

45. *ILL* (3 November 1928): xxix. Other Palmolive ads can be found ibid. (11 April 1931): xxi; *GRIN* (25 May 1934): 6; and *PS* (15 November 1935): 10. See also BHVP, Bon Marché agenda, 1931.

46. *ILL* (9 July 1932): xix.

47. For other general examples of such ads, see *ILL* (15 September 1928): xx; *GRIN* (29 January 1932): 8; *ILL* (16 December 1933): xxx; *GRIN* (26 January 1934): 8; *PS* (3 November 1935): 3; *GRIN* (14 May 1937): 12; and *ILL* (29 April 1939): xvi.

48. *IZ* (5 October 1933): 396. For some other general examples of German beauty ads, see *FZ*, LAB (7 September 1920): 4; *DAZ*, LAB (10 April 1926): n.p.; *VRW*, LAB (17 November 1926): n.p.; *MIP*, SBB (13 June 1935): 808; *VB* (25–26 September 1937): 23; *MIP*, SBB (24 March 1938): 396; and *VB* (27–29 May 1939): 24.

49. See, for example, *DAZ*, LAB (27 April 1926): n.p.; and *VB* (13 June 1934): n.p.

50. *DAZ*, LAB (9 April 1926): n.p. See also ibid. (23 May 1926): n.p.; and *VB* (3 June 1934): n.p.

51. *IZ* (10 June 1926): 763.

52. *VB* (29 July 1938): 12; emphasis shown in bold type in original. For another Laun ad, see ibid. (25–27 December 1936): 19.

53. Hau, *The Cult of Health and Beauty in Germany*, 33–44, 63–65, 101.

54. *GRM*, LAB (13 December 1927): n.p. See also *LV*, LAB (6 May 1921): n.p.; *SIMP* (27 April 1925): 62; *DAZ*, LAB (3 June 1926): n.p.; *GRM*, LAB (26 May 1932): n.p.; *VB* (14 June 1934): n.p.; *MIP*, SBB (24 January 1935): 99; *MIP*, SBB (4 April 1935): 435; and *VB* (3 June 1937): 20.

55. *IZ* (21 May 1936): 685. See also ibid. (12 October 1933): 423; *WM* (September 1934, advertising section): 13; *MIP*, SBB (28 March 1935): 407; *MIP*, SBB (10 December 1936): 1787; and *IZ* (16 March 1939): 350.

56. For a few examples of ads for skin care products from France, see *ILL* (7 July 1928): xxxix; *GRIN* (24 May 1929): 8; *GRIN* (27 May 1932): 13; *ILL* (17 February 1934): xvii; and *PS* (7 November 1935): 3. See also FORN, Magasins Réunis agenda, 1927, 54.

57. *VEN* (9 April 1937): 6.

58. *GRIN* (30 November 1928): 12.

59. *IZ* (3 March 1938): 294. See also *LV,* LAB (11 June 1921): n.p.; *NPZ,* LAB (10 April 1925): n.p.; *DAZ* (30 June 1926): n.p.; and *IZ* (26 October 1933): 488.

60. *IZ* (26 May 1938): 856; ellipsis in original.

61. *ILL* (7 April 1934): xxx. See also *GRIN* (26 July 1929): 12.

62. *ILL* (25 March 1939): xix; emphasis in original.

63. See, for instance, *SIMP* (8 March 1922): 677.

64. This ad appeared in *IZ* (2 August 1923): 81 and (9 August 1923): 88.

65. Stewart, *For Health and Beauty,* 9–11.

66. *MIP,* SBB (21 February 1935): 224.

67. *GRIN* (7 June 1929): 12.

68. Ibid. (16 February 1939): 14.

69. *LV,* LAB (6 June 1921): n.p.

70. *VB* (22 March 1935): n.p.

71. *GRIN* (14 June 1929): 8.

72. *VRW,* LAB (6 September 1930): n.p.

73. Martin, *Trois siècles de publicité en France,* 181–182, 299. See also Hultquist, "Americans in Paris," 472. So, too, was such medical or pseudomedical advertising prominent in Germany; see Reinhardt, *Von der Reklame zum Marketing,* 38.

74. See, for example, Goubert, *The Conquest of Water;* Hau, *The Cult of Health and Beauty in Germany;* and Stewart, *For Health and Beauty.*

75. BHVP, Bon Marché agenda, 1928, 82.

76. *VB* (20 December 1936): 20.

77. *DAZ,* LAB (18 April 1926): n.p.

78. *SIMP* (1 March 1922): 668.

79. *MAT,* LC (8 August 1922): 6. See also *AF* (20 May 1923): 6.

80. *GRIN* (16 February 1934): 8. See also *ILL* (7 May 1938): xxiv.

81. *WM* (November 1934, advertising section): 18.

82. *DAZ,* LAB (9 May 1926): n.p.

83. For some examples of these Melabon ads, which ran in the monthly publication *WM,* see (September 1934, advertising section): 10; (October 1934, advertising section): 5; (November 1934, advertising section): 19; and (December 1936, advertising section): 8. Along similar lines, see the Biomalz ad in *VRW,* LAB (30 November 1926): n.p.

84. *VEN* (19 June 1936): 12.

85. *AF* (10 August 1928): 5; emphasis in original. For another example that incorporates a child into an ad about a mother's health problems, see *PS* (14 November 1935): 7.

86. *VRW,* LAB (15 November 1926): n.p.

87. *LV,* LAB (9 August 1921): n.p.

88. For some general examples, see *GRIN* (26 July 1929): 12; *MAT,* LC (19 May 1931): 6; *ILL* (9 December 1933): xxxvi; *PS* (2 November 1935): 5; and *GRIN* (26 March 1937): 16 and (9 February 1939): 17. See also the advertisement for Depuratif Bleu from *Le Petit Parisien* from 15 October 1922 in ADP, Publicité (D 18 Z cart. 8), Folder Santé—Subfolder Pharmaciens.

89. ADP, Publicité Commerciale (6 AZ 1817). A similar issue is dealt with in a Tisane des Chartreux advertisement from 1939; see *ILL* (21 January 1939): x.

90. ADP, Publicité (D 18 Z cart. 8), Folder Santé—Subfolder Medecine et Pharmacopée. See also the previously mentioned 1936 brochure for Fluxine-Villefranche laboratories, which also contains an illustration relating to varicose veins; ADP, Publicité Commerciale (6 AZ 1817).

91. *ILL* (14 May 1938): xix. See also ibid. (6 April 1935): xxii and (11 March 1939): xviii.

92. *MAT*, LC (9 May 1921): 4.

93. *AF* (3 March 1921): 4.

94. Lubar has explored this gendering of expertise in the American context. See Lubar, "Men/Women/Production/Consumption," 30.

95. *VB* (12 June 1934): n.p. See also the ad for Togal tablets in *MIP*, SBB (3 January 1935): 17.

96. *PS* (8 November 1935): 6. See also the Ovomaltine ad in *GRIN* (21 January 1938): 12.

97. This advertisement appeared in both *AF* (21 June 1921): 4; and *OEU* (3 September 1921): n.p.

98. *ILL* (21 July 1928): xxvi.

99. ADP, Publicité Commerciale (6 AZ 1817).

100. For a few such German examples, see *VB* (10 January 1934): n.p.; *WM* (September 1934, advertising section): 18 and (November 1934, advertising section): 10; and *VB* (7 August 1938): 14 and (25 June 1939): 16.

101. *MAT*, LC (8 January 1921): 4.

102. Ibid. (27 June 1924): 6; emphasis in original. See also *ILL* (21 June 1930): xl; and a 1927 advertising flyer in ADP, Publicité (D 18 Z cart. 8), Folder Santé—Subfolder Medecins.

103. ADP, Publicité (D 18 Z cart. 8), Folder Santé—Subfolder Pharmaciens.

104. *AF* (2 September 1922): 4.

105. Ibid. (29 July 1922): 4.

106. For just a very small sample of these ads, see *ILL* (28 July 1928): xvi; *PS* (26 November 1935): 7; and *GRIN* (16 April 1937): 13 and (14 January 1938): 14. See also the advertisement from *Le Petit Parisien* from 15 October 1922 collected in ADP, Publicité (D 18 Z cart. 8), Folder Santé—Subfolder Pharmaciens.

107. *AF* (12 August 1920): 4.

108. For a few general examples of ads of this variety, see, for Germany, *DAZ*, LAB (16 April 1926): n.p.; *VRW*, LAB (13 December 1926): n.p.; and *VB* (5 March 1939): 24. For France, see *GRIN* (20 April 1934): 14; *PS* (22 November 1935): 3; and *ILL* (11 July 1936): xiv.

109. *VB* (21 February 1939): 10. Another Spalt tablets ad appears in *VB* (7 September 1937): 16.

110. *VB* (14 July 1935): n.p.

111. *DAZ* (25 October 1922): n.p.

112. *GRIN* (12 January 1934): 14.

113. *PS* (21 November 1935): 7.

114. For a few examples of this, see *AF* (27 March 1924): 6; and *GRIN* (13 May 1932): 10 and (7 September 1934): 14.

115. *PS* (4 November 1935): 7.

116. See, for instance, *GRIN* (18 May 1934): 16.

117. Not surprisingly, many of these testimonials were composed by advertisers, not actual customers. The more frequent appearance of such testimonials in French publicity can be attributed to the fact that, in Germany, the Nazi regime forbade the use of those that were not verifi-

ably authentic. See Berghoff, "Times Change and We Change with Them," 135; and de Grazia, *Irresistible Empire*, 275.

118. *PS* (21 November 1935): 7. See also *AF* (17 March 1923): 4; and *GRIN* (21 June 1929): 8.

119. *ILL* (13 April 1935): xxxiii. See also *AF* (26 March 1924): 4; and *PS* (4 November 1935): 7.

120. *ILL* (4 December 1937): xlii. See also *AF* (13 December 1927): 4.

121. *VRW,* LAB (6 December 1926): n.p.

122. *DAZ,* LAB (23 April 1926): n.p. See also *VRW,* LAB (23 November 1926): n.p.

123. *MIP,* SBB (7 February 1935): 169. See also *FZ,* LAB (31 August 1920): 6; and *GRM,* LAB (25 December 1927): n.p.

124. *VRW,* LAB (16 January 1927): n.p. See also *FZ,* LAB (20 September 1920): 3; and *VRW,* LAB (17 December 1926): n.p.

125. *ILL* (11 December 1937): xxxvi. See also *AF* (25 September 1920): 4; and *MAT,* LC (18 October 1923): 7.

126. *OEU* (11 October 1926): 5. See also *MAT,* LC (7 January 1920): 4 and (30 October 1922): 6; and *PS* (6 November 1935): 10.

127. *AF* (15 June 1923): 4. See also *MAT,* LC (26 May 1931): 6.

128. *GRIN* (4 May 1939): 14; emphasis in original.

129. Ibid.

130. Denman, "Visualizing the Nation," 189–197; and Sherman, "Monuments, Mourning and Masculinity in France after World War I." See also Peukert's analysis of the post–World War I "warrior male" discourse in Weimar Germany; Peukert, *The Weimar Republic,* 105–106.

FOUR. EVE'S CONQUEST OF THE STEERING WHEEL

1. FORN, Galeries Lafayette agenda, 1933, 11–12. A similar claim about the centrality of the automobile as symbol of female independence was made in an article in the *agenda* of the Grands Magasins du Louvre from 1926. See FORN, Grands Magasins du Louvre agenda, 1926, 85–90, esp. 87.

2. Zurbrugg, "Oh what a feeling!" 9.

3. Sachs, *For Love of the Automobile,* vii. See also Holden, "More Than a Marque," 28–39; and Möser, "World War I and the Creation of Desire for Automobiles in Germany," 210–215.

4. O'Sullivan, "Transports of Difference and Delight," 289. See also Holden, "More Than a Marque," 28–39; Möser, "World War I and the Creation of Desire for Automobiles in Germany," 200; Sachs, *For Love of the Automobile,* 91–92; and Scharff, *Taking the Wheel,* 165–169.

5. Rhys, *The Motor Industry,* 220–221.

6. Jones, *The Politics of Transport in Twentieth-Century France,* 24; Fridenson, "The Spread of the Automobile Revolution," 90; and Möser, "World War I and the Creation of Desire for Automobiles in Germany," 197–207.

7. Bellon, *Mercedes in Peace and War,* 14; Edelmann, *Vom Luxusgut zum Gebrauchsgegenstand,* 22–27; Jones, *The Politics of Transport in Twentieth-Century France,* 24; Laux, introduction to *The Automobile Revolution,* xiii–xvi; Möser, "World War I and the Creation of Desire for Automobiles in Germany," 208; and Rhys, *The Motor Industry,* 5, 220–221.

8. Laux, *The European Automobile Industry,* 74; Fridenson, "French Automobile Marketing,"

140; Fridenson, "The Spread of the Automobile Revolution," 103; Harp, *Marketing Michelin,* 192; and Rhys, *The Motor Industry,* 16.

9. Overy, "Cars, Roads, and Economic Recovery in Germany," 468; and Rhys, *The Motor Industry,* 16. See also Overy, "Heralds of Modernity," 65; and Scharff, *Taking the Wheel,* 112.

10. Laux, *The European Automobile Industry,* 76; Fridenson, "The Spread of the Automobile Revolution," 103–104.

11. Laux, *The European Automobile Industry,* 78, 100. See also Fridenson, "French Automobile Marketing," 133–134; and Fridenson, "The Spread of the Automobile Revolution," 103–104.

12. Fridenson, "French Automobile Marketing," 133.

13. Fridenson, "The Spread of the Automobile Revolution," 103; Laux, *The European Automobile Industry,* 82; and Reich, *The Fruits of Fascism,* 296. For more information on the operations of the Ford Motor Company across Europe, see Wilkins and Hill, *American Business Abroad.*

14. Eckermann, *World History of the Automobile,* 85; Fridenson, "The Spread of the Automobile Revolution," 107; Laux, *The European Automobile Industry,* 74; Overy, "Cars, Roads, and Economic Recovery in Germany," 468, 483; and Rhys, *The Motor Industry,* 16. See also Bellon, *Mercedes in Peace and War,* 14; and Edelmann, *Vom Luxusgut zum Gebrauchsgegenstand,* 14.

15. Laux, *The European Automobile Industry,* 89–90; Blaich, "The Development of the Distribution Sector in the German Car Industry," 95; Fridenson, "The Spread of the Automobile Revolution," 106–107; Möser, "World War I and the Creation of Desire for Automobiles in Germany," 195–196; and Overy, "Cars, Roads, and Economic Recovery in Germany," 466.

16. Blaich, "Why Did the Pioneer Fall Behind?" 154; and Eckermann, *World History of the Automobile,* 86. See also Edelmann, *Vom Luxusgut zum Gebrauchsgegenstand,* 61–69; Fridenson, "The Spread of the Automobile Revolution," 106; and Overy, "Cars, Roads, and Economic Recovery in Germany," 466–467.

17. Laux, *The European Automobile Industry,* 92; Ludvigsen, *Opel,* 46. See also Edelmann, *Vom Luxusgut zum Gebrauchsgegenstand,* 69–74; Fridenson, "Spread of the Automobile Revolution," 106; and Sachs, *For Love of the Automobile,* 42.

18. Edelmann, *Vom Luxusgut zum Gebrauchsgegenstand,* 115–118; Laux, *The European Automobile Industry,* 113; and Ludvigsen, *Opel,* 49.

19. Fridenson, "The Spread of the Automobile Revolution," 140; and Rhys, *The Motor Industry,* 15. See also Edelmann, *Vom Luxusgut zum Gebrauchsgegenstand,* 129–133; and Overy, "Cars, Roads, and Economic Recovery in Germany," 483.

20. Blaich, "Why Did the Pioneer Fall Behind?" 159; Edelmann, *Vom Luxusgut zum Gebrauchsgegenstand,* 168; Fridenson, "The Spread of the Automobile Revolution," 144; Overy, "Cars, Roads, and Economic Recovery in Germany," 468–469, 483; and Koshar, "Germans at the Wheel," 216. See also Eckermann, *World History of the Automobile,* 101; and Ludvigsen, *Opel,* 96.

21. Overy, "Cars, Roads, and Economic Recovery in Germany," 472–481.

22. Blaich, "Why Did the Pioneer Fall Behind?" 153–154; Eckermann, *World History of the Automobile,* 111; Laux, *The European Automobile Industry,* 112; Overy, "Cars, Roads, and Economic Recovery in Germany," 474, 480, 483; and Sachs, *For Love of the Automobile,* 54.

23. Overy, "Cars, Roads, and Economic Recovery in Germany," 472. See also Fridenson,

"The Spread of the Automobile Revolution," 144; and Laux, *The European Automobile Industry,* 93.

24. Laux, *The European Automobile Industry,* 93, 113–114.

25. Reich, *The Fruits of Fascism,* 112–119.

26. Berghoff, "Enticement and Deprivation," 177–178; Blaich, "Why Did the Pioneer Fall Behind?" 155–156; Edelmann, *Vom Luxusgut zum Gebrauchsgegenstand,* 202–208; Möser, "World War I and the Creation of Desire for Automobiles in Germany," 219–220; Reich, *The Fruits of Fascism,* 147–158; and Sachs, *For Love of the Automobile,* 59–62.

27. Overy, "Cars, Roads, and Economic Recovery in Germany," 468.

28. Rhys, *The Motor Industry,* 15–16. See also Eckermann, *World History of the Automobile,* 102.

29. Jones, *The Politics of Transport in Twentieth-Century France,* 55, 100. See also Harp, *Marketing Michelin,* 213.

30. Laux, *The European Automobile Industry,* 120, 124.

31. Ibid., 130.

32. Sachs, *For Love of the Automobile,* 32–33, 40–42.

33. Ibid., 40. See also Koshar, "Germans at the Wheel," 216.

34. Berghoff, "Enticement and Deprivation," 177.

35. Ibid., 178; Blaich, "Why Did the Pioneer Fall Behind?" 155–156.

36. Reich, *The Fruits of Fascism,* 157–158; Eckermann, *World History of the Automobile,* 121; and Laux, *The European Automobile Industry,* 116–117.

37. Zurbrugg, "Oh what a feeling!" 19–20.

38. Sachs, *For Love of the Automobile,* 92–97. De Certeau makes a related point about individual immobility on a train; see de Certeau, *The Practice of Everyday Life,* 111–114.

39. Sachs, *For Love of the Automobile,* 92–109. See also Overy, "Heralds of Modernity," 62–63, 71.

40. Roberts, for example, analyzes the ways in which cars represented an image of freedom and power for women in the immediate postwar years. Roberts, "Samson and Delilah Revisited," 674–675. See also Harp, *Marketing Michelin,* 220–221. For a good example of commentary with the same tenor in the United States, see Scharff, *Taking the Wheel,* 166–167, 171–173.

41. *OEU* (15 March 1925): 6.

42. *GRIN* (20 June 1930): 12.

43. Ibid. (22 August 1930): 12. See also the ad for window manufacturer Huet in *ILL* (4 July 1936): xvii.

44. *ILL* (4 October 1930): 113–116.

45. *GRIN* (12 July 1929): 10.

46. *OEU* (13 July 1927): 8. See also similar Monet and Goyon ads in *MAT,* LC (8 August 1923): 6; and *AF* (10 May 1927): 4. In addition, a Buick ad from 1928 invokes the theme that men will use an auto to travel to work; see *MAT,* LC (3 March 1928): 5.

47. *AF* (10 April 1927): 6.

48. *NPZ,* LAB (18 April 1930): n.p. The use of cars for business travel purposes was also raised in an ad featuring male figures in *DAZ,* LAB (12 December 1922): n.p.

49. *NPZ,* LAB (18 May 1930): n.p.

50. *VB* (18 February 1939): 10.

51. Ibid. (7 December 1936): 16.

52. *IZ* (3 May 1934): 547.

53. *DAZ,* LAB (4 May 1926): n.p.

54. For just a couple of examples, see *IZ* (30 January 1936): 161 and (12 March 1936): 328.

55. Koonz, *Mothers in the Fatherland,* 179.

56. Ibid., 196–198; Bleuel, *Sex and Society in Nazi Germany,* 67; Frevert, *Women in German History,* 222; Wilke and Wagner, "Family and Household," 143.

57. Greenfield, O'Connell, and Reid, "Gender, Consumer Culture and the Middle-Class Male," esp. 185, 192; Reekie, "Impulsive Women, Predictable Men," 365–372; Oldenziel, "Boys and Their Toys," esp. 86–87, 94–95; Oldenziel, *Making Technology Masculine,* 10–11; Scharff, *Taking the Wheel,* 119–126.

58. Scharff, *Taking the Wheel,* 119; see also 120–122. See also Oldenziel, "Boys and Their Toys," 94–95; and Sachs, *For Love of the Automobile,* 38.

59. *VB* (5 December 1936): 19. See also the Ford ad in *DAZ,* LAB (11 May 1926): n.p.; and the ad for Adler cars in *NPZ,* LAB (18 April 1930): n.p.

60. *VB* (25 June 1939): 9. See also the Ford ads in *DAZ,* LAB (7 April 1926): n.p. In addition, see the Auto Union ad in *VB* (10 June 1934): n.p.; and ads for Zündapp motorcycles in *VB* (2 June 1934): n.p. and (27–29 March 1937): 19.

61. *VB* (29 June 1937): 9.

62. Ibid. (9 June 1934, supplement): n.p.

63. *ILL* (7 October 1933): xlii.

64. *GRIN* (15 October 1937): 10. See also ads for Delage automobiles in *AF* (31 March 1921): 3; and *MAT,* LC (28 May 1921): 3.

65. ADP, Publicité (D 18 Z cart. 10), Folder Transports—Subfolder Automobiles. See also the ad for Oldsmobile in *MAT,* LC (8 August 1929): 7.

66. *VZ* (3 August 1933): n.p.

67. *VB* (22 August 1936): n.p.

68. FORN, Galeries Lafayette agenda, 1933, 14.

69. *ILL* (7 June 1930): xxxiii. There is a quite similar advertisement for Goodrich tires in *ILL* (31 May 1930): xli.

70. *VEN* (3 January 1936): 10; *VEN* (3 April 1936): 7; and *VEN* (29 May 1936): 8. See also the Buick ad in *ILL* (20 October 1928): xxxi.

71. This ad appeared in both *MAT,* LC (29 November 1925): 6; and *OEU* (29 November 1925): 6.

72. *GRIN* (27 April 1934): 6. See also the ad for Monet and Goyon motorized bikes in *MAT,* LC (23 May 1921): 4.

73. FORN, Grands Magasins du Louvre agenda, 1921, 89. See also BHVP, Bon Marché agenda, 1928, 101.

74. *ILL* (18 July 1936): ix; *GRIN* (2 July 1937): 6; *ILL* (9 July 1938): xiii.

75. *ILL* (3 October 1925): 358–359.

76. Scholars working in a variety of national contexts have noted this type of ideology; see, for instance, Greenfield, O'Connell, and Reid, "Gender, Consumer Culture and the Middle-

Class Male," 190; Reekie, "Impulsive Women, Predictable Men," 368–371; and Scharff, *Taking the Wheel,* 115.

77. *SIMP* (9 January 1928): 558.

78. *VB* (11 March 1939): 5. See also the cartoon in *IZ* (14 December 1933): 70.

79. *DAZ,* LAB (4 May 1926): n.p.

80. *GRIN* (2 August 1929): 12. See also the ad for Ford in *OEU* (23 October 1931): 3, which focuses on the vehicle's "docility."

81. *AF* (10 May 1927): 4. See also *OEU* (13 July 1927): 8.

82. *AF* (10 April 1927): 6.

83. *NPZ,* LAB (18 April 1930): n.p.

84. Ibid. (18 May 1930): n.p.

85. Mohun, "Laundrymen Construct Their World," 99. Oldenziel has demonstrated a similar discursive process at work with respect to American engineers and waged laborers, whereby the former asserted their technical authority over the latter, attempting to ensure their position of dominance over workers; see Oldenziel, *Making Technology Masculine,* 100–105.

86. Lungstrum, "*Metropolis* and the Technosexual Woman of German Modernity," 129. See also Horowitz and Mohun, introduction to *His and Hers,* 2; Oldenziel, "Boys and Their Toys," esp. 60–63, 94–95; Oldenziel, *Making Technology Masculine,* 141–147; and Reekie, "Impulsive Women, Predictable Men," 364–366.

87. Lungstrum, "*Metropolis* and the Technosexual Woman of German Modernity," 139.

88. *GRIN* (15 April 1932): 12.

89. Scharff, *Taking the Wheel,* 167.

90. *ILL* (4 October 1930): 113–116.

91. FORN, Grands Magasins du Louvre agenda, 1926, 88.

92. *GRIN* (20 May 1938): 8.

93. Goffman, *Gender Advertisements,* 37. See also Scharff, *Taking the Wheel,* 166–167.

94. *VB* (25 March 1939): 7.

95. For just a few examples, see the ads for Opel in *VZ* (17 August 1933): n.p. and (8 October 1934): n.p.; the ad for Daimler-Benz, ibid. (31 March 1935): n.p.; and the Hanomag ad, ibid. (30 January 1936, special issue): 30.

96. *VB* (22 August 1936): n.p.

97. *KZ,* LAB (19 January 1936): n.p.

98. Almost no French advertisements make any mention of the possibility of a test drive. While this could be due in part to differing customer service approaches in the two countries, I would attribute it more to the relatively high number of German auto ads for specific dealers; most French ads were for the auto companies as a whole.

99. *VB* (28 January 1936): n.p. See also the Adler ad in *NPZ,* LAB (18 May 1930): n.p.

100. Greenfield, O'Connell, and Reid, "Gender, Consumer Culture and the Middle-Class Male," 190; Parkin, *Food Is Love,* 16–17; Reekie, "Impulsive Women, Predictable Men," 368–371; Scharff, *Taking the Wheel,* 115.

101. ADP, Publicité (D 18 Z cart. 10), Folder Transports—Subfolder Automobiles.

102. *VB* (11 June 1939): 9.

103. *DAZ,* LAB (11 May 1926): n.p.

104. *WM* (March 1937): 1–8.

105. Simonton, *A History of European Women's Work,* 267.

106. Most numerous were ads for Esso Oil. For a few examples, see a series of ads that ran in late March 1937: *VB* (23 March 1937): 11, (24 March 1937): 5, and (31 March 1937): 10. See also *KZ,* LAB (15 December 1935): 9. Samples of ads for Shell Oil can be found in *VB* (21 October 1934): n.p. and (18 July 1938): 7. A Mobil Oil ad from *VB* (25–26 March 1937): 19 is typical of that company's marketing. A couple of ads for Standard Oil can be found in *VB* (10 June 1939): 9 and (16 June 1939): 9.

107. For a couple of examples, see the BP ad in *VRW,* LAB (22 August 1930): n.p.; and the ad for Esso Oil in *KZ,* LAB (2 November 1935): 3.

108. For just a few examples, see the Zenith carburetor ad in *AF* (6 July 1923): n.p.; the ad for Standard Oil in *OEU* (14 September 1927): 3; the Shell Oil ads in *OEU* (5 July 1929): 3, and *ILL* (13 August 1932): xi; and the ad for Esso Oil in *GRIN* (1 July 1938): 18.

109. For a few examples of this type, see the Shell Oil ads in *ILL* (4 June 1932): xxiii and (16 July 1932): xvii; as well as the ad for Mobil Oil in *GRIN* (20 April 1934): 11.

110. A couple of ads for Spido Oil provide good examples. See *GRIN* (13 May 1932): 10 and (3 June 1932): 10. Examples can also be found in Mobil Oil ads in *PS* (7 November 1935): 5 and (22 November 1935): 5. It was generally this type of advertisement, moreover, that was used when the product was not motor oil, but rather a different item related to auto maintenance. See, for example, the ad for Schrader tire-pressure gauges in *ILL* (28 June 1930): xxix. See also the advertising flyers for Peugeot motorcycles in ADP, Publicité (D 18 Z cart. 10), Folder Transports—Subfolder Cycles et Motos.

111. This is a Shell Oil ad from *ILL* (12 July 1930): xxi.

112. ADP, Publicité (D 18 Z cart. 10), Folder Transports—Subfolder Automobiles.

113. *GRIN* (26 March 1937): 13. See also the ad for Northeaster car horns from *ILL* (8 September 1928): xxi, which features a woman driver and makes a similar comment about consulting one's mechanic.

114. *GRIN* (25 June 1937): 18. See also the ad for Texaco Oil in *MAT,* LC (16 November 1928): 6; the Shell Oil ad in *ILL* (14 May 1932): xxv; and the Esso Oil ad in *GRIN* (14 May 1937): 20. One of the rare occasions in which women were pictured in such ads in Germany is likewise an ad for Esso that utilizes similar imagery; see *MIP,* SBB (28 April 1938): 591.

115. FORN, Grands Magasins du Louvre agenda, 1926, 85–90.

116. *ILL* (5 October 1929): 266.

117. Kuisel, *Seducing the French,* 233. See also Harp, *Marketing Michelin,* 187–188.

118. Beale, *The Modernist Enterprise,* 6–7; see also 11–47. See also de Grazia, *Irresistible Empire;* and Furlough, "Selling the American Way in Interwar France," 491–493, 502–503.

119. Beale, *The Modernist Enterprise,* 4–5. In a more general European context, see de Grazia, "Americanism for Export," 74–80; and de Grazia, "The Arts of Purchase," esp. 225.

120. Kuisel, *Seducing the French,* xii, 6.

121. Beale, *The Modernist Enterprise,* 80. See also Furlough, "Selling the American Way in Interwar France," 502–503.

122. Beale, *The Modernist Enterprise,* 71–82. See also Harp, *Marketing Michelin,* esp. 4–10, 189–200, 220–221.

123. Nolan, *Visions of Modernity*, esp. 5–11, 22–26, 109–120. See also de Grazia, *Irresistible Empire;* Schäfer, "Amerikanismus im Dritten Reich," 199–215; and Tower, "Ultramodern and Ultraprimitive," 94.

124. Eckermann, *World History of the Automobile*, 84.

125. de Grazia, "Americanism for Export," 80.

126. Nolan, *Visions of Modernity*, 70–75.

127. Herf, *Reactionary Modernism*, 2; see also 1–3, 16–18, 46–47, 217–227. See also de Grazia, *Irresistible Empire*, 21–22; Harvey, "Culture and Society in Weimar Germany," 291–295; and Nolan, *Visions of Modernity*, 9–11.

128. Herf, *Reactionary Modernism*, 47.

129. Sachs, *For Love of the Automobile*, 59.

130. Herf, *Reactionary Modernism*, 208. See also Möser, "World War I and the Creation of Desire for Automobiles in Germany," 215–218.

131. Qtd. in Herf, *Reactionary Modernism*, 196.

132. Berghoff has noted this phenomenon in a specifically German context. See Berghoff, "Enticement and Deprivation," esp. 167.

133. For a few examples, see *GRIN* (6 April 1934): 10; *PS* (9 November 1935): 16; and *GRIN* (23 April 1937): 13.

134. For just a few examples, see *AF* (8 October 1922): 4 and (11 February 1923): 6; and *GRIN* (19 December 1930): 14.

135. ADP, Publicité (D 18 Z cart. 10), Folder Transports—Subfolder Cycles et Motos. For examples of other auto ads that likewise invoked French manufacture, see the Rosengart ad in *GRIN* (19 October 1934): 18; and the Hotchkiss ad, ibid. (26 February 1932): 10.

136. *GRM,* LAB (11 December 1927): n.p. See also the Stoewer ad in *VRW,* LAB (18 September 1930): n.p.

137. *VB* (5 September 1937): 3. See also the BMW motorcycle ad in *DAZ,* LAB (4 April 1926): n.p.; and the Opel ad in *VB* (30 January 1936, special issue): 9.

138. *VB* (17 June 1934): n.p. See also the Auto Union ads in *VB* (2 June 1934): n.p. and (3 June 1934): n.p.; as well as the Mercedes-Benz ad in *KZ,* LAB (23 October 1938): n.p.

139. *ILL* (18 July 1936): ix.

140. *VB* (18 February 1939): 2. See also the Opel ad, ibid. (20 December 1938): 5, which is quite similar in imagery and tone, as is the ad for Mercedes-Benz in *MIP,* SBB (13 August 1936): 1120.

141. *VB* (3 August 1936): n.p. A 1930 Daimler-Benz ad likewise utilizes an image of the globe; see *VRW,* LAB (23 September 1930): n.p.

142. *KZ,* LAB (11 December 1938): n.p. See also the ad for Adler in *KZ,* LAB (15 December 1935): 19; and the ad for auto parts manufacturer SKF in *VB* (5 September 1937, supplement): 29.

143. For just a few examples, all from *GRIN,* see (20 May 1938): 12, (3 June 1938): 14, and (17 June 1938): 16, emphasis in original.

144. *VB* (15 June 1934): n.p. See also Mobil Oil advertisements in *VB* (5 July 1935): n.p. and (3 December 1938): 7. An ad for Shell Oil, ibid. (18 November 1938): 7, is comparable as well.

145. The reasons behind this merit further exploration. Whether due to the company's ef-

forts to get into the Nazi regime's good graces, its stronger position and hence greater frequency of advertising in Germany, or some other factor, this link to the nation in 1930s Germany was noticeably absent in Ford's advertising in France.

146. *VB* (12 June 1934): n.p.

147. Ibid. (18 February 1939): 8.

148. Ibid, (30 January 1936): n.p.

149. Reich, *The Fruits of Fascism,* 159.

150. *VB* (5 March 1939): 17. Generally speaking, however, incorporation of the swastika into advertisements in the Nazi era was quite rare, due to the legal restrictions on its use for advertising purposes. Berghoff explains that the Nazis were concerned that the flood of consumer goods emerging in the early 1930s with the Nazi emblem (including scrub brushes and playing cards) could demean Nazi symbols, thus leading to the passage of a law in May 1933 regulating the use of such symbols. See Berghoff, "Times Change and We Change with Them," 138–139.

151. *VB* (20 February 1939): 12.

152. Harp, *Marketing Michelin,* 221.

153. Nolan, *Visions of Modernity,* 124.

154. Ibid., 120–124.

155. Sachs, *For Love of the Automobile,* 91.

FIVE. AT WORK AND AT PLAY

1. McMillan, *Housewife or Harlot,* 125–126.

2. Karen Offen, "Body Politics," 140–143; and Sherman, "Monuments, Mourning and Masculinity in France after World War I," 89.

3. Dyer, *Population and Society in Twentieth-Century France,* 67. See also Offen, "Body Politics," 143–144; and Zerner, "De la couture aux presse," 9–11.

4. Peukert, *The Weimar Republic,* 86–87.

5. Boxer and Quataert, "Overview, 1890 to the Present," 245–246.

6. Ibid.

7. Ibid.; Frevert, *Women in German History,* 176–177; Petro, *Joyless Streets,* 70; and Peukert, *The Weimar Republic,* 96–97.

8. Stephenson, *Women in Nazi Germany,* 54; and Bridenthal, Grossmann, and Kaplan, "Women in Weimar and Nazi Germany," 25.

9. Koonz, *Mothers in the Fatherland,* 102; and Frevert, *Women in German History,* 217–218. See also Grossmann, *Reforming Sex,* 5–6.

10. Boxer and Quataert, "Overview, 1890 to the Present," 246; Czarnowski, "The Value of Marriage for the *Volksgemeinschaft,*" 100–101; and Mouton, *Nurturing the Nation,* 56–60. Czarnowski and Mouton note that such loans were contingent on the couple being deemed "fit" for marriage.

11. Boxer and Quataert, "Overview, 1890 to the Present," 248–249; Stephenson, *Women in Nazi Society,* 98; and Stephenson, *Women in Nazi Germany,* 53–54.

12. Koonz, *Mothers in the Fatherland,* 179.

13. Bridenthal, Grossmann, and Kaplan, "Women in Weimar and Nazi Germany," 25;

Koonz, *Mothers in the Fatherland*, 196–198; Stephenson, *Women in Nazi Society,* 99–103; and Bleuel, *Sex and Society in Nazi Germany,* 62–68. See also Kessler, *"Die deutsche Frau,"* 23–25. Frevert has noted an important exception, however, in that the regime continued to oppose and restrict the presence of women as public employees and in some professional occupations; see Frevert, *Women in German History,* 219–220.

14. Boxer and Quataert, "Overview, 1890 to the Present," 248–249; Stephenson, *Women in Nazi Society,* 98; and Stephenson, *Women in Nazi Germany,* 53–54.

15. Bridenthal, Grossmann, and Kaplan, "Women in Weimar and Nazi Germany," 25; and Mouton, *Nurturing the Nation,* 61.

16. Frevert, *Women in German History,* 177.

17. Ibid. See also Peukert, *The Weimar Republic,* 96.

18. See Boxer and Quataert, "Overview, 1890 to the Present," 245–246; Frevert, *Women in German History,* 178; Peukert, *The Weimar Republic,* 96–97; and Wilke and Wagner, "Family and Household," 132–133.

19. Offen, "Body Politics," 143–144; Reynolds, *France between the Wars,* 92–95; Singer, "Technology and Social Change," 325; Tilly and Scott, *Women, Work, and Family,* 149–151, 157–162; and Zerner, "De la couture aux presses," 16–20.

20. Offen, "Body Politics," 143–144. See also McMillan, *Housewife or Harlot,* 119–121; and Tilly and Scott, *Women, Work, and Family,* 157, 162. In addition, there was a widespread perception that, if economic conditions deteriorated precipitously, such female employees would be much more easily expendable than their male counterparts. See McMillan, *Housewife or Harlot,* 119. See also Weber, *The Hollow Years,* 83. Indeed, in that context it is noteworthy that ads depicting women as employees did not appear regularly until the very last years of the 1920s, when some semblance of broader economic order had been restored.

As in Germany, women who tried to enter into occupations still culturally constructed as masculine were far less successful; yet in contrast to Germany, their high visibility, caused by the social anxiety they created, masked the small numbers of women who actually broke into the ranks of masculine-dominated jobs, such as doctors and lawyers. See Roberts, "Rationalization, Vocational Guidance and the Reconstruction of Female Identity in Post-war France," 369; and Weber, *The Hollow Years,* 82. See also Zerner, "De la couture aux presses," 20–25.

21. *OEU* (2 September 1929): 6. See also *AF* (2 January 1929): 3.

22. *OEU* (8 October 1930): 7. See also *MAT,* LC (16 November 1932): 6.

23. *OEU* (8 October 1930): 7.

24. *La République* (22 July 1932): 4.

25. See, for instances, *IZ* (18 April 1935): 530 and (19 November 1936): 720.

26. *MIP,* SBB (4 April 1935): 442.

27. *La République* (5 August 1932): 4.

28. Allen has discussed hostility across Western Europe toward working married women, especially mothers; see Allen, *Feminism and Motherhood in Western Europe,* 149–159. Moreover, France had a high proportion of married women engaged in waged employment compared to other European states; see Clark, "The Primary Education of French Girls," 421.

29. Roberts, "Rationalization, Vocational Guidance and the Reconstruction of Female Identity in Post-war France," 369–371. See also Clark, "The Primary Education of French Girls," 421; and McMillan, *Housewife or Harlot,* 118–119.

30. See, for instance, *OEU* (29 September 1927): 6; *MAT,* LC (29 September 1927): 3; and *OEU* (8 September 1929): 6.

31. *SIMP* (16 September 1934): 295. See also *IZ* (28 September 1933): 342.

32. See, for example, Cross, *A Social History of Leisure since 1600,* 193–196. See also Baranowski and Furlough, introduction to *Being Elsewhere,* 5–6, who specifically treat the relationship between consumerism and tourism.

33. Baranowski and Furlough, introduction to *Being Elsewhere,* 8; Hau, *The Cult of Health and Beauty in Germany,* 177; Koshar, *German Travel Cultures,* 71. See also Reinartz, *Sport in Hamburg,* 187–189; and Sachse, "Freizeit zwischen Betrieb und Volksgemeinschaft," 305–328.

34. For instance, see Koshar, *German Travel Cultures,* 71. See also Harvey, "Culture and Society in Weimar Germany," 288.

35. Baranowski, "Strength through Joy," 224; and Koshar, *German Travel Cultures,* 123–124. See also Baranowski, *Strength through Joy.*

36. See, for example, Merritt, "Strength through Joy," 74–77.

37. Koshar, *German Travel Cultures,* esp. 13, 71, 101, 109–110, 116–117. See also Baranowski, "Strength through Joy," 213.

38. Mackaman, *Leisure Settings,* 123–124; and Mackaman, "The Tactics of Retreat," esp. 36.

39. See Cross, "Vacations for All," 599–601; Furlough, "Making Mass Vacations," 249; and Jackson, "Le temps des loisirs," 226–236. See also Boyer, *Le tourisme,* 148–155; Cacérès, *Loisirs et travail du moyen âge à nos jours,,* 187–190; and Rauch, *Vacances en France,* 9–10.

40. Holt, "Sport, the French, and the Third Republic," 294; and Holt, *Sport and Society in Modern France,* 11–12.

41. The European term "football," rather than the American "soccer," will be used throughout this chapter.

42. Holt, *Sport and Society in Modern France,* 5. Along similar lines, Fieschi discusses the increasing presence and visibility of sport in interwar French daily life in everything from press coverage to shop windows; see Fieschi, *Histoire du sport français,* 77. It has also been argued, however, that truly widespread participation in sport in France did not come to fruition until the Popular Front mandated paid vacations; see Saillard, "Le vêtement de sport," 7–8.

43. See, for instance, Peukert, *The Weimar Republic,* 175–176. At the same time, it should be noted, some scholars have somewhat qualified this assertion. See Eisenberg, "Massensport in der Weimarer Republik," 137–177.

44. Holt, *Sport and Society in Modern France,* 3–4. See also Arnaud, "Sportifs de tous les pays . . . !" 20–21; and Holt, "Sport, the French, and the Third Republic," 289, 297–298.

45. Hartmann-Tews and Luetkens, "The Inclusion of Women into the German Sport System," 54; Peukert, *The Weimar Republic,* 175–176; and Pfister and von der Lippe, "Women's Participation in Sports and the Olympic Games in Germany and Norway," 33.

46. Becker, "Sportsmen in the Machine World," 165.

47. MacCannell, *The Tourist,* 3.

48. Ibid., 1.

49. Baranowski and Furlough, introduction to *Being Elsewhere,* 1, 8; Löfgren, *On Holiday,* 267–273; and Urry, *Consuming Places,* 163–164.

50. Koshar, "Seeing, Traveling, and Consuming," 4.

51. Baranowski and Furlough, introduction to *Being Elsewhere,* 21.

52. MacCannell, *The Tourist,* 13. Koshar makes a similar claim in a specifically German context; see Koshar, *German Travel Cultures,* 203.

53. Pfister et al., "Women and Football," 1–2, 19–20; Pfister and Hartmann-Tews, "Women and Sport," 1, 10; and Terret, "Femmes, sport, identité et acculturation," 46–48. See also Kinnaird, Kothari, and Hall, "Tourism," 5; Löfgren, *On Holiday,* 100; and Mauer, "Tourismus im Visier der 'Gender'-Debatte," esp. 153–156.

54. Pfister and Hartmann-Tews, "Women and Sport," 11.

55. Pfister et al., "Women and Football," 19–20. See also Hau, *The Cult of Health and Beauty in Germany,* 182; and Melling, "Cultural Differentiation, Shared Aspiration," 28, 40–41.

56. Carr, "Sport and Party Ideology in the Third Reich," 4–6; Frame, "Gretchen, Girl, Garçonne?" 29–31; Guttmann, *Women's Sports,* 184; Naul, "History of Sport and Physical Education in Germany," 25; Pfister, "Conflicting Femininities," 93–94; Pfister, "Sport for Women," 169–170; and Terret, "Femmes, sport, identité et acculturation," 42–44.

57. Pfister, "Breaking Bounds," 107; and Pfister, "The Medical Discourse on Female Physical Culture in Germany," 191–198. For evidence regarding similar medical justifications in France, see Terret, "Femmes, sport, identité et acculturation," 43–44.

58. Hargreaves, *Heroines of Sport,* 2; Hargreaves, *Sporting Females,* 169–171; Hartmann-Tews and Luetkens, "The Inclusion of Women into the German Sport System," 54; Hau, *The Cult of Health and Beauty in Germany,* 63–64, 181–182; Pfister and von der Lippe, "Women's Participation in Sports and the Olympic Games in Germany and Norway," 34; and Willis, "Women in Sport in Ideology," 122–123.

59. Müller, "Turnen und Sport im sozialen Wandel," 131; and Pfister et al, "Women and Football," 12–13.

60. Pfister, "Conflicting Femininities," 101–102.

61. It should be noted that scholars have shown that women's sporting participation did increase in the interwar years. In the French case, see, for example, Holt, "Sport, the French, and the Third Republic," esp. 297; and Terret, "Femmes, sport, identité et acculturation," 42–46. With respect to Germany, see Müller, "Turnen und Sport im sozialen Wandel," 131–132, 136; Pfister, "Sport for Women," 168–169; and Pfister and von der Lippe, "Women's Participation in Sports and the Olympic Games in Germany and Norway," 34. See also Eisenberg, "Massensport in der Weimarer Republik," 158–162. See also Guttmann, *Women's Sports,* 160–161, which discusses the high level of participation in sports by working-class German women, particularly single women.

62. The example of Weimar has been much less analyzed in this regard, perhaps because its exclusion from the international sports scene for a considerable part of its existence muted the enunciation of a strong connection between national prestige and sport.

63. Guttmann, *Women's Sports,* 183. For discussions of the role of Americanism in sport, see Becker, "Weimarer Sportrepublik," 183–184, 199–206; Becker, "Sportsmen in the Machine World," 154–155; and Krüger, "We are sure to have found the true reasons for the American superiority in sports," 53–62.

64. Pfister, "Conflicting Femininities," 92–93.

65. Arnaud, "French Sport and the Emergence of Authoritarian Regimes," esp. 114–119; Arnaud, "Sportifs de tous les pays . . . !" 13–14; and Holt, "Interwar Sport and Interwar Relations," 210–211. See also Spivak, "Prestige national et sport," 184–185.

66. Arnaud, "French Sport and the Emergence of Authoritarian Regimes," 115. See also Guttmann, *Women's Sports*, 165; and Krüger, "The Role of Sport in German International Politics," 80–81.

67. Arnaud, "French Sport and the Emergence of Authoritarian Regimes," esp. 116–119; and Spivak, "Prestige national et sport," 185–186. The fear of German athletic triumphs may have been well founded, for as Krüger notes, at the first postwar Olympics at which the Germans competed, in 1928, they won the second-most medals of any country at the games; see Krüger, "The Role of Sport in German International Politics," 83.

68. For a few examples, see *OEU* (6 August 1921): n.p.; *AF* (15 February 1929): 3; *MAT*, LC (17 June 1929): 6; FORN, Nouvelles Galeries "A La Ménagère" agenda, 1923; the 1925 Printemps catalog in ADP, Publicité Commerciale (D 18 Z cart. 7), Folder Le Printemps, 1916–1927, 12; and the 1934 catalog of the Bazar de l'Hôtel de Ville in BNF, Bazar de l'Hôtel de Ville, catalogues, 1910–, 25. At the same time, the extent to which tennis was gendered as a sport that was suitable for both men and women can be seen in a couple of images that show men and women playing tennis together; see, for example, FORN, Printemps agenda, 1923, 135; and BHVP, Bon Marché agenda, 1928, 117.

69. This assertion was made, in fact, in the 1928 *agenda* of the Bon Marché; see BHVP, Bon Marché agenda, 1928, 25. Still, there were occasional ads featuring women and skiing; for a couple of examples, see *AF* (6 December 1927): 4; and *ILL* (27 November 1937): xxi.

70. For just a few examples, see *DAZ*, LAB (14 November 1922): n.p.; *IZ* (30 January 1936): 136; *VB* (2 December 1936): 23; *KZ*, LAB (29 January 1939): n.p.

71. For instance, see *NPZ*, LAB (15 June 1930): n.p.; *GRM*, LAB (5 June 1932): n.p.; *VB* (9 June 1937): 19; and *IZ* (17 June 1937): 817. In French imagery, women are sometimes shown in the water, although another common strategy in French advertising, particularly in ads for cameras, was to picture women standing on a diving board over an often unseen pool of water; for some examples, see *OEU* (2 August 1923): n.p.; BHVP, Bon Marché agenda, 1928, 124, 128; *OEU* (28 July 1932): 8; and *GRIN* (24 June 1938): 14.

72. For a few examples from France, see *GRIN* (17 May 1929): 10; BMD, Dossier Golf; FORN, Magasins Réunis agenda, 1927, 12; and BHVP, Bon Marché agenda, 1928, 179. For a German example, see *IZ* (14 March 1935): 320.

73. Durry, "Le combat des femmes," 301; Fieschi, *Histoire du sport français*, 71–72; Guttmann, *Women's Sports*, 157–159; Rearick, *The French in Love and War*, 50, 147–148; Savignon, "La mode sous influence sport," 16–17; and Weber, *The Hollow Years*, 157–159.

74. For instance, see Rearick, *The French in Love and War*, 147–148.

75. See various press clippings about Lenglen collected in BMD, Dossier Tennis (1924–1986); and BMD, Dossier Sports.Généralité (1889–1940).

76. BMD, Dossier Tennis (1924–1986).

77. Ibid.

78. Even at that, acceptance of women's sporting activities involving national prestige developed slowly in the interwar years, as evidenced by continued resistance to women's inclusion in the Olympic Games. See, for instance, Durry, "Le combat des femmes," 304–305; Guttmann, *Women's Sports*, 164–169; Hargreaves, *Sporting Females*, 211–219; Pfister and von der Lippe, "Women's Participation in Sports and the Olympic Games in Germany and Norway," 31–32; and Terret, "Femmes, sport, identité et acculturation," 47.

79. See, for instance, for Germany, *LV,* LAB (2 July 1921): n.p.; and *VRW,* LAB (13 December 1926): n.p. For a few French examples, see the 1931 catalog of the Bazar de l'Hôtel de Ville in BNF, Bazar de l'Hôtel de Ville, catalogues, 1910–, 4; and BHVP, Bon Marché agenda, 1928, 40, 50, 132.

80. *GRIN* (13 August 1937): 12.

81. Ibid. (28 May 1937): 16.

82. BHVP, Bon Marché agenda, 1928, 76.

83. *VRW,* LAB (8 August 1930): n.p.

84. The hurdler can be found in *VB* (14 July 1935): n.p. The rugby players appeared in *VB* (28 July 1935): n.p.

85. *DAZ,* LAB (9 December 1922): n.p.

86. Ibid. (14 December 1922): n.p.

87. *LV,* LAB (18 June 1921): n.p.

88. *VB* (11 March 1937): 18.

89. *Notre Temps* (18 December 1932): n.p.

90. BHVP, Bon Marché agenda, 1928, 73.

91. As Savignon asserts, French fashion designers during the interwar years, such as Chanel, likewise adhered to that message; see Savignon, "La mode sous influence sport," 15–16. See also Saillard, "Le vêtement de sport," esp. 9–10.

92. For a couple of examples, see *GRIN* (23 July 1937): 8 and (12 January 1939): 10. German examples were similar, though not as numerous. For one example, see the women's page *"Das Reich der Frau"* in *KZ,* LAB (31 December 1935): n.p., where there is a discussion of women's sports as related to fashion (though without any illustrations of it).

93. FORN, Grands Magasins du Louvre agenda, 1921, 85–90.

94. Ibid., Galeries Lafayette agenda, 1924, 444.

95. BMD, Dossier Golf.

96. Ibid.

97. BMD, Dossier Tennis (1924–1986).

98. BMD, Dossier Sports.Généralité (1899–1940). Nonetheless, it should be noted that some of the listed women were participants in more masculine-defined sports, and that some of them were listed as having outside occupations as well, although these still tended to be more feminine-gendered jobs such as typist or social worker.

99. BMD, Dossier Sports.Généralité (1899–1940).

100. *IZ* (20 May 1926): 677.

101. Pfister et al, "Women and Football," 18; and Willis, "Women in Sport in Ideology," 121–122.

102. *AF* (27 May 1927): 3. See also ibid. (18 July 1928): 3; and *OEU* (6 August 1929): 4.

103. *OEU* (19 July 1927): 4.

104. Pfister, "The Medical Discourse on Female Physical Culture in Germany," 191.

105. Willis, "Women in Sport in Ideology," 122.

106. See Koshar, *German Travel Cultures,* esp. 71–73; Mackaman, *Leisure Settings;* and Young, *"La Vieille France* as Object of Bourgeois Desire," 170.

107. Koshar, *German Travel Cultures,* 132–134, 158–159. See also Confino and Koshar, "Régimes of Consumer Culture," 149.

108. See Baranowski and Furlough, introduction to *Being Elsewhere,* 14–16.

109. Jackson, "Le temps des loisirs," 226. See also Cacérès, *Loisirs et travail du moyen âge à nos jours,* 187–194; and Rauch, *Vacances en France,* 9–10, 97–102.

110. Cross, *A Social History of Leisure since 1600,* 175–176; and Jackson, "Le temps des loisirs," 231.

111. Baranowski, "Strength through Joy," 215–217; Confino and Koshar, "Régimes of Consumer Culture," 149; Löfgren, *On Holiday,* 241–243; and Merritt, "Strength through Joy," 67–75.

112. See, for example, Kinnaird et al, "Tourism," 18–19; Koshar, *German Travel Cultures,* 96; Koshar, "What ought to be seen," 325–326; and Löfgren, *On Holiday,* esp. 137–138, 148–151, 269–271.

113. MacCannell, *The Tourist,* 3.

114. For example, see MacCannell, *The Tourist,* 13; and Urry, *The Tourist Gaze,* 104–112.

115. Koshar, "What ought to be seen," 339.

116. Baranowski and Furlough, introduction to *Being Elsewhere,* esp. 7–8, 14–15.

117. Baranowski, "Strength through Joy," esp. 213–223.

118. Merritt, "Strength through Joy," esp. 71–77. See also Baranowski and Furlough, introduction to *Being Elsewhere,* 14–15, which notes the existence of such ideology in a context beyond Nazi Germany.

119. Koshar, *German Travel Cultures,* 112–113.

120. Harp, *Marketing Michelin,* 225–238.

121. Young, "*La Vieille France* as Object of Bourgeois Desire," 170–183. See also Cross, "Vacations for All," 599; Jackson, "Le temps des loisirs," 232; Rauch, *Vacances en France,* 85–93, 252–253; and Rearick, *The French in Love and War,* 157–158.

122. For Germany, see *FZ,* LAB (11 August 1920): 4; *DAZ,* LAB (25 November 1922): n.p.; *NPZ,* LAB (12 April 1925): n.p.; *GRM,* LAB (11 December 1927): n.p.; *VZ* (23 August 1933): n.p.; *MIP,* SBB (10 January 1935): 49; *VB* (2 September 1937): 8; and *KZ,* LAB (15 January 1939): n.p. For a few examples from France, see *MAT,* LC (3 September 1920): 4; *ILL* (28 July 1928): xiv; *GRIN* (24 January 1930): 10; *ILL* (14 April 1934): xxviii; and (20 August 1938): vii.

123. *GRIN* (2 August 1929): 12.

124. *MAT,* LC (10 August 1922): 6.

125. *OEU* (15 August 1927): 3.

126. *KZ,* LAB (2 October 1938): n.p. See also *VZ* (2 July 1933): n.p.; and *VB* (26 January 1936): n.p.

127. *SIMP* (9 September 1934): 283.

128. Baranowski and Furlough, introduction to *Being Elsewhere,* 14–15; Löfgren, *On Holiday,* 153–154, 182–184; Rearick, *The French in Love and War,* 154–157; Sachs, *For Love of the Automobile,* 152–157; and Young, "*La Vieille France* as Object of Bourgeois Desire," 170, 184.

129. Young, "*La Vieille France* as Object of Bourgeois Desire," 176. In a different context, Felski has likewise noted the gendering of modernity as masculine in contrast to femininity as emblematic of tradition; see Felski, *The Gender of Modernity,* esp. 1–3, 35–60.

130. Baranowski and Furlough, introduction to *Being Elsewhere,* 5.

131. *VZ* (23 July 1933): n.p.

132. Ibid. (25 August 1933): n.p.

133. Ibid. (12 March 1936): 328. Another Baden-Baden ad, though one without any visual images, can be found in *FZ*, LAB (7 August 1920): 3.

134. *ILL* (9 July 1938): xvi. See also *GRIN* (9 March 1939): 14.

135. *ILL* (21 July 1928): xxvi.

136. Ibid. (20 May 1939): 109.

137. Baranowski, "Strength through Joy," 218; and Löfgren, *On Holiday,* 240–243. See also Rauch, *Les vacances,* esp. 58–60.

138. For some general examples of such ads, see *MAT,* LC (13 July 1923): 6; and *OEU* (9 August 1923): n.p., (4 July 1929): 8, and (14 August 1929): 6.

139. *MAT* (24 July 1931): 7. For examples of similarly themed Kodak ads, see *OEU* (28 July 1921): n.p.; and *MAT,* LC (5 July 1923): 8.

140. BHVP, Bon Marché agenda, 1928, 123. Some such advertisements did depict fatherly figures as well, but in most cases the visual focus remained on the mother. This was true of a 1924 Kodak ad in which a woman is pictured holding a camera, while around her are several smaller images, intended to represent the photographs the woman has taken on her vacation. These smaller images also incorporate familial imagery, including some images of a father with the mother and children, but the original, dominant image of the woman with the camera is the unmistakable visual focus of the advertisement; see, for instance, FORN, Nouvelles Galeries "A La Ménagère" agenda, 1923; *MAT,* LC (19 June 1924): 6; and *OEU* (11 July 1929): 8. Other images, though much less commonplace, depict women who have neither children nor a husband with them; see *OEU* (7 July 1921): n.p.; *AF* (11 July 1928): 4; *MAT,* LC (19 June 1931): 7; and *GRIN* (12 March 1937): 14.

141. For some general examples of ads of this variety, see *WM* (September 1934, advertising section): 17; *IZ* (25 July 1935): 120; and *VB* (24 June 1937): 18.

142. See, for instance, *VZ* (12 July 1933): n.p.; and *VB* (7 June 1934): n.p.

143. See *IZ* (16 July 1936): 97, (29 July 1937): 157, and (22 June 1939): 927.

144. Ibid. (8 June 1939): 856.

145. Indeed, Sachs suggests that tourism first became an item of mass consumption thanks in large part to the easy mobility provided by the automobile; Sachs, *For Love of the Automobile,* 151–157.

146. This irony has been noted by Harp, *Marketing Michelin,* 264–265. See also Sachs, *For Love of the Automobile,* 150–151.

147. Koshar, *German Travel Cultures,* 117–118; and Koshar, "Germans at the Wheel," 217.

148. *VZ* (7 July 1933): n.p.

149. *VB* (10 September 1937): 16.

150. Herf, *Reactionary Modernism,* 204–207. See also Koshar, *German Travel Cultures,* 118–119. For more on the connection of leisure, aesthetic ideals, and industrial development, see Schütz, "Zur Modernität des 'Dritten Reiches,'" 116–136.

151. *ILL* (12 July 1930): xxv. Löfgren has examined the role of the automobile in facilitating family-oriented vacations both in Europe and the United States; Löfgren, *On Holiday,* 63–64.

152. *La République* (10 July 1930): 4.

153. *ILL* (31 March 1934): xxiii. See also *AF* (9 April 1927): 3; *ILL* (20 October 1928): xxxi; and *GRIN* (31 May 1929): 12.

154. *ILL* (4 April 1931): xxix. On a related note, Brown has explored the controversy surrounding the erection of roadside advertising signs by oil companies in Europe, including a brief mention of Shell's removal of its signs in France, to which this ad refers. Brown suggests that the move may have been partially motivated by heavy taxation on such signage in France. See Brown, "Cultivating a 'Green' Image," 347–365, esp. 359–360. In Nazi Germany, moreover, the state imposed heavy restrictions on roadside advertising, thus largely eliminating such signage from 1933 onward. See Berghoff, "Times Change and We Change with Them," 135–136; and de Grazia, *Irresistible Empire,* 275.

155. BHVP, Bon Marché agenda, 1928, 168.

APPENDIX

1. Albert, "La presse française de 1871 à 1940," 456, 457–458.

2. Ibid., 511, 519–520, 527–532.

3. Ibid., 591, 590.

4. Goubert, *The Conquest of Water,* 120–121; and Stewart, *For Health and Beauty,* 60.

5. Albert, "La presse française de 1871 à 1940," 597–598; Goubert, *The Conquest of Water,* 120–121; and Stewart, *For Health and Beauty,* 60.

6. Albert, "La presse française de 1871 à 1940," 564–568, 511, 576–577, 563–564.

7. Ibid., 511, 524. See also Martin, *Trois siècles de publicité en France,* 229.

8. Albert, "La presse française de 1871 à 1940," 522, 525–526. See also Martin, *Trois siècles de publicité en France,* 229–231.

9. Martin, *Trois siècles de publicité en France,* 231–234.

10. Albert, "La presse française de 1871 à 1940," 526.

11. Hale, *The Captive Press in the Third Reich,* 3, 143. See also Welch, *The Third Reich,* 34–35.

12. Eksteins, *The Limits of Reason,* 74.

13. Ibid. See also Hale, *The Captive Press in the Third Reich,* 1; and Pross, *Zeitungsreport,* 48.

14. Eksteins, *The Limits of Reason,* 114.

15. Ibid., 74; Hale, *The Captive Press in the Third Reich,* 3; Koszyk, *Deutsche Presse,* 369; Pross, *Zeitungsreport,* 81; and Welch, *The Third Reich,* 38–39.

16. Eksteins, *The Limits of Reason,* 266–267; Hale, *The Captive Press in the Third Reich,* 83–90, 265–267; and Welch, *The Third Reich,* 34–37. See also Pross, *Zeitungsreport,* 95–102.

17. Eksteins, *The Limits of Reason,* 286–291; Hale, *The Captive Press in the Third Reich,* 76–83; and Welch, *The Third Reich,* 34–35. See also Koszyk, *Deutsche Presse,* 258; and Pross, *Zeitungsreport,* 48.

18. Eksteins, *The Limits of Reason,* 267–275, 281. See also Hale, *The Captive Press in the Third Reich,* 156.

19. Hale, *The Captive Press in the Third Reich,* 30–31; and Koszyk, *Deutsche Presse,* 381–382.

20. Eksteins, *The Limits of Reason,* 85; Hale, *The Captive Press in the Third Reich,* 40–41, 59; Koszyk, *Deutsche Presse,* 367–368; Pross, *Zeitungsreport,* 63; and Welch, *The Third Reich,* 36.

21. Koszyk, *Deutsche Presse,* 240. See also Pross, *Zeitungsreport,* 49.

22. Eksteins, *The Limits of Reason,* 91; and Hale, *The Captive Press in the Third Reich,* 277. See also Koszyk, *Deutsche Presse,* 135–159.

23. Eksteins, *The Limits of Reason,* 283–284.

24. Ibid., 129, viii–ix, 25–27, 125–130, 136, 283–284; and Koszyk, *Deutsche Presse,* 216–219, 268–269.

25. Eksteins, *The Limits of Reason,* 303–304; Hale, *The Captive Press in the Third Reich,* 290; and Koszyk, *Deutsche Presse,* 269–270.

26. Koszyk, *Deutsche Presse,* 179–183. See also Pross, *Zeitungsreport,* 57.

27. Koszyk, *Deutsche Presse,* 179–183; and Sherayko, "Selling the Modern," 171.

28. Koszyk, *Deutsche Presse,* 302; see also 290–302. See also Pross, *Zeitungsreport,* 62–63.

29. Hale, *The Captive Press in the Third Reich,* 62. See also Koszyk, *Deutsche Presse,* 303–309; and Pross, *Zeitungsreport,* 42–45.

30. Eksteins, *The Limits of Reason,* viii–ix, 22–23, 111–112, 136, 283–284; Koszyk, *Deutsche Presse,* 251–258; and Pross, *Zeitungsreport,* 49.

31. Eksteins, *The Limits of Reason,* 117, 121, 286, 294–295, 314.

BIBLIOGRAPHY

PRIMARY SOURCES

Newspapers and Periodicals

Action Française, L'
Gringoire
Illustration, L'
Illustrirte Zeitung
Notre Temps
Oeuvre, L'
Paris-Soir
République, La
Simplicissimus
Vendredi
Völkischer Beobachter
Vossische Zeitung
Westermanns Monatshefte

Archives de Paris

Publicité Commerciale (6 AZ 1817)

Publicité Commerciale (D 18 Z cart. 7)
Folder Bazar de l'Hotel de Ville, 1913–1931
Folder Belle Jardinière, 1862–1931

Folder Bon Marché, 1847–1933
Folder Galeries Lafayette, 1912–1933
Folder Le Louvre, 1877–1933
Folder Le Printemps, 1916–1927
Folder Palais de la Nouveauté, 1925–1927
Folder Samaritaine, 1910–1933

Publicité (D 18 Z cart. 8)
Folder Alimentation (Produits d')
Folder Félix Potin, 1868–1933
Folder Santé
    Subfolder Medecine et Pharmacopée
    Subfolder Medecins
    Subfolder Pharmaciens

Publicité (D 18 Z cart. 9)
Folder Bonneteries
Folder Habillement
    Subfolder Tailleurs
Folder Installation
    Subfolder Electricité, Gaz, Téléphone
    Subfolder Entretien, Désinfection

Publicité (D 18 Z cart. 10)
Folder Transports
    Subfolder Automobiles
    Subfolder Cycles et Motos

Bibliothèque Forney, Paris

Bon Marché agenda, 1933, 1938
Galeries Lafayette agenda, 1924, 1928, 1929, 1932, 1933
Grands Magasins du Louvre agenda, 1921, 1922, 1924, 1926
Magasins Réunis agenda, 1927
Nouvelles Galeries "A La Ménagère" agenda, 1923
Printemps agenda, 1920–1926, 1929, 1932, 1934, 1936–1938

Bibliothèque Historique de la Ville de Paris

Bon Marché agenda, 1920, 1922, 1923, 1925, 1928, 1931, 1932, 1934
Galeries Lafayette agenda, 1923, 1938

Printemps, catalogue publicitaire, 1929
Printemps, catalogue, 1930

Bibliothèque Marguerite Durand, Paris

Dossier Golf
Dossier Maîtresse de Maison
Dossier Publicité (1912–1981)
    Folder 1912–1921
Dossier Sports.Généralité (1899–1940)
Dossier Tennis (1924–1986)

Bibliothèque Nationale de France (site François-Mitterrand), Paris

Bazar de l'Hotel de Ville, catalogues, 1910–
Galeries Lafayette agenda, 1934
Grands Magasins du Louvre, documents publicitaires, 1925–
Grands Magasins Royal Haussman, catalogues, 1930–
La Mode et L'Ameublement Au Bon Marché, 1920
Magasins Réunis Rive Gauche, catalogues, 1926–
Trois Quartiers, documents publicitaires, 1925–

Landesarchiv Berlin

Deutsche Allgemeine Zeitung
Frankfurter Zeitung
Germania
Kreuz-Zeitung
Leipziger Volkszeitung
Neue Preussische Zeitung (*Kreuz-Zeitung*)
Vörwarts

Library of Congress, Washington, D.C.

Le Matin

Staatsbibliothek zu Berlin

Münchner Illustrierte Presse

SECONDARY SOURCES

Abrams, Lynn, and Elizabeth Harvey. "Gender and Gender Relations in German History." Introduction to *Gender Relations in German History: Power, Agency and Experience from the Sixteenth to the Twentieth Century,* edited by Abrams and Harvey. Durham: Duke University Press, 1997.

Accampo, Elinor A. "Private Life, Public Image: Motherhood and Militancy in the Self-Construction of Nelly Roussel, 1900–1922." In *The New Biography: Performing Femininity in Nineteenth-Century France,* edited by Jo Burr Margadant. Berkeley and Los Angeles: University of California Press, 2000.

Albert, Pierre. "La presse française de 1871 à 1940." In *Histoire générale de la presse française,* vol. 3, *De 1871 à 1940,* edited by Claude Bellanger, Jacques Godechot, Pierre Guiral, and Fernand Terrou. Paris: Presses Universitaires de France, 1972.

Allen, Ann Taylor. *Feminism and Motherhood in Western Europe, 1890–1970: The Maternal Dilemma.* New York: Palgrave Macmillan, 2005.

Arnaud, Pierre. "French Sport and the Emergence of Authoritarian Regimes, 1919–1939." In *Sport and International Politics,* edited by Pierre Arnaud and James Riordan. London: Routledge, E & FN Spon, 1998.

———. "Sportifs de tous les pays . . . !" In *Les origines du sport ouvrier en Europe,* edited by Arnaud. Paris: Éditions L'Harmattan, 1994.

Auffret, Marc. *La France de l'entre deux guerres, 1919–1939.* Paris: Culture, art, loisirs, 1972.

Badinter, Elisabeth. *Mother Love: Myth and Reality: Motherhood in Modern History.* New York: Macmillan, 1981.

Baranowski, Shelley. *Strength through Joy: Consumerism and Mass Tourism in the Third Reich.* Cambridge: Cambridge University Press, 2004.

———. "Strength through Joy: Tourism and National Integration in the Third Reich." In *Being Elsewhere: Tourism, Consumer Culture, and Identity in Modern Europe and North America,* edited by Baranowski and Ellen Furlough. Ann Arbor: University of Michigan Press, 2001.

Baranowski, Shelley, and Ellen Furlough. Introduction to *Being Elsewhere: Tourism, Consumer Culture, and Identity in Modern Europe and North America,* edited by Baranowski and Furlough. Ann Arbor: University of Michigan Press, 2001.

Barlow, Tani E., Madeleine Due Yong, Uta G. Poiger, Priti Ramamurthy, Lynn M. Thomas, and Alys Eve Weinbaum. "The Modern Girl around the World: A Research Agenda and Preliminary Findings." *Gender and History* 17 (2005): 245–294.

Beale, Marjorie A. *The Modernist Enterprise: French Elites and the Threat of Modernity, 1900–1940.* Stanford: Stanford University Press, 1999.

Becker, Frank. "Sportsmen in the Machine World: Models for Modernization in Weimar Germany." *International Journal of the History of Sport* 12 (1995): 153–168.

——. "Weimarer Sportrepublik: Deutungsangebote für die Demokratie." *Archiv für Kulturgeschichte* 78 (1996): 179–206.

Bellon, Bernard P. *Mercedes in Peace and War: German Automobile Workers, 1903–1945.* New York: Columbia University Press, 1990.

Berenson, Edward. *The Trial of Madame Caillaux.* Berkeley and Los Angeles: University of California Press, 1992.

Berghoff, Hartmut. "Enticement and Deprivation: The Regulation of Consumption in Pre-War Nazi Germany." In *The Politics of Consumption: Material Culture and Citizenship in Europe and America,* edited by Martin Daunton and Matthew Hilton. New York: Berg, 2001.

——. "'Times Change and We Change with Them': The German Advertising Industry in the Third Reich—Between Professional Self-Interest and Political Repression." In *The Emergence of Modern Marketing,* edited by Roy Church and Andrew Godley. London: Frank Cass, 2003.

Bessel, Richard. *Germany after the First World War.* Oxford: Clarendon Press, 1993.

Blaich, Fritz. "The Development of the Distribution Sector in the German Car Industry." In *Development of Mass Marketing: The Automobile and Retailing Industries,* edited by Akio Okochi and Koichi Shimokawa. Tokyo: Tokyo University Press, 1980.

——. "Why Did the Pioneer Fall Behind? Motorisation in Germany between the Wars." In *The Economic and Social Effects of the Spread of Motor Vehicles: An International Centenary Tribute,* edited by Theo Barker. London: Macmillan, 1987.

Bleuel, Hans Peter. *Sex and Society in Nazi Germany.* Translated by J. Maxwell Brownjohn. Philadelphia: Lippincott, 1973.

Bock, Gisela. "Racism and Sexism in Nazi Germany: Motherhood, Compulsory Sterilization, and the State." In *When Biology Became Destiny: Women in Weimar and Nazi Germany,* edited by Renate Bridenthal, Atina Grossmann, and Marion Kaplan. New York: Monthly Review Press, 1984.

Bowden, Sue, and Avner Offer. "The Technological Revolution that Never Was: Gender, Class, and the Diffusion of Household Appliances in Interwar England." In *The Sex of Things: Gender and Consumption in Historical Perspective,* edited by Victoria de Grazia. Berkeley and Los Angeles: University of California Press, 1996.

Boxer, Marilyn J., and Jean H. Quataert. "Overview, 1890 to the Present." In *Connecting Spheres: European Women in a Globalizing World, 1500 to the Present,* by Boxer, Quataert, et al. New York: Oxford University Press, 2000.

Boyer, Marc. *Le tourisme.* Paris: Éditions du Seuil, 1982.

Breuilly, John. "The National Idea in Modern German History." In *German History since 1800,* edited by Mary Fulbrook. London: Arnold, 1997.

Bridenthal, Renate. "Class Struggle around the Hearth: Women and Domestic Service in the Weimar Republic." In *Towards the Holocaust: The Social and Economic Collapse of the Weimar Republic,* edited by Michael N. Dobkowski and Isidor Walliman. Westport, Conn.: Greenwood, 1983.

Bridenthal, Renate, Atina Grossmann, and Marion Kaplan. "Women in Weimar and Nazi Germany." Introduction to *When Biology Became Destiny: Women in Weimar and Nazi Germany,* edited by Bridenthal, Grossmann, and Kaplan. New York: Monthly Review Press, 1984.

Brown, Robert. "Cultivating a 'Green' Image: Oil Companies and Outdoor Publicity in Britain and Europe, 1920–1936." *Journal of European Economic History* 22 (1993): 347–365.

Cacérès, Bénigno. *Loisirs et travail du moyen âge à nos jours.* Paris: Éditions du Seuil, 1973.

Carr, G. A. "Sport and Party Ideology in the Third Reich." *Canadian Journal of History of Sport and Physical Education* 5 (1974): 1–9.

Chessel, Marie-Emmanuelle. "Die Werbefachleute in Frankreich in der Zeit zwischen den beiden Weltkriegen: Geschichte einer Professionalisierung?" *Jahrbuch für Wirtschaftsgeschichte* 1 (1997): 79–92.

———. *La publicité: Naissance d'une profession, 1900–1940.* Paris: CNRS, 1998.

———. "Une methode publicitaire americaine?: Cadum dans la France de l'entre deux guerres." *Enterprises et Histoire* 11 (1996): 61–76.

Clark, Linda L. "The Primary Education of French Girls: Pedagogical Prescriptions and Social Realities, 1880–1940." *History of Education Quarterly* 21 (1981): 411–428.

Coffin, Judith G. *The Politics of Women's Work: The Paris Garment Trades, 1750–1915.* Princeton: Princeton University Press, 1996.

Confino, Alon, and Rudy Koshar. "Régimes of Consumer Culture: New Narratives in Twentieth-Century German History." *German History* 19 (2001): 135–161.

Cova, Anne. *Maternité et droits des femmes en France (XIXe-XXe siècles).* Paris: Anthropos, 1997.

Cowan, Ruth Schwartz. "The Industrial Revolution in the Home." In *The Social Shaping of Technology,* 2nd ed., edited by Donald MacKenzie and Judy Wajcman. Buckingham: Open University Press, 1999.

———. *More Work for Mother: The Ironies of Household Technology from the Open Hearth to the Microwave.* New York: Basic, 1983.

Coward, Rosalind. *Female Desires: How They Are Sought, Bought, and Packaged.* New York: Grove Press, 1985.

Cross, Gary S. *A Quest for Time: The Reduction of Work in Britain and France, 1840–1940.* Berkeley and Los Angeles: University of California Press, 1989.

———. *A Social History of Leisure since 1600.* State College, Pa.: Venture, 1990.

———. "Vacations for All: The Leisure Question in the Era of the Popular Front." *Journal of Contemporary History* 24 (1989): 599–621.

Crossick, Geoffrey, and Serge Jaumain. "The World of the Department Store: Distribution, Culture and Social Change." In *Cathedrals of Consumption: The European Department Store, 1850–1939,* edited by Crossick and Jaumain. Brookfield, Vt.: Ashgate, 1999.

Czarnowski, Gabriele. "'The Value of Marriage for the *Volksgemeinschaft*': Policies towards Women and Marriage under National Socialism." In *Fascist Italy and Nazi Germany: Comparisons and Contrasts,* edited by Richard Bessel. Cambridge: Cambridge University Press, 1996.

David, Henry P., Jochen Fleischhacker, and Charlotte Höhn. "Abortion and Eugenics in Nazi Germany." *Population and Development Review* 14 (1988): 81–112.

de Certeau, Michel. *The Practice of Everyday Life.* Translated by Steven F. Rendall. Berkeley and Los Angeles: University of California Press, 1984.

de Grazia, Victoria. "Americanism for Export." *Wedge* 7–8 (1985): 74–81.

———. "The Arts of Purchase: How American Publicity Subverted the European Poster, 1920–1940." In *Remaking History,* edited by Barbara Kruger and Phil Mariani. Seattle: Bay Press, 1989.

———. *Irresistible Empire: America's Advance through 20th-Century Europe.* Cambridge: Belknap Press, Harvard University Press, 2005.

Delbourg-Delphis, Marylène. *Le chic et le look: Histoire de la mode feminine et des moeurs de 1850 à nos jours.* Paris: Hachette, 1981.

Denman, Mariatte C. "Visualizing the Nation: Madonnas and Mourning Mothers in Postwar Germany." In *Gender and Germanness: Cultural Productions of Nation,* edited by Patricia Herminghouse and Magda Mueller. Providence: Berghahn, 1997.

Domansky, Elisabeth. "Militarization and Reproduction in World War I Germany." In *Society, Culture, and the State in Germany, 1870–1930,* edited by Geoff Eley. Ann Arbor: University of Michigan Press, 1996.

Downs, Laura Lee. *Manufacturing Inequality: Gender Division in the French and British Metalworking Industries, 1914–1939.* Ithaca: Cornell University Press, 1995.

Durry, Jean. "Le combat des femmes et l'évolution des structures." Chap. 11 in *L'histoire en mouvements: Le sport dans la société française (XIXe-XXe siècle),* edited by Ronald Hubscher. Paris: Armand Colin, 1992.

Dyer, Colin. *Population and Society in Twentieth-Century France.* New York: Holmes and Meier, 1978.

Eckermann, Erik. *World History of the Automobile.* Translated by Peter L. Albrecht. Warrendale, Pa.: Society of Automotive Engineers, 2001.

Edelmann, Heidrun. *Vom Luxusgut zum Gebrauchsgegenstand: Die Geschichte der Verbreitung von Personenkraftwagen in Deutschland.* Frankfurt am Main: Verband der Automobilindustrie, 1989.

Eisenberg, Christiane. "Massensport in der Weimarer Republik: Ein statistischer Überblick." *Archiv für Sozialgeschichte* 33 (1993): 137–177.

Eksteins, Modris. *The Limits of Reason: The German Democratic Press and the Collapse of Weimar Democracy.* Oxford: Oxford University Press, 1975.

Felski, Rita. *The Gender of Modernity.* Cambridge: Harvard University Press, 1995.

Fieschi, Jean Toussaint. *Histoire du sport français de 1870 à nos jours.* Paris: PAC, 1983.

Fourny, Jean-François. "Discours de la mode des années trente aux années quatre-vingt-dix." *Contemporary French Civilization* 16 (1992): 214–230.

Frame, Lynne. "Gretchen, Girl, Garçonne? Weimar Science and Popular Culture in Search of the Ideal New Woman." In *Women in the Metropolis: Gender and Modernity in Weimar Culture,* edited by Katharina von Ankum. Berkeley and Los Angeles: University of California Press, 1997.

Frevert, Ute. "Gender in German History." Translated by Polly Kienle. In *German History since 1800,* edited by Mary Fulbrook. London: Arnold, 1997.

———. *Women in German History: From Bourgeois Emancipation to Sexual Liberation.* Translated by Stuart McKinnon-Evans. Oxford: Berg, 1988.

Fridenson, Patrick. "French Automobile Marketing, 1890–1979." In *Development of Mass Marketing: The Automobile and Retailing Industries,* edited by Akio Okochi and Koichi Shimokawa. Tokyo: Tokyo University Press, 1980.

———. "Some Economic and Social Effects of Motor Vehicles in France since 1890." In *The Economic and Social Effects of the Spread of Motor Vehicles: An International Centenary Tribute,* edited by Theo Barker. London: Macmillan, 1987.

———. "The Spread of the Automobile Revolution, 1914–1945." Pt. 2 of *The Automobile Revolution: The Impact of an Industry,* by Jean-Pierre Bardou, Jean-Jacques Chanaron, Fridenson, and James M. Laux. Chapel Hill: University of North Carolina Press, 1982.

Frost, Robert L. "Machine Liberation: Inventing Housewives and Home Appliances in Interwar France." *French Historical Studies* 18 (1993): 109–130.

Furlough, Ellen. "Making Mass Vacations: Tourism and Consumer Culture in France, 1930s to 1970s." *Comparative Studies in Society and History* 40 (1998): 247–286.

———. "Selling the American Way in Interwar France: *Prix Uniques* and the Salons des Arts Ménagers." *Journal of Social History* 26 (1993): 491–519.

Gagnon, Paul A. "La Vie Future: Some French Responses to the Technological Society." *Journal of European Studies* 6 (1976): 172–189.

Gilbert, Sandra M. "Soldier's Heart: Literary Men, Literary Women, and the Great War." *Signs* 8 (1983): 422–450.

Giles, Judy. "A Home of One's Own: Women and Domesticity in England, 1918–1950." *Women's Studies International Forum* 16 (1993): 239–253.

Goffman, Erving. *Gender Advertisements.* Cambridge: Harvard University Press, 1979.

Goldstein, Carolyn. "From Service to Sales: Home Economics in Light and Power, 1920–1940. *Technology and Culture* 38 (1997): 121–152.

Gorman, Lyn, and David McLean. *Media and Society in the Twentieth Century: A Historical Introduction.* Oxford: Blackwell, 2003.

Goubert, Jean-Pierre. *The Conquest of Water: The Advent of Health in the Industrial Age.* Translated by Andrew Wilson. Princeton: Princeton University Press, 1989.

Grayzel, Susan R. *Women's Identities at War: Gender, Motherhood, and Politics in Britain and France during the First World War.* Chapel Hill: University of North Carolina Press, 1999.

Greenfield, Jill, Sean O'Connell, and Chris Reid. "Gender, Consumer Culture and the Middle-Class Male, 1918–1939." In *Gender, Civic Culture and Consumerism: Middle-Class Identity in Britain, 1800–1940,* edited by Alan Kidd and David Nicholls. Manchester: Manchester University Press, 1999.

Gronberg, Tag. "Beware Beautiful Women: The 1920s Shopwindow Mannequin and a Physiognomy of Effacement." *Art History* 20 (1997): 375–396.

Grossmann, Atina. "*Girlkultur* or Thoroughly Rationalized Female: A New Woman in Weimar Germany?" In *Women in Culture and Politics: A Century of Change,* edited by Judith Friedlander, Blanche Wiesen Cook, Alice Kessler-Harris, and Carroll Smith-Rosenberg. Bloomington: Indiana University Press, 1986.

———. *Reforming Sex: The German Movement for Birth Control and Abortion Reform, 1920–1950.* Oxford: Oxford University Press, 1995.

———. "The New Woman and the Rationalization of Sexuality in Weimar Germany." In *Powers of Desire: The Politics of Sexuality,* edited by Ann Snitow, Christine Stansell, and Sharon Thompson. New York: Monthly Review Press, 1983.

Guenther, Irene V. "Nazi 'Chic'? German Politics and Women's Fashions, 1915–1945." *Fashion Theory* 1 (1997): 29–58.

Gunn, Simon. "The Public Sphere, Modernity and Consumption: New Perspectives on the History of the English Middle Class." In *Gender, Civic Culture and Consumerism: Middle-Class Identity in Britain, 1800–1940,* edited by Alan Kidd and David Nicholls. Manchester: Manchester University Press, 1999.

Gustavus, Christa. "WKS—Wulf Konrad Schwerdtfeger." In *Berliner Chic: Mode von 1820 bis 1990,* edited by Christine Waidenschlager. Berlin: Stiftung Stadtmuseum Berlin, 2001.

Guttmann, Allen. *Women's Sports: A History.* New York: Columbia University Press, 1991.

Hale, Oron J. *The Captive Press in the Third Reich.* Princeton: Princeton University Press, 1964.

Hales, Barbara. "Woman as Sexual Criminal: Weimar Constructions of the Criminal Femme Fatale." In *Women in German Yearbook 12: Feminist Studies in German Literature and Culture,* edited by Sara Friedrichsmeyer and Patricia Herminghouse. Lincoln: University of Nebraska Press, 1996.

Hardyment, Christina. *From Mangle to Microwave: The Mechanization of Household Work.* Cambridge, England: Polity, 1988.

Hargreaves, Jennifer. *Heroines of Sport: The Politics of Difference and Identity.* London and New York: Routledge, 2000.

——. *Sporting Females: Critical Issues in the History and Sociology of Women's Sports.* London and New York: Routledge, 1994.

Harp, Stephen L. *Marketing Michelin: Advertising and Cultural Identity in Twentieth-Century France.* Baltimore: Johns Hopkins University Press, 2001.

Hartmann-Tews, Ilse, and Sascha Alexandra Luetkens. "The Inclusion of Women into the German Sport System." In *Sport and Women: Social Issues in International Perspective,* edited by Hartmann-Tews and Gertrud Pfister. New York: Routledge, 2003.

Harvey, Elizabeth. "Culture and Society in Weimar Germany: The Impact of Modernism and Mass Culture." In *German History since 1800,* edited by Mary Fulbrook. London: Arnold, 1997.

Hau, Michael. *The Cult of Health and Beauty in Germany: A Social History, 1890–1930.* Chicago: University of Chicago Press, 2003.

Hausen, Karin. "Mother's Day in the Weimar Republic." Translated by Miriam Frank with Erika Busse Grossmann. In *When Biology Became Destiny: Women in Weimar and Nazi Germany,* edited by Renate Bridenthal, Atina Grossmann, and Marion Kaplan. New York: Monthly Review Press, 1984.

——. "Mothers, Sons, and the Sale of Symbols and Goods: The 'German Mother's Day,' 1923–33." In *Interest and Emotion: Essays on the Study of Family and Kinship,* edited by Hans Medick and David Warren Sabean. Cambridge: Cambridge University Press, 1984.

Heinze, Karen. "'Schick, selbst mit beschränkten Mitteln!' Die Anleitung zur alltäglichen Distinktion in einer Modezeitschrift der Weimarer Republik." *Werkstatt-Geschichte* 7 (1994): 9–17.

Herf, Jeffrey. *Reactionary Modernism: Technology, Culture, and Politics in Weimar and the Third Reich.* Cambridge: Cambridge University Press, 1984.

Hermand, Jost. "*All Power to the Women:* Nazi Concepts of Matriarchy." *Journal of Contemporary History* 19 (1984): 649–667.

Holden, Len. "More Than a Marque. The Car as Symbol: Aspects of Culture and Ideology." In *The Motor Car and Popular Culture in the 20th Century,* edited by David Thoms, Holden, and Tim Claydon. Brookfield, Vt.: Ashgate, 1998.

Holt, Richard. "Interwar Sport and Interwar Relations: Some Conclusions." In *Sport and International Politics,* edited by Pierre Arnaud and James Riordan. London: Routledge, E & FN Spon, 1998.

——. "Sport, the French, and the Third Republic." *Modern and Contemporary France* 6 (1998): 289–299.

——. *Sport and Society in Modern France.* Hamden, Conn.: Archon, 1981.

Horowitz, Roger, and Arwen Mohun. Introduction to *His and Hers: Gender, Consumption, and Technology,* edited by Horowitz and Mohun. Charlottesville: University Press of Virginia, 1998.

Hosgood, Christopher P. "Mrs Pooter's Purchase: Lower-Middle-Class Consumerism and the Sales, 1870–1914." In *Gender, Civic Culture and Consumerism: Middle-Class Identity in Britain, 1800–1940,* edited by Alan Kidd and David Nicholls. Manchester: Manchester University Press, 1999.

Hultquist, Clark Eric. "Americans in Paris: The J. Walter Thompson Company in France, 1927–1968." *Enterprise and Society* 4 (2003): 471–501.

Huss, Marie-Monique. "Pronatalism in the Inter-war Period in France." *Journal of Contemporary History* 25 (1990): 39–68.

Jackson, Julian. *The Popular Front in France: Defending Democracy, 1934–38.* Cambridge: Cambridge University Press, 1988.

———. "'Le temps des loisirs': Popular Tourism and Mass Leisure in the Vision of the Front Populaire." In *The French and Spanish Popular Fronts: Comparative Perspectives,* edited by Martin S. Alexander and Helen Graham. Cambridge: Cambridge University Press, 1989.

Jenson, Jane. "Gender and Reproduction: Or, Babies and the State." *Studies in Political Economy* 20 (1986): 9–46.

Jones, Joseph. *The Politics of Transport in Twentieth-Century France.* Montreal: McGill-Queen's University Press, 1984.

Kent, Susan Kingsley. *Making Peace: The Reconstruction of Gender in Interwar Britain.* Princeton: Princeton University Press, 1993.

Kessler, Hannelore. *"Die deutsche Frau": Nationalsozialistische Frauenpropaganda im "Völkischen Beobachter."* Cologne: Pahl-Rugenstein Verlag, 1981.

Kinnaird, Vivian, Uma Kothari, and Derek Hall. "Tourism: Gender Perspectives." In *Tourism: A Gender Analysis,* edited by Kinnaird and Hall. New York: Wiley, 1994.

Klaus, Alisa. "Depopulation and Race Suicide: Maternalism and Pronatalist Ideologies in France and the United States." In *Mothers of a New World: Maternalist Politics and the Origins of Welfare States,* edited by Seth Koven and Sonya Michel. New York: Routledge, 1993.

Klinksiek, Dorothee. *Die Frau im NS-Staat.* Stuttgart: Deutsche Verlags-Anstalt, 1982.

Knodel, John E. *The Decline of Fertility in Germany, 1871–1939.* Princeton: Princeton University Press, 1974.

Koonz, Claudia. *Mothers in the Fatherland: Women, the Family, and Nazi Politics.* New York: St. Martin's Press, 1987.

Koshar, Rudy. "Germans at the Wheel: Cars and Leisure Travel in Interwar Germany." In *Histories of Leisure,* edited by Rudy Koshar. New York: Berg, 2002.

———. *German Travel Cultures.* New York: Berg, 2000.

———. "Seeing, Traveling, and Consuming: An Introduction." In *Histories of Leisure,* edited by Koshar. New York: Berg, 2002.

———. "'What ought to be seen': Tourists' Guidebooks and National Identities in Modern Germany and Europe." *Journal of Contemporary History* 33 (1998): 323–340.

Koszyk, Kurt. *Deutsche Presse, 1914–1945.* Pt. 3, *Geschichte der deutschen Presse.* Berlin: Colloquium Verlag, 1972.

Krüger, Arnd. "The Role of Sport in German International Politics, 1918–1945." In *Sport and International Politics,* edited by Pierre Arnaud and James Riordan. London: Routledge, E & FN Spon, 1998.

———. "'We are sure to have found the true reasons for the American superiority in sports': The Reciprocal Relationship between the United States and Germany in Physical Culture and Sport." In *Turnen and Sport: The Cross-Cultural Exchange,* edited by Roland Naul. New York: Waxmann, 1991.

Kudlien, Fridolf. "The German Response to the Birth-Rate Problem during the Third Reich." *Continuity and Change* 5 (1990): 225–247.

Kuisel, Richard F. *Seducing the French: The Dilemma of Americanization.* Berkeley and Los Angeles: University of California Press, 1993.

Lacey, Kate. "Driving the Message Home: Nazi Propaganda in the Private Sphere." In *Gender Relations in German History: Power, Agency and Experience from the Sixteenth to the Twentieth Century,* edited by Lynn Abrams and Elizabeth Harvey. Durham: Duke University Press, 1997.

———. *Feminine Frequencies: Gender, German Radio, and the Public Sphere, 1923–1945.* Ann Arbor: University of Michigan Press, 1996.

Laird, Pamela Walker. *Advertising Progress: American Business and the Rise of Consumer Marketing.* Baltimore: Johns Hopkins University Press, 1998.

Laux, James M. *The European Automobile Industry.* New York: Twayne, 1992.

———. Introduction to *The Automobile Revolution: The Impact of an Industry,* by Jean Pierre Bardou, Jean-Jacques Chanaron, Patrick Fridenson, and Laux. Chapel Hill: University of North Carolina Press, 1982.

Lears, Jackson. *Fables of Abundance: A Cultural History of Advertising in America.* New York: Basic, 1994.

Lees, Lynn Hollen. "Safety in Numbers: Social Welfare Legislation and Fertility Decline in Western Europe." In *The European Experience of Declining Fertility, 1850–1970: The Quiet Revolution,* edited by John R. Gillis, Louise A. Tilly, and David Levine. Oxford: Blackwell, 1992.

Lefko, Stefana. "'Truly Womanly' and 'Truly German': Women's Rights and National Identity in *Die Frau.*" In *Gender and Germanness: Cultural Productions of Nation,* edited by Patricia Herminghouse and Magda Mueller. Providence: Berghahn, 1997.

Leiss, William, Stephen Kline, and Sut Jhally. *Social Communication in Advertising: Persons, Products and Images of Well-Being.* 2nd ed. New York: Routledge, 1990.

Lerman, Nina E., Arwen Palmer Mohun, and Ruth Oldenziel. "The Shoulders We Stand On and the View from Here: Historiography and Directions for Research." *Technology and Culture* 38 (1997): 9–30.

———. "Versatile Tools: Gender Analysis and the History of Technology." *Technology and Culture* 38 (1997): 1–8.

Light, Alison. *Forever England: Femininity, Literature and Conservatism between the Wars.* New York: Routledge, 1991.

Livi Bacci, Massimo. *The Population of Europe: A History.* Translated by Cynthia De Nardi Ipsen and Carl Ipsen. Oxford: Blackwell, 1999.

Löfgren, Orvar. *On Holiday: A History of Vacationing.* Berkeley and Los Angeles: University of California Press, 1999.

Loreck, Hanne. "Das Kunstprodukt 'Neue Frau' in den zwanziger Jahren." In *Mode der 20er Jahre,* edited by Christine Waidenschlager with Christa Gustavus. Tübingen: Ernst Wasmuth Verlag, 1993.

Lubar, Steven. "Men/Women/Production/Consumption." In *His and Hers: Gender, Consumption, and Technology,* edited by Roger Horowitz and Arwen Mohun. Charlottesville: University Press of Virginia, 1998.

Ludvigsen, Karl. *Opel: Wheels to the World.* Princeton: Princeton Publishing, 1975.

Lungstrum, Janet. "*Metropolis* and the Technosexual Woman of German Modernity." In *Women in the Metropolis: Gender and Modernity in Weimar Culture,* edited by Katharina von Ankum. Berkeley and Los Angeles: University of California Press, 1997.

MacCannell, Dean. *The Tourist: A New Theory of the Leisure Class.* New York: Schocken, 1989.

Mackaman, Douglas Peter. *Leisure Settings: Bourgeois Culture, Medicine, and the Spa in Modern France.* Chicago: University of Chicago Press, 1998.

———. "The Tactics of Retreat: Spa Vacations and Bourgeois Identity in Nineteenth-Century France." In *Being Elsewhere: Tourism, Consumer Culture, and Identity in Modern Europe and North America,* edited by Shelley Baranowski and Ellen Furlough. Ann Arbor: University of Michigan Press, 2001.

Maier, Charles S. *Recasting Bourgeois Europe: Stabilization in France, Germany, and Italy in the Decade after World War I.* Princeton: Princeton University Press, 1975.

Marchand, Roland. *Advertising the American Dream: Making Way for Modernity, 1920-1940.* Berkeley and Los Angeles: University of California Press, 1985.

Marschalck, Peter. *Bevölkerungsgeschichte Deutschlands im 19. und 20. Jahrhundert.* Frankfurt am Main: Suhrkamp, 1984.

Martin, Marc. *Trois siècles de publicité en France.* Paris: Éditions Odile Jacob, 1992.

Martin, Martine. "Ménagère: Une profession? Les dilemmes de l'entre deux guerres." *Le Mouvement Social* 140 (1987): 89–106.

Mason, Tim. "Women in Germany, 1925–1940: Family, Welfare and Work. Part I." *History Workshop* 1 (1976): 74–113.

Mauer, Mechtild. "Tourismus im Visier der 'Gender'-Debatte." *Voyage* 2 (1998): 153–160.

McBride, Theresa. *The Domestic Revolution: The Modernisation of Household Service in England and France, 1820–1920.* New York: Holmes and Meier, 1976.

McCracken, Grant. *Culture and Consumption: New Approaches to the Symbolic Character of Consumer Goods and Activities.* Bloomington: Indiana University Press, 1988.

McDonald, Kenneth. "Creating a 'Nazi Style': The German Fashion Institute and State Efforts to Influence Fashion in the 1930s." *Proceedings of the South Carolina Historical Association* (2000): 51–62.

McMillan, James. *Housewife or Harlot: The Place of Women in French Society, 1870–1940.* New York: St. Martin's Press, 1981.

Melling, Alethea. "Cultural Differentiation, Shared Aspiration: The Entente Cordiale of International Ladies' Football, 1920–45." In *Sport in Europe: Politics, Class, Gender,* edited by J. A. Mangan. London: Frank Cass, 1999.

Merritt, Michael A. "Strength through Joy: Regimented Leisure in Nazi Germany." In *Nazism and the Common Man: Essays in German History (1929–1939),* edited by Otis C. Mitchell, 2nd ed. Washington, D.C.: University Press of America, 1981.

Merron, Jeff. "Putting Foreign Consumers on the Map: J. Walter Thompson's Struggle with General Motors' International Advertising Account in the 1920s." *Business History Review* (1999): 465–502.

Meyer, Sibylle. "The Tiresome Work of Conspicuous Leisure: On the Domestic Duties of the Wives of Civil Servants in the German Empire (1871–1918)." Translated by Lyndel Butler. In *Connecting Spheres: European Women in a Globalizing World, 1500 to the Present,* by Marilyn J. Boxer, Jean H. Quataert, et al. Oxford: Oxford University Press, 2000.

Mohun, Arwen Palmer. "Laundrymen Construct Their World: Gender and the Transformation of a Domestic Task to an Industrial Process." *Technology and Culture* 38 (1997): 97–120.

Mort, Frank. "Paths to Mass Consumption: Historical Perspectives." Introduction to *Commercial Cultures: Economies, Practices, Spaces,* edited by Peter Jackson, Michelle Lowe, Daniel Miller, and Mort. New York: Berg, 2000.

Möser, Kurt. "World War I and the Creation of Desire for Automobiles in Germany." In *Getting and Spending: European and American Consumer Societies in the Twentieth Century,* edited by Susan Strasser, Charles McGovern, and Matthias Judt. Cambridge: Cambridge University Press, 1998.

Mouton, Michelle. *From Nurturing the Nation to Purifying the Volk: Weimar and Nazi Family Policy, 1918–1945.* Cambridge: Cambridge University Press, 2007.

Müller, Martin L. "Turnen und Sport im sozialen Wandel: Körperkultur in Frankfurt am Main während des Kaiserreichs und der Weimarer Republik." *Archiv für Sozialgeschichte* 33 (1993): 107–136.

Naul, Roland. "History of Sport and Physical Education in Germany, 1800–1945." In

Sport and Physical Education in Germany, edited by Naul and Ken Hardman. New York: Routledge, 2002.

Nolan, Mary. "'Housework Made Easy': The Taylorized Housewife in Weimar Germany's Rational Economy." *Feminist Studies* 16 (1990): 549–577.

———. *Visions of Modernity: American Business and the Modernization of Germany.* Oxford: Oxford University Press, 1994.

———. "Work, Gender and Everyday Life: Reflections on Continuity, Normality and Agency in Twentieth-Century Germany." In *Stalinism and Nazism: Dictatorships in Comparison,* edited by Ian Kershaw and Moshe Lewin. Cambridge: Cambridge University Press, 1997.

Nye, Robert A. *Crime, Madness, and Politics in Modern France: The Medical Concept of National Decline.* Princeton: Princeton University Press, 1984.

Offen, Karen. "Body Politics: Women, Work and the Politics of Motherhood in France, 1920–1950." In *Maternity and Gender Policies: Women and the Rise of European Welfare States, 1880s–1950s,* edited by Gisela Bock and Pat Thane. London and New York: Routledge, 1991.

Ogden, Philip E., and Marie-Monique Huss. "Demography and Pronatalism in France in the Nineteenth and Twentieth Centuries." *Journal of Historical Geography* 8 (1982): 283–298.

Oldenziel, Ruth. "Boys and Their Toys: The Fisher Body Craftsman's Guild, 1930–1968, and the Making of a Male Technical Domain." *Technology and Culture* 38 (1997): 60–96.

———. *Making Technology Masculine: Men, Women and Modern Machines in America, 1870–1945.* Amsterdam: Amsterdam University Press, 1999.

O'Sullivan, Tim. "Transports of Difference and Delight: Advertising and the Motor Car in Twentieth-Century Britain." In *The Motor Car and Popular Culture in the 20th Century,* edited by David Thoms, Len Holden, and Tim Claydon. Brookfield, Vt.: Ashgate, 1998.

Overy, Richard J. "Cars, Roads, and Economic Recovery in Germany, 1932–8." *Ecomomic History Review* 28 (1975): 466–483.

———. "Heralds of Modernity: Cars and Planes from Invention to Necessity." In *Fin de Siècle and Its Legacy,* edited by Mikulas Teich and Roy Porter. Cambridge: Cambridge University Press, 1990.

Parkin, Katherine J. *Food Is Love: Food Advertising and Gender Roles in Modern America.* Philadelphia: University of Pennsylvania Press, 2006.

Pedersen, Susan. "Catholicism, Feminism, and the Politics of the Family during the Late Third Republic." In *Mothers of a New World: Maternalist Politics and the Origins of Welfare States,* edited by Seth Koven and Sonya Michel. New York: Routledge, 1993.

———. *Family, Dependence, and the Origins of the Welfare State: Britain and France, 1914–1945.* Cambridge: Cambridge University Press, 1993.

Peiss, Kathy. "Making Faces: The Cosmetics Industry and the Cultural Construction of Gender, 1890–1930." *Genders* 7 (1990): 143–169.

Petersen, Vibeke Rützou. *Women and Modernity in Weimar Germany: Reality and Its Representation in Popular Fiction.* New York: Berghahn, 2001.

Petro, Patrice. *Joyless Streets: Women and Melodramatic Representation in Weimar Germany.* Princeton: Princeton University Press, 1989.

Peukert, Detlev J. K. *The Weimar Republic: The Crisis of Classical Modernity.* Translated by Richard Deveson. New York: Hill and Wang, 1992.

Pfister, Gertrud. "Breaking Bounds: Alice Profé, Radical and Emancipationist." In *Freeing the Female Body: Inspirational Icons,* edited by J.A. Mangan and Fan Hong. London: Frank Cass, 2001.

———. "Conflicting Femininities: The Discourse on the Female Body and the Physical Education of Girls in National Socialism." *Sport History Review* 28 (1997): 89–107.

———. "The Medical Discourse on Female Physical Culture in Germany in the 19th and Early 20th Centuries." *Journal of Sport History* 17 (1990): 183–198.

———. "Sport for Women." In *Sport and Physical Education in Germany,* edited by Roland Naul and Ken Hardman. New York: Routledge, 2002.

Pfister, Gertrud, and Gerd von der Lippe. "Women's Participation in Sports and the Olympic Games in Germany and Norway—A SocioHistorical Analysis." *Journal of Comparative Physical Education and Sport* 16 (1994): 30–41.

Pfister, Gertrud, and Ilse Hartmann-Tews. "Women and Sport in Comparative and International Perspectives: Issues, Aims and Theoretical Approaches." In *Sport and Women: Social Issues in International Perspective,* edited by Hartmann-Tews and Pfister. New York: Routledge, 2003.

Pfister, Gertrud, Kari Fasting, Sheila Scraton, and Benilde Vázquez. "Women and Football—A Contradiction? The Beginnings of Women's Football in Four European Countries." In *Sport in Europe: Politics, Class, Gender,* edited by J. A. Mangan. London: Frank Cass, 1999.

Pine, Lisa. *Nazi Family Policy, 1933–1945.* New York: Berg, 1997.

———. "Women and the Family." In *Weimar and Nazi Germany: Continuities and Discontinuities,* edited by Panikos Panayi. Harlow, England: Longman, 2001.

Pollay, Richard. "The Subsiding Sizzle: A Descriptive History of Print Advertising, 1900–1980." *Journal of Marketing* 49 (1985): 24–37.

Pross, Harry. *Zeitungsreport: Deutsche Presse im 20. Jahrhundert.* Weimar: Verlag Hermann Böhlaus Nachfolger, 2000.

Rauch, André. *Les vacances.* Paris: Presses Universitaires de France, 1993.

———. *Vacances en France de 1830 à nos jours.* Paris: Hachette, 1996.

Reagin, Nancy R. "Comparing Apples and Oranges: Housewives and the Politics of Consumption in Interwar Germany." In *Getting and Spending: European and American Consumer Societies in the Twentieth Century,* edited by Susan Strasser,

Charles McGovern, and Matthias Judt. Cambridge: Cambridge University Press, 1998.

———. *A German Women's Movement: Class and Gender in Hanover, 1880–1933*. Chapel Hill: University of North Carolina Press, 1995.

———. "*Marktordnung* and Autarkic Housekeeping: Housewives and Private Consumption under the Four-Year Plan, 1936–1939." *German History* 19 (2001): 162–184.

Rearick, Charles. *The French in Love and War: Popular Culture in the Era of the World Wars*. New Haven: Yale University Press, 1997.

Reekie, Gail. "Impulsive Women, Predictable Men: Psychological Constructions of Sexual Difference in Sales Literature to 1930." *Australian Historical Studies* 24 (1991): 359–377.

Reich, Simon. *The Fruits of Fascism: Postwar Prosperity in Historical Perspective*. Ithaca: Cornell University Press, 1990.

Reinartz, Klaus. *Sport in Hamburg: Die Entwicklung der freien Selbstorganisation und der öffentlichen Verwaltung des modernen Sports von 1816 bis 1933*. Hoya, Germany: Niedersächsischen Institut für Sportgeschichte, 1997.

Reinhardt, Dirk. *Von der Reklame zum Marketing: Geschichte der Wirtschaftswerbung in Deutschland*. Berlin: Akademie Verlag, 1993.

Reynolds, Siân. *France between the Wars: Gender and Politics*. New York: Routledge, 1996.

Rhys, D. G. *The Motor Industry: An Economic Survey*. London: Butterworths, 1972.

Ribeiro, Aileen. *The Art of Dress: Fashion in England and France, 1750 to 1820*. New Haven: Yale University Press, 1995.

———. *Fashion in the French Revolution*. London: Batsford, 1988.

Rice, Jenny, and Carol Saunders. "'Mini Loves Dressing Up': Selling Cars to Women." In *The Motor Car and Popular Culture in the 20th Century*, edited by David Thoms, Len Holden, and Tim Claydon. Brookfield, Vt.: Ashgate, 1998.

Roberts, Mary Louise. *Civilization without Sexes: Reconstructing Gender in Postwar France, 1917–1927*. Chicago: University of Chicago Press, 1994.

———. "Prêt-à-déchiffrer: La mode de l'après-guerre et la 'nouvelle histoire culturelle.'" Translated by Jean-Michel Galano. *Le Mouvement Social* 174 (1996): 57–73.

———. "Rationalization, Vocational Guidance and the Reconstruction of Female Identity in Post-War France." *Proceedings of the Annual Meeting of the Western Society for French History* 20 (1993): 367–381.

———. "Samson and Delilah Revisited: The Politics of Women's Fashion in 1920s France." *American Historical Review* 98 (1993): 657–684.

Rosenhaft, Eve. "Women in Modern Germany." In *Modern Germany Reconsidered, 1870–1945*, edited by Gordon Martel. New York: Routledge, 1992.

Rupp, Leila J. "Mother of the *Volk*: The Image of Women in Nazi Ideology." *Signs* 3 (1977): 362–379.

Sachs, Wolfgang. *For Love of the Automobile: Looking Back into the History of Our De-*

sires. Translated by Don Reneau. Berkeley and Los Angeles: University of California Press, 1992.

Sachse, Carola. "Freizeit zwischen Betrieb und Volksgemeinschaft: Betriebliche Freizeitpolitik im Nationalsozialismus." *Archiv für Sozialgeschichte* 33 (1993): 305–328.

Saillard, Olivier. "Le vêtement de sport: Le vêtement moderne!" In *Mode et Sport: Musée de la Mode, 9 juin-16 août 1998.* Marseille: Musées de Marseille, 1998.

Savignon, Jéromine. "La mode sous influence sport: Quelques aspects de la laïcisation du vêtement de sport dans la mode féminine, 1920–1998." In *Mode et sport: Musée de la Mode, 9 juin-16 août 1998.* Marseille: Musées de Marseille, 1998.

Schäfer, Hans Dieter. "Amerikanismus im Dritten Reich." In *Nationalsozialismus und Modernisierung,* edited by Michael Prinz and Rainer Zitelmann. Darmstadt, Germany: Wissenschaftliche Buchgesellschaft, 1991.

Scharff, Virginia. *Taking the Wheel: Women and the Coming of the Motor Age.* New York: Free Press, 1991.

Schug, Alexander. "Wegbereiter der modernen Absatzwerbung in Deutschland: Advertising Agencies und die Amerikanisierung der deutschen Werbebranche in der Zwischenkriegszeit." *WerkstattGeschichte* 34 (2003): 29–52.

Schütz, Erhard. "Zur Modernität des 'Dritten Reiches.'" *Internationales Archiv für Sozialgeschichte der deutschen Literatur* 20 (1995): 116–136.

Schwartz, Vanessa R. *Spectacular Realities: Early Mass Culture in Fin-de-Siècle Paris.* Berkeley and Los Angeles: University of California Press, 1998.

Scott, Joan Wallach. "Gender: A Useful Category of Historical Analysis." In *Gender and the Politics of History.* New York: Columbia University Press, 1988.

Seccombe, Wally. "Men's 'Marital Rights' and Women's 'Wifely Duties': Changing Conjugal Relations in the Fertility Decline." In *The European Experience of Declining Fertility, 1850–1970: The Quiet Revolution,* edited by John R. Gillis, Louise A. Tilly, and David Levine. Oxford: Blackwell, 1992.

Sherayko, Gerard. "Selling the Modern: The New Consumerism in Weimar Germany." Ph.D. diss., Indiana University, 1996.

Sherman, Daniel J. "Monuments, Mourning and Masculinity in France after World War I." *Gender and History* 8 (1996): 82–107.

Showalter, Elaine. *Sexual Anarchy: Gender and Culture at the Fin de Siècle.* New York: Viking Penguin, 1990.

Simonton, Deborah. *A History of European Women's Work, 1700 to the Present.* New York: Routledge, 1998.

Singer, Barnett. "Technology and Social Change: The Watershed of the 1920's." *Proceedings of the Annual Meeting of the Western Society for French History* 4 (1976): 321–329.

Sneeringer, Julia. "The Shopper as Voter: Women, Advertising, and Politics in Post-Inflation Germany." *German Studies Review* 27 (2004): 476–501.

Spivak, Marcel. "Prestige national et sport: Cheminement d'un concept, 1890–1936." *Relations Internationales* 38 (1984): 175–191.

Spree, Reinhard. "The German Petite Bourgeoisie and the Decline of Fertility: Some Statistical Evidence from the Late 19th and Early 20th Centuries." *Historical Social Research* 22 (1982): 15–49.

Stearns, Peter N. *Consumerism in World History: The Global Transformation of Desire.* New York: Routledge, 2001.

———. "Stages of Consumerism: Recent Work on the Issues of Periodization." *Journal of Modern History* 69 (1997): 102–117.

Steele, Valerie. *Paris Fashion: A Cultural History.* Oxford: Oxford University Press, 1988.

Stephenson, Jill. "Propaganda, Autarky and the German Housewife." In *Nazi Propaganda: The Power and the Limitations,* edited by David Welch. Totowa, N.J.: Barnes and Noble Books, 1983.

———. "'Reichsbund der Kinderreichen': The League of Large Families in the Population Policy of Nazi Germany." *European Studies Review* 9 (1979): 350–375.

———. "Women, Motherhood, and the Family in the Third Reich." In *Confronting the Nazi Past: New Debates on Modern German History,* edited by Michael Burleigh. New York: St. Martin's Press, 1996.

———. *Women in Nazi Germany.* Harlow, England: Longman, 2001.

———. *Women in Nazi Society.* New York: Harper and Row, Barnes and Noble Books, 1975.

Stewart, Mary Lynn. *For Health and Beauty: Physical Culture for Frenchwomen, 1880s–1930s.* Baltimore: Johns Hopkins University Press, 2001.

Strasser, Susan. *Satisfaction Guaranteed: The Making of the American Mass Market.* Washington: Smithsonian Institution Press, 1989.

Teitelbaum, Michael S., and Jay M. Winter. *The Fear of Population Decline.* Orlando: Academic Press, 1985.

Terret, Thierry. "Femmes, Sport, Identité et Acculturation (Premiere Moitié du 20ème Siècle)." *Stadion* 26 (2000): 41–53.

Thebaud, Françoise. *Quand nos grand-mères donnaient la vie: La maternité en France dans l'entre-deux-guerres.* Lyon: Presses Universitaires de Lyon, 1986.

Thomas, Graham, and Christine Zmroczek. "Household Technology: The 'Liberation' of Women from the Home?" In *Family and Economy in Modern Society,* edited by Paul Close and Rosemary Collins. London: Macmillan, 1985.

Tiersten, Lisa. *Marianne in the Market: Envisioning Consumer Society in Fin-de-Siècle France.* Berkeley and Los Angeles: University of California Press, 2001.

Tilly, Louise A., and Joan W. Scott. *Women, Work, and Family.* New York: Holt, Rinehart and Winston, 1978.

Tower, Beeke Sell. "'Ultramodern and Ultraprimitive': Shifting Meanings in the Imagery of Americanism in the Art of Weimar Germany." In *Dancing on the Volcano: Essays on the Culture of the Weimar Republic,* edited by Thomas W. Kniesche and Stephen Brockmann. Columbia, S.C.: Camden House, 1994.

Urry, John. *Consuming Places.* New York: Routledge, 1995.

———. *The Tourist Gaze: Leisure and Travel in Contemporary Societies.* London: Sage, 1990.

Usborne, Cornelie. *The Politics of the Body in Weimar Germany: Women's Reproductive Rights and Duties.* Ann Arbor: University of Michigan Press, 1992.

van der Will, Wilfried. "Culture and the Organization of National Socialist Ideology, 1933 to 1945." In *German Cultural Studies: An Introduction,* edited by Rob Burns. Oxford: Oxford University Press, 1995.

Vinken, Barbara. *Die deutsche Mutter: Der lange Schatten eines Mythos.* Munich: Piper Verlag, 2001.

von Ankum, Katharina, ed. *Women in the Metropolis: Gender and Modernity in Weimar Culture.* Berkeley and Los Angeles: University of California Press, 1997.

Waidenschlager, Christine. "Berliner Mode der zwanziger Jahre zwischen Couture und Konfecktion." In *Mode der 20er Jahre,* edited by Waidenschlager with Christa Gustavus. Tübingen: Ernst Wasmuth Verlag, 1993.

Weber, Donald. "Selling Dreams: Advertising Strategies from *grands magasins* to Supermarkets in Ghent, 1900–1960." In *Cathedrals of Consumption: The European Department Store, 1850–1939,* edited by Geoffrey Crossick and Serge Jaumain. Brookfield, Vt.: Ashgate, 1999.

Weber, Eugen. *The Hollow Years: France in the 1930s.* New York: Norton, 1994.

Weindling, Paul. *Health, Race, and German Politics between National Unification and Nazism, 1870–1945.* Cambridge: Cambridge University Press, 1989.

Welch, David. *The Third Reich: Politics and Propaganda.* New York: Routledge, 1993.

Werner, Françoise. "Du ménage à l'art ménager: L'evolution du travail ménager et son écho dans la presse feminine française de 1919 à 1939." *Le Mouvement Social* 129 (1984): 61–87.

Weyrather, Irmgard. *Muttertag und Mutterkreuz: Der Kult um die "deutsche Mutter" im Nationalsozialismus.* Frankfurt am Main: Fischer Taschenbuch Verlag, 1993.

Wiggershaus, Renate. *Frauen unterm Nationalsozialismus.* Wuppertal: Peter Hammer Verlag, 1984.

Wilke, Gerhard, and Kurt Wagner. "Family and Household: Social Structures in a German Village between the Two World Wars." In *The German Family: Essays on the Social History of the Family in Nineteenth- and Twentieth-Century Germany.* Totowa, N.J.: Barnes and Noble Books, 1981.

Wilkins, Mira, and Frank Ernest Hill. *American Business Abroad: Ford on Six Continents.* Detroit: Wayne State University Press, 1964.

Williams, James C. "Getting Housewives the Electric Message: Gender and Energy

Marketing in the Early Twentieth Century." In *His and Hers: Gender, Consumption, and Technology,* edited by Roger Horowitz and Arwen Mohun. Charlottesville: University Press of Virginia, 1998.

Williamson, Judith. *Decoding Advertisements: Ideology and Meaning in Advertising.* New York: Marion Boyars, 1978.

Willis, Paul. "Women in Sport in Ideology." In *Sport, Culture and Ideology,* edited by Jennifer Hargreaves. London: Routledge and Kegan Paul, 1982.

Winter, J. M. "War, Family, and Fertility in Twentieth-Century Europe." In *The European Experience of Declining Fertility, 1850–1970: The Quiet Revolution,* edited by John R. Gillis, Louise A. Tilly, and David Levine. Oxford: Blackwell, 1992.

Young, Patrick. "*La Vieille France* as Object of Bourgeois Desire: The Touring Club de France and the French Regions, 1890–1918." In *Histories of Leisure,* edited by Rudy Koshar. New York: Berg, 2002.

Zdatny, Steven. "Hair and Fashion, 1910–1920: A Coiffeur's History of a Critical Decade." *Proceedings of the Annual Meeting of the Western Society for French History* 24 (1997): 335–345.

———. "La mode à la garçonne, 1900–1925: Une histoire sociale des coupes de cheveux." *Le Mouvement Social* 174 (1996): 23–56.

Zerner, Sylvie. "De la couture aux presses: l'emploi féminin entre les deux guerres." *Le Mouvement Social* 140 (1987): 9–25.

Zurbrugg, Nicholas. "'Oh what a feeling!'—The Literatures of the Car." In *The Motor Car and Popular Culture in the 20th Century,* edited by David Thoms, Len Holden, and Tim Claydon. Brookfield, Vt.: Ashgate, 1998.

INDEX

Illustrations are denoted by italic page numbers.

108, 121–31, 143, 175; as unable to understand technology fully, 50–51, 123–31, 139,
175; linked to nature and tradition, 62, 64,
82–83, 148, 156, 162–63, 169–70, 172; and
national identity, 73, 137–39; fashions of,
79, 81–82, 85–86, 120; imperative of beauty
for, 87–94; as fundamentally unhealthy,
94–102; and automobiles, 109–10, 114–31
passim, 137–39, 163, 168; as passive receivers
of technology from men, 120, 123, 125–26,
137, 143; and sports, 148–59 *passim;* and
tourism, 162–72 *passim. See also* Housewifery; "Modern woman"; Motherhood
Work. *See* Labor
World War I: sense of emasculation caused
by, 1–3; impact on gender roles, 1–3, 7, 48,

56; gender concerns created by, 1–3, 25, 48,
74; women's roles during, 1–3, 52; restoring gender order following, 2–3, 48; wom-
en's employment during, 2, 7–8, 25; demographic concerns deriving from, 47, 56, 58;
and diminution of patriarchal authority,
48, 74; impact on family model, 56–57, 64;
gender imbalance in population caused by,
80, 140; impact on automobile industry,
110; mentioned, 6–9, 14, 17, 28–29, 54, 87,
103, 113, 146, 157, 172, 182
World War II, 27, 58, 113, 173, 182
Wrigley candies, ads for, 105–106

Zenith carburetors, ads for, 217n
Zündapp motorcycles, ads for, 215n